Dec 2004
Book group

John A Sapp

Mr Kenneth Horst
PO Box 1199
Meadow Vista CA 95722-1199

Whatever

Happened

to the Soul?

DreamSeeker Mag
"Voices from the Soul"

D0981645

THEOLOGY AND THE SCIENCES

Kevin J. Sharpe, Series Editor

TITLES IN THE SERIES

Whatever Happened to the *Soul?*

Scientific and Theological Portraits of Human Nature

Edited by
Warren S. Brown
Nancey Murphy
and H. Newton Malony

FORTRESS PRESS   MINNEAPOLIS

WHATEVER HAPPENED TO THE SOUL?
Scientific and Theological Portraits of Human Nature

Where not otherwise indicated, Scripture quotations are from the New Revised Standard Version Bible, copyright © 1989 by the Division of Christian Education of the National Council of the Churches of Christ in the United States of America. Used with permission.

Cover photo: Patient's art from *Botschaft der Träume,* courtesy of Dr. Gaetano Benedetti and Vandenhoeck & Ruprecht, Göttingen.

Library of Congress Cataloging-in-Publication Data

Whatever happened to the soul? : scientific and theological portraits of human nature / edited by Warren S. Brown, Nancey Murphy, and H. Newton Malony.
    p.   cm.
    Includes bibliographical references and index.
    ISBN 0-8006-3141-2 (alk. paper)
    1. Man (Christian theology)   2. Religion and science.   3. Soul.
  I. Brown, Warren S., 1944- . II. Murphy, Nancey C. III. Malony, H. Newton.
BT702.W43   1998
233'.5—dc21
                                         98-37943
                                            CIP

The paper used in this publication meets the minimum requirements of American National Standard for Information Sciences—Permanence of Paper for Printed Library Materials, ANSI Z329.48-1984.

Manufactured in the U.S.A.   AF1-3141

02   01   00   3   4   5   6   7   8   9   10

To Janet,

*whose body-soul has been assailed
but not overcome
by either quadriplegia or cancer;*

whose faith radiates glory to God.

Contents

Contributors

RAY S. ANDERSON, Professor of Theology and Ministry at Fuller Theological Seminary in Pasadena, California, is the author of numerous books and articles, including *The Soul of Ministry: Forming Leaders for God's People* (1997), *Self Care: A Theology of Personal Empowerment and Spiritual Healing* (1995), and *On Being Human: Essays in Theological Anthropology* (1992).

V. ELVING ANDERSON, Professor Emeritus of Genetics at the University of Minnesota, is past president of Sigma Xi, the Scientific Research Society, and other scientific societies. He has published articles and contributed to books on genetic factors in human behavioral problems and breast cancer and on ethical issues in genetics and other areas of biology. His current research interest is gene mapping in epilepsy.

FRANCISCO J. AYALA, Donald Bren Professor of Biological Sciences at the University of California, Irvine, is a member of the President's Committee of Advisors on Science and Technology. He has been president and chairman of the board of the American Association for the Advancement of Science. He has published twelve books and more than 600 papers on evolutionary biology and the philosophy of science.

WARREN S. BROWN JR. is Professor in the Graduate School of Psychology at Fuller Theological Seminary and Director of the Lee Edward Travis Institute for Biopsychosocial Research. He is also an Adjunct Professor in the Department of Psychiatry at the UCLA School of Medicine and a member of the UCLA Brain Research Institute. He has published numerous scientific articles on brain function and higher cognitive processes in humans.

JOEL B. GREEN, Associate Dean and Professor of New Testament Interpretation at Asbury Theological Seminary, is the author or editor of thirteen books, including most recently *The Gospel of Luke* in the *International Commentary on the New Testament Series* (1997). Until recently, he served on the faculty of the American Baptist Seminary of the West/Graduate Theological Union, Berkeley.

MALCOLM JEEVES is president of the Royal Society of Edinburgh, Scotland's National Academy of Science and Letters, and Honorary Research

Professor of Psychology, University of St. Andrews, Scotland. Formerly editor-in-chief of *Neuropsychologia*, past chairman of the International Neuropsychological Symposium, he is author of many scientific papers on neuropsychology as well as books relating science and Christian beliefs. Recent works include *Mind Fields* (1994), *Human Nature at the Millennium* (1997), and *Science, Life and Christian Belief* (with R. J. Berry) (1998).

H. NEWTON MALONY is Senior Professor in the Graduate School of Psychology at Fuller Theological Seminary, where he was director of programs in the integration of psychology and theology for many years. He has written widely on the implications of findings in the social/behavioral/physical sciences for the tasks of counseling and ministry. In his dual professional role as an ordained United Methodist minister, he has been interested in the implications of these matters for pastoral work as well as professional functioning.

NANCEY MURPHY is Professor of Christian Philosophy at Fuller Theological Seminary, Pasadena, California. She is a member of the Board of Directors of the Center for Theology and the Natural Sciences in Berkeley, California. Her recent books include *Anglo-American Postmodernity* (1997), *On the Moral Nature of the Universe: Theology, Cosmology, and Ethics* (with G. F. R. Ellis, 1996), and *Beyond Liberalism and Fundamentalism* (1996).

STEPHEN G. POST is Professor of Biomedical Ethics, Philosophy, and Religion at Case Western Reserve University. His book *The Moral Challenge of Alzheimer Disease* (1995) deals systematically with questions of theology and the human self. He was associate editor of the five-volume *Encyclopedia of Bioethics* (second edition, 1995). Post holds his doctorate from the University of Chicago Divinity School in theology and ethics.

Preface

In August of 1997 an article appeared in a leading American scientific journal that described a trend toward a warming of the relationship between science and faith.[1] Thawing of a previously icy relationship was seen on the side of science in the promotion of a science/faith dialogue within the American Association for the Advancement of Science and in the formation of study centers such as the Center for Theology and Natural Science in Berkeley. Within religion, a warming of relationships was seen in a more liberal official view of evolution on the part of the Roman Catholic Church, as well as the fact that this book was to be published out of work done at Fuller Theological Seminary, known for its conservative evangelicalism.

Indeed, *Whatever Happened to the Soul?* is an attempt to establish a perspective on human nature that would allow for greater resonance between science and faith. We have tried to describe the nature of humans from the perspective of disciplines ranging from biology to theology in a way that is reconcilable and congruent. Our attempt has been, in every case, to achieve descriptions that both represent the current state of knowledge in the discipline and harmonize with the descriptions from the other disciplines. In order to increase by a few degrees the warming relationship between science and faith, we have attempted to sound a multi-disciplinary resonant chord (to mix metaphors).

Our core theme—the key of the resonant chord—is a monistic, or holistic, view of humans. In order to avoid confusion with reductionistic or materialistic forms of monism, which we do not wish to espouse, as well as to denote a particular form of monism, we have chosen the label "nonreductive physicalism" to represent our common perspective. Thus, statements about the physical nature of human beings made from the perspective of biology or neuroscience are about *exactly the same entity* as statements made about the spiritual nature of persons from the point of view of theology or religious traditions. We would disavow the opinion that human science speaks about a physical being, while theology and religion speak about a spiritual essence or soul.

While some of the issues dealt with in this book have fostered acrimonious debate in the past, this book is *not* meant to be contentious. We have written from the perspective that views soul as a functional capacity of a complex physical organism, rather than a separate spiritual essence that somehow inhabits a body. We have adopted this position because we believe it is the best way to incorporate and reconcile all the various sources of available data. There is,

---

1. Gregg Easterbrook, "Science and God: A Warming Trend?" *Science* 277 (1997): 890-893.

however, no way to provide absolute proof that dualist theories are false. Therefore, we honor the opinions of those who disagree with our premise. Our primary attempt at being convincing has been our effort to achieve consistency and congruence across domains of knowledge regarding human nature.

The inspiration for this project came from discussions surrounding lectures on the integration of psychology (in this case, neuropsychology) and theology given by Malcolm Jeeves (University of St. Andrews) in January of 1995 at the Graduate School of Psychology at Fuller Theological Seminary.[2] Malcolm had urged that a cross-disciplinary book on human nature was needed. Such a book needed to do for the dialogue between faith and the scientific fields of human biology and psychology what *Portraits of Creation* by Van Till, Snow, Stek, and Young had attempted to do for the dialogue between Christian faith and the fields of cosmology and geology. It was decided that the Fuller group (Brown, Murphy, and Malony) should spearhead an effort to bring together a group to do this work.[3]

Critical to the accomplishment of our task has been a generous grant from the John Templeton Foundation. This grant allowed the authors of this volume to gather for three different two-day conferences to discuss our disciplines, the dominant view of human nature that is implied, and the philosophical and theological issues that emerge. On these three occasions we were able to describe to one another the view of human nature that arises from the current body of scholarly work in our particular discipline and to receive extensive comment, criticism, and discussion from colleagues representing other disciplines. We believe that these meetings allowed this book to have greater coherence and unity than are typically the case for multi-authored works.

Each chapter in this book was extensively critiqued by an expert in the particular discipline who was not a part of our author group but whose perspectives were sufficiently broad to allow an understanding of the intentions of this project. In this way we attempted to insure that the perspective voiced in each chapter not only harmonizes with those presented in other chapters, but is consistent with the best knowledge in the particular discipline. We would like

2. Malcolm A. Jeeves, *Human Nature at the Millennium: Reflections on the Integration of Psychology and Christianity* (Grand Rapids: Baker, 1997).
3. Different perspectives on human nature have implications for the physical, psychological, and spiritual care of persons. A chapter written by H. Newton Malony dealing with this important issue was originally included in the development of this book but was ultimately omitted to keep the focus more specifically on theology and science. The chapter by Malony entitled "Counseling Body/Soul Persons" has been published in the *International Journal for the Psychology of Religion* 8, no. 3 (1998).

to thank the following individuals for their efforts and suggestions, which markedly enhanced the quality of this book: R. J. Berry (University College, London), Dan Blazer (School of Medicine, Duke University), Arthur Peacocke (Exeter College, Oxford), Ted Peters (Pacific Lutheran Theological Seminary), Marianne Meye Thompson (Fuller Theological Seminary), Fraser Watts (Queens College, Cambridge), David Washburn (Sonny Carter Life Sciences Laboratory, University of Georgia), William C. Spohn (Department of Religious Studies, Santa Clara University), and Herbert Benson (Harvard University School of Medicine). The authors would also like to thank those who have helped in the practical tasks of managing this project and preparing this book, specifically Linda Rojas and Dan Palomino. Finally, we wish to thank Marilyn Thomsen, who has done so much in publicity and public relations to make sure this project does not disappear in the forest of the many academic books published each year.

Chapter One

Human Nature:
Historical, Scientific, and Religious Issues

Nancey Murphy

THE PURPOSE OF THIS BOOK

Are human beings composed of two parts, a material body and a nonmaterial mind or soul? Or are humans purely physical beings? This ancient philosophical question serves as a point of intersection between a variety of scientific developments and a variety of theological concerns. Because of this intersection, there is potential for conflict. Many Christians, and believers of other faiths as well, hold (or at least assume) a dualist account. Some Christians believe that body-soul dualism is an essential part of Christian teaching.

However, many scientists and philosophers today suppose that the person is but one substance—a physical body. Evolutionary biology and genetics both suggest our continuity with other life forms. The most striking recent evidence for such a view comes from current advances in cognitive science and the various neurosciences. One way to represent its significance is to point out that neuroscience has in a sense *completed* the Darwinian revolution, bringing not only the human body but the human mind as well, into the sphere of scientific investigation. In particular, nearly all of the human capacities or faculties once attributed to the *soul* are now seen to be functions of the brain. Localization studies—that is, finding the regional structure or distributed system in the brain responsible for such things as language, emotion, and decisionmaking—provide especially strong motivation for saying that it is the brain that is responsible for these capacities, not some immaterial entity associated with the body. In Owen Flanagan's terms, it is the brain that is the *res cogitans*—the thinking thing.[1]

1. Owen Flanagan, *The Science of Mind*, 2d ed. (Cambridge, Mass.: MIT Press, 1991), 318.

Is there *essential* conflict here? Our answer is no. This book explores the nature of the human person from a variety of perspectives: scientific, philosophical, biblical, theological, and ethical. The goal of the book is to demonstrate the possibility of an account of human nature that satisfies the demands of these many disciplines—to show that the portraits sketched from these various disciplinary perspectives may all in fact be of the same "person." Each chapter in its own way points toward a view of the person that we call "nonreductive physicalism." "Physicalism" signals our agreement with the scientists and philosophers who hold that it is not necessary to postulate a second metaphysical entity, the soul or mind, to account for human capacities and distinctiveness. "Nonreductive," indicates our rejection of contemporary philosophical views that say that the person is "nothing but" a body. That is, many physicalist accounts of the person are also reductive: they aim to show that human behavior can be *exhaustively* explained by means of genetics or neurobiology. So the difficult issue is to explain how we can claim that we *are* our bodies, yet without denying the "higher" capacities that we think of as being essential for our humanness: rationality, emotion, morality, free will, and, most important, the capacity to be in relationship with God. This we hope to accomplish in the following chapters.

The purpose of this chapter is to provide some historical background to the issues here considered and to provide a map of the relations among the chapters that follow. The book's brief Conclusion reflects in greater depth on the convergence of the chapters.

Western views of the nature of the person have been influenced by philosophical theories, religious views (especially Christian), and, in the modern era, by the sciences. Thus, the historical survey that follows takes up these various sources.

ANCIENT PHILOSOPHY

It has become common in some theological circles to make a sharp distinction between the Hebrew Scriptures' "holistic" account of the person and Greek dualism.[2] This is an oversimplification on a number of counts, not least of which is the fact that the philosophers of Greece and Rome were not at all united on these issues.[3] It is difficult to think our way back to these ancient sources; we have a fairly precise concept of the material, which allows for a

2. See, for example, Oscar Cullmann, "Immortality of the Soul or Resurrection of the Dead?" in *Immortality and Resurrection,* ed. Krister Stendahl (New York: Macmillan, 1958), 9-53; see also below, "Developments in Theology and Biblical Studies."
3. See Green, chapter 7.

sharp distinction between the material and the nonmaterial. However, one of the contentious issues in ancient philosophy was the nature of matter itself. For many Greek thinkers reality was conceived as a hierarchy of beings exhibiting varying degrees of materiality. One important conflict in ancient philosophy, then, concerned the question whether the soul belonged to this gradation of material realities. The Stoics regarded the human soul as but an aspect of an all-pervading cosmic *logos;* Epicureans provided an atomist-materialist account of the soul.

The two philosophers who have had the greatest impact on Christian theology are Plato and Aristotle. While Plato's account is indeed dualistic, it is not clear that Aristotle's account should be so regarded. Plato (427?-348 B.C.E.) described the person as an immortal soul imprisoned in a mortal body. The soul is tripartite and hierarchically organized. There is an analogy between the harmonious functioning of the soul and that of the ideal state. The appetitive or impulsive element of the soul is analogous to the lowest class in society, the consumers. Reason is the highest element and corresponds to the ruling class. In between is an element corresponding to the soldier-police. The name for this element, *thumos,* may be translated "spirit" (in the sense in which a horse has spirit). The proper coordination of these three elements or faculties constitutes human well-being.

Plato's concept of the soul was related to his "otherworldly" view of reality. During much of his career he held the doctrine of the *Forms* or *Ideas*—the view that concepts have a real existence and are eternal. He argued from the fact that people possess knowledge of these concepts or Forms without being taught that they must have come to know them by acquaintance before birth. Thus, the rational part of the soul pre-exists the body, dwelling in the transcendent realm of the Forms, and returns there at death.

In his mature position, Aristotle (384-322 B.C.E.) thought of the soul not as an entity, but more as a life principle—that aspect of the person that provides the powers or attributes characteristic of the human being. Plants and animals have souls as well—nutritive and sensitive souls, which give them the powers to grow and reproduce and to move and perceive, respectively. Human souls are organized hierarchically and incorporate the nutritive and sensitive powers, but in addition provide rational powers. He illustrates the relation of soul to body with an analogy: if the eye were a complete animal, sight would be its soul. Because the soul is a principle of the functioning of the body, it would follow that the soul dies with the body. However, a vestige of Aristotle's earlier, Platonic dualism remains in his speculation that perhaps one aspect of rationality (*Nous*) survives death. But even if this is the case, this does not amount to personal immortality, since *Nous* is an impersonal rational faculty.

Aristotle's conception of the soul and body fits well into his general "hylo-morphic" conception of reality. All material things are composed of matter and form. Form is an immanent principle that gives things their essential charac-teristics and powers. The soul is but one type of form. Although Aristotle uses the same term (*form*) as Plato, it is important to stress the differences between their views. Aristotle's forms are not pre-existent, transcendent entities, as were Plato's. Since for Aristotle the soul is a form, this difference matters a great deal in his concept of the person and makes it questionable whether Aristotle's view should be considered an instance of body-soul dual*ism* at all.

In general, what we see in Greek philosophical speculation is the recogni-tion that human beings have some remarkable capabilities all their own (such as doing mathematics and philosophy) and others that they share with animals (sensation). It did not seem possible to attribute these powers to matter—to the body—and so philosophers developed theories about an additional component of the person to account for them. Since living persons have all of these pow-ers and corpses do not, the soul is also taken to be the life principle.

EARLY CHRISTIAN SOURCES

It would be reasonable to begin this section with an account of scriptural teaching on the nature of the person. However, this is one of the most vexing issues in the discussion, in part because our current questions were not the questions of the writers of Scripture, but also because of a long history of pro-jecting onto the texts interpretations and even translations that reflect later writers' concerns and assumptions. So this issue will be treated *indirectly* in the penultimate section of this chapter, where recent history of conflicting inter-pretations of Scripture are surveyed.[4]

Tertullian (160-220) followed the Stoics in teaching that the human soul is corporeal and is generated with the body. Origin (185-254) followed Plato in teaching that the soul is incorporeal and eternal, pre-existing the body. After the time of Jerome (c. 347-420) the soul was generally thought to be created at the time of conception.

Augustine (354-430) has probably been the most influential teacher on these matters because of his legacy in both Protestant and Catholic theology and because of his importance in the development of Christian spirituality. Augustine's conception of the person is a modified Platonic view: a human being is an immortal (not eternal) soul using (not imprisoned in) a mortal body. The soul is tripartite (and thus an image of the Trinity) and hierarchi-cally ordered. However, the "parts" are slightly different from those recognized

4. For a more adequate account, see Green, chapter 7.

by Plato. Our modern conception of the will is an Augustinian notion, and for Augustine the will is superior to the intellect.

Foreshadowed in Augustine's thought is the modern problem of causal interaction. If the soul is to the body as an agent to a tool, then it is inconsistent to say that the body affects the soul. Consequently Augustine was never able to give a satisfactory account of sensory knowledge. Augustine's notion that one knows one's own soul directly will have striking repercussions in modern epistemology.

Augustine was much influenced by the Neoplatonists, who had incorporated Platonic philosophy into religious systems emphasizing the care and development of the soul as the means of salvation. Augustine and other early theologians bequeathed this emphasis on the soul to subsequent spiritual writers. It is by cultivating the higher faculties of the soul (and often by repressing the lower faculties and the body) that one develops the capacity for knowledge of and relation to God.

In the writings of Thomas Aquinas (1225-1274) we have the most systematic development of an Aristotelian alternative to the largely Platonic accounts influenced by Augustine. Thomas took up both Aristotelian hylomorphic metaphysics and Aristotle's thesis that the soul is the form of the body.

Thomas had an elaborate account of the hierarchically ordered faculties or powers of the soul, which he developed by asking, first, what activities humans engage in and, second, what operative powers are needed to *explain* such actions. He then drew conclusions about the essential nature of the soul from this list of powers. It will be worthwhile summarizing these faculties here, as they are relevant to the current topic of brain localization studies.

The "lowest" powers of the human soul, shared with plants and animals, are the vegetative faculties of nutrition, growth, and reproduction. Next higher are the sensitive faculties, shared with animals, and including the exterior senses of sight, hearing, smell, taste, and touch, and the four "interior senses," called *sensus communis, phantasia* (imagination), *vis aestimativa,* and *vis memorativa* (memory). The *sensus communis* is the faculty that distinguishes and collates the data from the exterior senses—for example, associating the bark and the brownness of the fur with the same dog. The *vis aestimativa* allows for apprehensions that go beyond sensory perception, for example, apprehending the fact that something is useful or friendly or unfriendly. This sensitive level of the soul also provides for the power of locomotion and for lower aspects of appetite—the ability to be attracted to sensible objects. This appetitive faculty is further subdivided between a simple tendency toward or away from what is sensed as good or evil, and a more complex inclination to meet bodily needs or threats with appropriate responses: attack, avoidance, or acquiescence. Together these appetitive faculties (all still at the sensitive level) provide for eleven kinds of emotion: love, desire, delight, hate, aversion, sorrow, fear, daring, hope, despair, and anger.

The rational faculties, according to Thomas, are distinctively human: passive and active intellect and will. The will is a higher appetitive faculty whose object is the good. Since God is ultimate goodness, this faculty is ultimately directed toward God. The two faculties of the intellect enable abstraction, grasping or comprehending the abstracted universals, judging, and remembering. Morality is a function of attraction to the good combined with rational judgment as to what the good truly consists in. The intellect rather than the will is (in general) the more noble faculty in Thomas's system.

For Augustine, the immortality of the soul was a given, but the unity of the person always remained a problem. For Thomas, in contrast, the unity of the person was a given, and immortality became a problem. While Thomas believed that his Aristotelian conception of soul helped Christians appreciate the doctrine of the resurrection of the body, he still needed an account of the immortality of the (individual, personal) soul, since he believed that there needed to be a soul *to which* the body would be restored at the general resurrection. Thus, he devised an extremely complex argument for the immortality of the human soul (but not animal or plant souls), based on the unity of the soul and the rational soul's capacity to know the natures of all other bodies.

EARLY MODERN SCIENCE

Galileo (1564-1642) is famous for his role in the Copernican revolution. However, he played a comparable role in a development that has had equally revolutionary consequences: the substitution of a corpuscular or atomist conception of matter for ancient and medieval hylomorphism. The revolution in astronomy called for adjustments in physics and chemistry, and even in theology, ethics, and political theory. Atomism in metaphysics and physics eventually affected chemistry, psychology, the social sciences, and, indirectly, theology.[5] The animosity toward any sort of teleology that one still encounters in contemporary philosophy of biology seems to be residual heat from the explosive collision of these two worldviews.

No less were there consequences in philosophy. René Descartes (1596-1650) is considered the originator of modern philosophy. We can see why he

---

5. See Nancy Murphy, *Beyond Liberalism and Fundamentalism: How Modern and Postmodern Philosophy Set the Theological Agenda* (Valley Forge, Pa.: Trinity Press International, 1996), chapter 3; and *idem*, *Anglo-American Postmodernity: Philosophical Perspectives on Science, Religion, and Ethics* (Boulder, Colo.: Westview Press, 1997), chapter 1.

would turn away from the (still-official) Catholic account of the soul as the substantial *form* of the body and propose a radical substance dualism more akin to Platonism when we recall that Descartes was also involved in the atomist revolution in physics.[6] Descartes distinguished two basic kinds of realities, extended substance (*res extensa*) and thinking substance (*res cogitans*); the latter included angels and human minds.

Notice the shift from "souls" to "minds." Latin has two words, *anima* and *animus*, each translated "soul," but *animus* is also translated "mind," while *anima* is also translated as the principle of life. English-language philosophy has used the term "mind" rather than "soul" in most cases.

The shift from hylomorphism to atomism and substance dualism created what is now seen by many to be an insoluble problem: mind–body interaction. Whereas for Aristotle and his followers the mind/soul was but one instance of form, in modern thought the mind becomes something of an anomaly in an otherwise purely material world of nature. Furthermore, the very conception of matter has changed. Before, matter and form had been correlative concepts—matter was that which had the potential to be activated by form. Matter (at least as unformed, prime matter) was entirely passive. For early moderns, matter is also passive, inert. But now, instead of being moved by immanent forms, it is moved by external forces—physical forces. Now there is a dilemma: hold on to the immateriality of mind, and there is then no way to account for its supposed ability to move the body; interpret it as a quasi-physical force and its effects ought to be measurable and quantifiable as is any other force in nature. But nothing of the latter enters into modern physics.

Lest one conclude that the problems of mind-body interaction are merely the result of too crude a view of physical interactions in early modern physics, it is important to note that contemporary physics presents comparable complications. Now, as Owen Flanagan points out, the problem has to do with the law of conservation of matter and energy:

> If Descartes is right that a nonphysical mind can cause the body to move, for example, we decide to go to a concert and go, then physical energy must increase in and around our body, since we get up and go to the concert. In order, however, for physical energy to increase in any system, it has to have been transferred from some other physical system. But the mind, according to Descartes, is not a physical system and therefore it does not have any energy to transfer. The mind cannot account for the fact that our body ends up at the concert.

6. Joel Green notes that Descartes' radical substance dualism has so influenced current thinking on these issues that we tend to read Plato himself with Cartesian presuppositions. See chapter 7.

If we accept the principle of the conservation of energy we seem committed either to denying that the nonphysical mind exists, or to denying that it could cause anything to happen, or to making some very implausible ad hoc adjustments in our physics. For example, we could maintain that the principle of conservation of energy holds, but that every time a mind introduces new energy into the world—thanks to some mysterious capacity it has—an equal amount of energy departs from the physical universe—thanks to some perfectly orchestrated mysterious capacity the universe has.[7]

It is worth mentioning briefly the epistemological problems created by this metaphysical shift. For Aristotelians, sensory knowledge resulted from the transference of the form of the thing perceived into the intellect of the perceiver, whose mind was, literally, in-*formed* by exactly that which makes the object to be what it is. Thus, exact knowledge of the essences of things was possible on the basis of very little observation. Perceptual *error* is what needed explanation.

In a world composed of atoms, sensation must result from the impinging of atoms on the sensory membranes, and then from coded information conveyed to the brain (and for dualists thence to the mind). Ideas in the mind are no longer identical to the forms inherent in things, but mere representations produced by a complicated process of transmission, encoding, and decoding. Thus arises modern skepticism with regard to sense perception.[8]

Descartes' solution was to begin with the Augustinian notion that we know our own souls/minds directly.[9] But for early modern philosophers that is *all* we know directly. Descartes reassured himself of the possibility of (indirect) knowledge of the external world by arguing that a benevolent creator would not have constructed us so as to be constantly deceived.

PHILOSOPHY OF MIND

There have been psychophysical monists of various sorts throughout the modern period: Descartes's contemporary, Thomas Hobbes (1588-1679) was a materialist, who described thinking as "motions about the head" and emotions as "motions about the heart." George Berkeley (1685-1753) took the opposite tack and resolved all of reality into ideas (perceptions). However, the most

7. Flanagan, *The Science of the Mind,* 21.
8. See Theo C. Meyering, *Historical Roots of Cognitive Science: The Rise of a Cognitive Theory of Perception from Antiquity to the Nineteenth Century* (Dordrecht: Kluwer Academic Publishers, 1989).
9. Owen Flanagan uses results from current neuroscience to call into question this philosophical assumption concerning the priority of self-knowledge. See *The Science of the Mind,* 194-200.

common position throughout the earlier years of the modern period has been dualism. Yet, ever since Descartes proposed the pineal gland as the locus of mind-brain interaction, the problem of the relation of the mind and body has occupied philosophers. A variety of solutions to the problem of causal interaction has been tried.

Psychophysical parallelism is the view that physical events cause physical events, that mental events cause mental events, and that the *appearance* of causal interaction between the mental and the physical is an illusion created by the fact that there is a pre-established harmony between these two independent causal chains. This harmony is either established at the beginning by God or is the result of constant divine interventions. Gottfried Wilhelm Leibniz (1646-1716) was one proponent of this theory. Its inspiration is said to have come from observation that clocks on various towers throughout the city kept the same time yet had no causal influence on one another. This position was never widely accepted and lost its appeal with the growing atheism of modern philosophy. As Owen Flanagan says, "to have to introduce God to explain the workings of the mind, however, is to introduce a big Spirit in order to get rid of the perplexities of a world of little spirits, and to magnify the complications one presumably set out to reduce."[10]

Another attempt to solve the problem of mental causation is epiphenomenalism. This is the theory that conscious mental life is a causally inconsequential byproduct of physical processes in the brain. This position has two drawbacks. First, why should causation from the physical to the mental be thought any less problematic than from the mental to the physical? Second, there seems to be overwhelming evidence for interaction. These objections are not thought fatal, however, and some say that there is now solid scientific evidence for the thesis. We shall have to examine it in more detail later.[11]

As a consequence both of the problems with mind-body interaction and of the scientific developments to be surveyed below, the balance has shifted in philosophy of mind from dualism to a variety of forms of materialism or physicalism.

Logical behaviorism, widely discussed roughly between the 1930s and early 1960s, claimed that talk of mental phenomena is a shorthand (and misleading) way of talking about actual and potential behavior. Gilbert Ryle (1900-1976) ridiculed the Cartesian mind as "the ghost in the machine," claiming that the

10. Ibid., 64. I concur with Flanagan that this is not an attractive solution. The same conception of matter that created the problem of mind-body interaction creates equal difficulties for an account of divine action. See my *Beyond Liberalism and Fundamentalism*, chapter 3.

11. See Murphy, chapter 6 of this volume; and Flanagan, *The Science of the Mind*, 344-348.

view of the mind as a substance or object rests on a "category mistake" of assuming that because "mind" is a noun there must be an object that it names. While Ryle's critique of dualism is widely accepted as definitive, it has not proved possible to translate language about the mind into language about behavior and dispositions.

A still-current option is the mind-brain identity thesis. There are various versions: the *mind* is identical with the brain; mental *properties* (such as the property of being in pain, or believing some proposition to be true) are identical with physical properties; or mental *events* are identical with brain events. The first of these is an infelicitous expression of the identity thesis since it makes the very mistake for which Ryle criticized the dualists.

An important distinction in philosophy of mind is that between "type identity" and "token identity." Token identity is the thesis that every particular mental event or property is identical with *some* physical event or other; type identity is a stronger thesis to the effect that every type of mental event is identical with a type of physical event. So, for instance, a type of sensation, such as pain, is identical with a particular type of neuron firing. Type identity entails the reducibility of the mental descriptions to physical descriptions. Flanagan says:

> The implication that follows from the latter assumption is this: if type-type identity theory is true then reduction of psychology to neuroscience will eventually be possible. It is easy to see why reduction requires that all the concepts of the science to be reduced be translatable into the concepts of the reducing science. These translations are called "bridge laws" and once they are in place reduction merely involves replacing, synonym for synonym. Type-type identity statements, of course, are precisely the necessary bridge laws.[12]

This strong identity thesis may be unobjectionable in cases such as pain sensations, but it runs into problems with higher-order mental states such as believing some proposition. When conjoined with the thesis that brain events obey causal laws, type identity implies not only that beliefs could be redescribed in purely neurological language, but also that our beliefs are caused by neurophysiological laws. Some philosophers are perfectly sanguine about this outcome and in fact look forward to the day when neuroscience replaces our "folk psychology."[13] Others, however, object that such an account makes nonsense of our views that beliefs are (ordinarily) held for reasons rather than out of causal necessity.

12. Ibid., 218.
13. For example, see Paul M. Churchland, "Eliminative Materialism and Propositional Attitudes," *Journal of Philosophy* 78 (1981): 67-90; and Patricia Smith Churchland, "A Perspective on Mind-Brain Research," *Journal of Philosophy* 77 (1980): 185-207.

The distinction between type and token identity theories makes it possible, however, to state the difference between reductive and nonreductive materialism or physicalism. A variety of philosophers have held that the functioning brain is indeed the seat of mental capacities, and so every mental event is identical to *some* physical event.[14] Yet, because there are no type identities between the mental and the physical (no psychophysical laws), the mental cannot be reduced to the physical. Donald Davidson's "anomalous monism" is the best-known current version of nonreductive physicalism. He claims that there are no strict laws at the mental level; beliefs are related instead by principles of rationality. Because there *are* causal laws at the physical level, beliefs must be only token identical with brain states. The reductionist might reply to Davidson that he is simply assuming that we are not deceived about the "anomalous" nature of mental life and thus has begged the question of the relation of the mental to the physical. Fortunately, this apparent standoff between reductionist and nonreductionist philosophical positions may be susceptible to resolution by scientific advances combined with further philosophical analysis.

RECENT SCIENCE

Biology

Darwinian evolution has had an impact on contemporary culture comparable to that of the revolution in physics and astronomy that heralded the beginning of modern science. One of many issues it raised was that of continuity between humans and (other) animals. One effect was to provide additional reason to question any form of body-soul or body-mind dualism.

The rejection of hylomorphism represented by the development of modern physics meant the rejection of animal (and plant) souls, understood as the substantial forms of their bodies. Descartes described animals in purely material terms. Against this background, the recognition of human kinship with and development from lower animals warranted the conclusion, in the eyes of many, that humans, too, are purely material.

Many theologians evaded this materialist conclusion by granting that the human body is a product of biological evolution but maintaining that God creates a soul for each individual at conception. This intellectual maneuver runs into difficulties, however, when we ask when the *human* species appeared. Contemporary biologists now offer a very complex account of human origins in which there is no clear distinction between animals and humans. Were our first hominid ancestors human, or are only modern humans truly human, or

14. I suggest that the better way to make this point is to say that every mental event is *realized* by some physical event, not identical to it. See Murphy, this volume chapter 6.

did the change take place somewhere in between? What about hominid species that are not in the direct line of descent to modern humans?[15] To claim that humans alone have the gift of a soul seems to force an arbitrary distinction where there is much evidence for continuity.

If human distinctiveness cannot be attributed to the unique possession of a soul or immaterial mind, in what *does* it consist? This has become an intriguing philosophical and theological issue—one likely to benefit from continuing scientific investigation of actual similarities and differences between ourselves and the other higher primates.[16] The issue of human distinctiveness is a major theme of this volume.

Development of the science of genetics has contributed to the discussion of human nature initiated by the theory of evolution. Not only did the biochemical explanation of heredity solidify the evolutionary account of human origins; it also contributed new evidence for human continuity with the other species, since all other life forms possess DNA, and there may not be *any* genes unique to the human species.[17]

Genetics has posed new challenges to traditional accounts of human nature, as well, in that a number of authors have claimed to provide accounts of distinctively human traits, such as morality, in purely biological terms. Sociobiologists identify behavior among lower animals, even insects, as "altruistic," for example, a bird whose cry warns the flock of danger and at the same time exposes it to greater risk of capture. This behavior—and by implication, human altruism as well—is explained in terms of its survival value not for the individual but for the individual's particular configuration of genes. So what appears on the surface as morally commendable behavior is actually the outworking of "the selfish gene."[18]

The specter of genetic determinism arises in a variety of areas of behavior. Twin studies have shown that there is even a genetic element influencing religious behavior.[19]

So radical claims are being made for the relevance of developments in biology over the past century and a half for our portraits of human nature, claims that need to be examined critically.[20]

15. See Ayala, chapter 2 this volume.
16. See Ayala, chapter 2; Jeeves, chapter 4; and Brown, chapter 5 of this volume.
17. See V. E. Anderson, chapter 3 this volume.
18. This is Richard Dawkins's term. See *The Selfish Gene* (Oxford: Oxford University Press, 1989).
19. K. R. Truett et al., "A Model System for Analysis of Family Resemblance in Extended Kinship of Twins," *Behavior Genetics* 24, no. 1 (1994): 35-49.
20. See especially Ayala, chapter 2 of this volume; and V. E. Anderson, chapter 3 this volume.

Sciences of the Mind

Scientific advances bearing on the nature of the mind have been so numerous in recent years that it will be impossible to do justice to them here.[21] My strategy will be to note some of the relevant sciences and to mention examples of findings that have a bearing on the issues at hand. Three major fields of study are the neurosciences, cognitive science, and the study of artificial intelligence.

A major part of current neuroscience research involves mapping the regions of the brain (neuroanatomy) and studying the functions of the various regions (neurophysiology). Studies of this sort intersect, in fascinating ways, the philosophical issues canvassed above. First, they provide dramatic evidence for physicalism. As neuroscientists associate more and more of the faculties once attributed to mind or soul with the functioning of specific regions or systems of the brain it becomes more and more appealing to say that it is in fact the brain that performs these functions. It is important to note that this evidence will never amount to proof: it will always be possible for the dualist to claim that these functions belong to the mind and that mental events are merely *correlated* with events in particular regions of the brain.

Early localization research was largely dependent upon the study of patients with localized brain damage due to strokes or tumors. Deficits in mental and social functioning could be recorded and later, after an autopsy, correlated with the location of lesions. With the development of CAT scans (computerized axial tomography) it has become possible to study correlations between structural abnormalities and behavior of people while they are alive. MRI scans (magnetic resonance imaging) now provide more detailed pictures, more easily revealing locations of brain damage. PET scans (positron emission tomography) allow research correlating localized brain activity with the performance of specialized cognitive tasks.

These varied techniques have allowed for the localization of a vast array of cognitive functions. For example, Broca's area in the left frontal region and Wernicke's area in the temporal lobe are involved in language. Furthermore, more specifically located lesions can selectively affect the person's command of color vocabulary, common nouns, highly specific nouns, and proper names.[22] There are also, apparently, social regions of the brain, for example, those allowing for facial recognition and perception of emotion. Victims of localized damage may show "affective agnosia," the inability to recognize emotions.[23]

---

21. See Jeeves, chapter 4 of this volume.
22. Paul Churchland, *The Engine of Reason, the Seat of the Soul: A Philosophical Journey into the Brain* (Cambridge, Mass.: MIT Press, 1995), 159-160. This is a very accessible account of current brain research and includes philosophical treatment of important issues as well.
23. See Jeeves, chapter 4 of this volume.

"Cognitive science" is the name for a cluster of disciplines aimed at under-standing mental functioning: motor control, perception, recognition, language, memory, and reasoning. Cognitive science received a great impetus from the development of computers; one approach to cognitive science consists in com-puter modeling of mental processes.

At one time cognitive science was quite independent of neurological research. The assumption was that just as one could understand computer soft-ware and the inputs and outputs of a computer without knowing the physics of the hardware, so too mental inputs and outputs could be understood inde-pendently of knowledge of the neural "hardware." However, it turns out that the kind of computer hardware one has makes a difference to the kinds of functions that can be performed by a computer. This suggests that cognitive theorists' accounts of mental operations must be consistent with neurobiolo-gists' accounts of our physical systems.

A striking advance in cognitive science came in the shift from an account of reasoning modeled on serial computation to one based on "connectionism," "parallel distributed processing," and "neural networks." The old model of cog-nitive functioning postulated a central processing unit that performs *serial* computations over *mental representations;* thinking is manipulating symbols according to a stored program that contains *rules* for the transformation of these symbolic representations.

There are problems with this model: First, some kinds of mental operations, such as mathematical computations, can be performed easily by computers designed to operate in this manner. However, there are a number of tasks (such as recognition of faces) that humans can perform instantly and that such a com-puter could perform only very slowly, if at all. Second, most human reasoning is "fuzzier" than what can be modeled by a computer programmed with for-mal rules. Finally, serial processing is unrealistic biologically. Brain tissue is sub-ject to many instances of small, irreparable damage; the loss of a single con-nection in a central processing unit of a serial computer is highly likely to result in serious dysfunction. Yet humans can suffer a great deal of brain damage, for example, due to aging, without noticeable decrease in cognitive abilities.

The solution to the problems of speed and susceptibility to breakdown is to hypothesize that the brain functions by means of a vast number of *parallel processing systems,* which then feed into a more central processor for more global computation and dissemination. Owen Flanagan describes shortcomings of the old model and explains the features of *distribution* and *connectivity* in an engaging manner, so I shall quote him at length:

> [The old models] have several shortcomings. First, they are ultimately, despite
> certain tempting analogies . . . biologically unrealistic, and this is for a host

of reasons. For present purposes, the most important . . . is that there is no anatomical area of the brain . . . where memories of every kind are stored. There is no single brain area that plays the role that the ubiquitous box labeled "long-term memory" plays in standard flow charts of the mind.

Not only is the capacity to remember different kinds of things distributed throughout the brain rather than dependent on one large localized memory store, but some evidence suggests that even within each domain there is no specific anatomical location that plays the role of storing, on a permanent basis, things that are memorable in that domain. Not only is there no all-purpose memory warehouse in the brain; there are no smallish, domain-specific long-term memory stores either. There are no stores stocked with memories, period.

Consider face recognition. The metaphor of the well-run office with permanent files might lead us to imagine that what happens when one recognizes a familiar face is that my superspeedy and superefficient secretarial homunculus fetches my face files and searches for a match with the one before it. Since damage to the right parietal lobe can produce prosopagnosia—the inability to recognize or remember faces, possibly even to see faces as such—one might hypothesize that such damage destroys the files or the fetcher. Unfortunately, no facts about the brain support this way of thinking about the process. Even for those of us with intact parietal lobes, there is nothing in the relevant parts of the brain that is anything like a file full of pictures of faces I have known, nor is there any processor to play the role of the secretarial homunculus. A familiar face activates a complex but characteristic pattern of neural activity. The brain is *disposed* to activation of a certain sort when a familiar face appears.

Memories exist as dispositions, not as permanent states or files. Memories, inactive or active, are *distributed* in two respects. First, when inactive, they exist only as dispositions to activation spread throughout different areas of the brain. The nature of particular distributions depends on the nature and strengths of various connections among systems of neurons. Second, remembering just is the activation of the relevant populations of neurons distributed through many layers of the brain.[24]

This new theory of cognitive processes has enabled the computer modeling of a surprising number of mental operations, including the learning of English pronunciation, discrimination of human faces from other objects, and even identification of emotions represented by facial expressions.[25]

24. Flanagan, *The Science of the Mind,* 232-233.
25. The most readable account of these accomplishments I have found is Paul Churchland, *The Engine of Reason.* See also Gerald M. Edelman, *Bright Air, Brilliant Fire: On the Matter of the Mind* (New York: Basic Books, 1992).

Science and the Soul

As a means of summarizing the impact of scientific developments on contemporary conceptions of the person, it may be enlightening to review the various human faculties attributed by Thomas Aquinas to the soul and mention some of the scientific developments relevant to each.

First, the soul, for Thomas and most ancient and medieval thinkers, was the life principle. Today, the most common criterion for death is "brain death," that is, the cessation of all neural activity.

The functions of the nutritive or vegetative soul included growth, nutrition, and reproduction. These processes are fairly well understood now in biological terms, especially since the discovery of DNA. The brain is significantly involved here, in that neurochemicals play a large role in appetite and sex drive; pituitary hormones control growth.

The functions of the animal soul were locomotion and a variety of senses and appetites. Locomotion is now known to be controlled by cortical and subcortical brain processes and by the efferent nervous system.

Great progress has been made in tracing the processes involved in sensation. For example, signals are transmitted from two different kinds of light-sensitive cells in the retina, through a series of processors, to the visual cortex. Smell involves signals from six different kinds of receptor cells to the olfactory lobes.

The task Thomas assigned to the "interior sense" called the *sensus communis,* the ability to synthesize input from the various external senses, is now studied by neuroscientists as "the binding problem."

Thomas's "interior sense" of memory has been much researched. As described above, (long-term) memory is now conceived of as the result of patterns of connections within the neural network. Short-term memory is believed to be enabled by a system of "recurrent pathways" such that information is processed, then recycled and fed into the process again. The hippocampus is involved in converting short-term into long-term memory, but how this happens is not yet known.

Also mentioned above is the localization of specific sorts of memory. For example, different regions are involved in language memory, with separate locations being responsible for verb access, proper name access, common noun access, and color terms. For another example, the parietal lobes and portions of the inferior temporal areas are involved in memory of faces.

PET scans make it possible to record localized elevations of neuronal activity. Paul Churchland reports an experiment in which his wife, Patricia, was asked to perform a task involving her visual *imagination.* The activity in her visual cortex was elevated exactly during the time she was doing the exercise, but not to the same extent as when she received external visual stimulation. Paul Churchland hypothesizes that visual imagination involves the systematic stimulation of the visual cortex "by way of *recurrent* axonal pathways descending from elsewhere in the brain."[26]

Thomas's *vis aestimativa* included the ability to distinguish between the friendly and the unfriendly, the useful and the useless. One clear instance of this is our ability to read others' emotions. While there does not seem to be a single location responsible for this capacity, there are patients whose brain damage has resulted in its loss. "Boswell" suffers from extensive lesions to the frontal pole of both temporal lobes and to the underpart of the frontal cortex. One among many of his mental deficits is the inability to perceive emotion. Churchland reports:

> I watched as Boswell was shown a series of dramatic posters advertising sundry Hollywood movies. He was asked to say what was going on in each. One of them showed a man and a woman, in close portrait, confronting one another angrily. The man's mouth was open in a plainly hostile shout. Boswell, without evident discomfort or dismay, explained that the man appeared to be *singing* to the woman.[27]

Thomas's sensitive appetite was responsible for emotions such as desire, delight, sorrow, despair. Studies of the etiology of mental illnesses involving inappropriate affect have shown a significant role for neurotransmitters such as dopamine and serotonin.

The higher mental faculties that Thomas attributed to the rational soul are further from being understood. However, all of them involve language, and so even if we do not understand *how* they depend on brain functioning, we know *that* they do because of the close association of linguistic abilities with specific brain areas, especially Wernicke's area and Broca's area.

The appetitive function attributed to the rational soul was, for Thomas, the ground of moral behavior. In chapter 4, Malcolm Jeeves reports a famous case of brain damage, that of a railway employee by the name of Phineas Gage. As a result of a metal rod piercing his brain, Gage's "aspirations, his ethics and morals, were altered."

The foregoing is a brief sketch of a few of the points at which biology, neuroscience, and cognitive science have provided accounts of the dependence on physical processes of *specific* faculties once attributed to the soul. Now, some readers might comment at this point that in all of this discussion of mental capacities the most important element has been overlooked: consciousness. Of course nearly all of the mental functions mentioned above are largely conscious, but, one might say, this still does not explain consciousness.

26. Churchland, *The Engine of Reason*, 157.
27. Ibid., 179.

And, in fact, it is consciousness that *is* the mind (or soul). There are two prominent attitudes in current literature regarding consciousness. One is well represented by the title of Daniel Dennett's book, *Consciousness Explained*.[28] The other point of view is that of philosophers such as Thomas Nagel, designated by their opponents as the "new mysterians,"[29] who claim that consciousness is essentially inexplicable. A middle position might be more reasonable. In previous centuries life was equally as mysterious as consciousness is now. It was thought that it could only be explained by invoking a "vital force." However, in recent years it has been possible to study ever simpler life forms and to list the minimal ingredients that go into the distinction between the living and the nonliving: self-boundedness, self-generation, and self-perpetuation of an entity as a consequence of its dynamic interchange with its surroundings.[30] The fact that we can observe the continuities between simplest life forms and nonliving predecessors, on the one hand, and between those simple forms and increasingly complex organisms on the other gives us a sense of *understanding* life, as well as being able to list its necessary and sufficient conditions.

Approaches like Dennett's set out to list the necessary and sufficient conditions for consciousness. In order to have a sense of *understanding* how the conscious can arise from the nonconscious we might need to survey the spectrum from the first rudimentary form of sentience up to our own. Unfortunately, whereas it is possible to study simpler life forms "from the outside" and learn their biological features, it is not possible to study simpler life forms "from the inside," experiencing their more primitive forms of consciousness. The question, then, is whether it is possible in imagination to retrace the steps from the beginning and thus to demystify consciousness.

To sum up, science has provided a massive amount of evidence suggesting that we need not postulate the existence of an entity such as a soul or mind in order to explain life and consciousness. Furthermore, philosophers have argued cogently that the belief in a substantial mind or soul is the result of confusion arising from how we talk. We have been misled by the fact that "mind" and "soul" are nouns into thinking that there must be an object to which these terms correspond. Rather, we say that a person is intelligent, and by this we mean that the person behaves or has the disposition to behave in certain ways; we do not mean to postulate the existence of a substance, intelligence. Similarly, when we say a person has a mind, we might better understand this to mean

28. Boston: Little, Brown, and Co., 1991.
29. Owen Flanagan apparently coined this term.
30. Gail Raney Fleishaker, "Three Models of a Minimal Cell," in *Prebiotic Self Organization of Matter,* eds. C. Ponnamperuma and F. R. Erlich (n.p.: A. Deepak Publishing, 1990), 235.

that the person displays a broad set of actions, capacities, and dispositions. Authors of some of the following chapters make a parallel move with regard to the soul.

What difference do all of these developments make from a theological perspective? In the following sections we consider some recent developments in theological accounts of the human person, and then survey related theological or doctrinal issues.

DEVELOPMENTS IN THEOLOGY AND BIBLICAL STUDIES

It appears that the question of the metaphysical makeup of the human person has not been perceived, throughout the course of Christian history, as a matter central to Christian teaching; the issue has arisen at several major turning points in church history but for the rest it has been relegated to the status of background assumption. Two points at which it became prominent have already been mentioned: the first was the adaptation of Christian teaching to the gentile world, and here assorted Greek and Roman philosophical positions were adopted and adapted. The second point was the Aristotelian revival in the Middle Ages, occasioning writings such as those of Thomas Aquinas.

For all of its repercussions elsewhere in theology, the Reformation seems not to have brought this issue to the forefront. Controversies regarding purgatory led to disputes about the "intermediate state" between death and the final resurrection. Martin Luther and some of the Radical Reformers argued that the soul either dies with the body or "sleeps" until the general resurrection; Calvin wrote a treatise titled *Psychopannychia* (1542) to contest such views. Yet even those who argued for the death of the soul were obviously presupposing a dualistic conception of the person.

The development of biblical criticism and critical church history in the modern period has again required examination of presuppositions concerning the nature of the person. Critical church history has provided moderns with a sense of the historical development of thought, which allows questions to arise in a new way about the consistency of present church teachings with those of the Bible.

Historical criticism of the Bible itself has had a major impact on modern conceptions of the person, but there have been contradictory tendencies. In the eighteenth and especially the nineteenth centuries many New Testament scholars cast doubt on the historicity of Jesus' resurrection.[31] Skepticism about res-

31. Among the most prominent was D. F. Strauss in *The Life of Jesus Critically Examined* (1835).

urrection led to increased emphasis among theologians on the immortality of the soul as the basis for Christian hope in an afterlife. Immanuel Kant's transcendental proof of the soul's immortality surely reinforced this move.

Meanwhile biblical scholars began to question whether body-soul dualism was in fact the position to be found in Scripture. One important contribution here was the work of H. Wheeler Robinson, an Old Testament scholar whose book *The Christian Doctrine of Man* went through three editions and eight printings between 1911 and 1952. Robinson argues that "the Hebrew idea of personality is that of an animated body, not (like the Greek) that of an incarnated soul." Surveying the Synoptic Gospels and the Pauline and Johannine writings, he argues that the psychological terminology and ideas of the New Testament are largely continuous with the Old Testament in conceiving of the person as a unity rather than dualistically. However, he also says that the most important advance in the New Testament is the belief that the essential personality (whether called the *psyche* or the *pneuma*) survives bodily death. This soul or spirit may be temporarily disembodied, but it is not complete without the body, and its continued existence after bodily death is dependent upon God rather than a natural endowment of the soul. So despite his claim that understanding of the history of anthropological dogma requires attention to the points of contrast and conflict between Hebrew and Greek conceptions of human nature, the contrasts in Robinson's own account between New Testament and Platonic conceptions turn out not to be so great as they might first appear.

Theological thinking on these issues around the time Robinson wrote can only be described as confused. This can be seen by comparing related entries in reference works from early in the twentieth century. In *The New Schaff-Herzog Encyclopedia of Religious Knowledge* (1910) there is a clear consensus on a dualist account of scriptural teaching.[32] C. A. Beckwith in "Biblical Conceptions of Soul and Spirit" claims that "the human soul is indeed bound to corporeality, yet it survives death because it possesses the Spirit of God as its immanent principle of life," and states that *soma* is opposed to *psyche* as *sarx* is to *pneuma* (11:12–14). In the same reference work, E. Schaeder describes resurrection in terms of God's giving new bodies to risen souls (9:496–497). G. Runze in "Immortality" claims that soul and body were sharply distinguished in the New Testament and that at death the soul rests in God until it receives a new glorified body (5:459, 462).

Yet in a slightly earlier work, *A Dictionary of the Bible* (1902), two sharply opposed views appear.[33] J. Laidlaw in his article on "Soul" says that through-

32. Samuel Macauley Jackson, ed. (New York and London: Funk and Wagnalls Company, 1910).
33. James Hastings, ed. (Edinburgh: T. & T. Clark, 1902).

out most of the Bible, "soul" is simply equivalent to the life embodied in living creatures (4:608). E. R. Bernard's article on "resurrection," however, describes resurrection as "the clothing of the soul with a body which has to be reconstituted," and points out that "the only self which we know is a self constituted of a body as well as a soul" (4:236).

This tendency to juxtapose incompatible accounts of biblical teaching continued through the middle of the century, when several new factors gave the issue greater prominence. One was the rise of neo-orthodox theology after World War I. Karl Barth and others made a sharp distinction between Hebraic and Hellenistic conceptions, and strongly favored the former. Barth also contributed to recognition of the centrality of the resurrection to Christian teaching. The biblical theology movement in the mid-twentieth century continued to press for the restoration of earlier, Hebraic understandings of Christianity.

A decisive contribution was Rudolf Bultmann's claim in his *Theology of the New Testament* that Paul uses *soma* to characterize the human person as a whole.[34] The following year John A. T. Robinson published *The Body: A Study in Pauline Theology*.[35] Although he was much influenced by H. Wheeler Robinson, we can see that the meaning of "holistic" anthropology has shifted decisively: whereas the earlier Robinson found a qualified dualism in Paul's writings—what some authors call "holistic dualism"—in Bultmann's and the later Robinson's view, Paul's teaching (as well as the Old Testament) is thoroughly physicalist.

A casual survey of the literature of theology and biblical studies throughout this century, then, shows a gradual replacement of a dualistic account of the person along with a view of the afterlife as immortality of the soul, first, by a recognition of the holistic character of biblical conceptions of the person, often while still presupposing temporarily separable "parts," and then by a holistic but also physicalist account of the person. One way of highlighting this shift is to note that in *The Encyclopedia of Religion and Ethics* (1909-1921) there is a lengthy article on "soul" and no entry for "resurrection."[36] In *The Anchor Bible Dictionary* (1992) there is no entry for "soul" but a very long set of articles on "resurrection."[37]

The foregoing picture of twentieth-century thought is an oversimplification, however, for several reasons. First, this century has seen the development in American Protestantism of two fairly distinct theological traditions. The account given above traces developments in what we may loosely call the lib-

---

34. Rudolf Bultmann, *Theology of the New Testament,* vol. 1 (New York: Scribner, 1951).
35. John A. T. Robinson, *The Body: A Study in Pauline Theology* (London: SCM, 1952).
36. James Hastings, ed. (New York: Charles Scribner's Sons, 1909-1921).
37. David Noel Freedman, ed. (New York: Doubleday, 1992).

eral tradition. Meanwhile, however, the tendency among conservatives has been to maintain a dualist (or trichotomist) account of the person, but also to stress resurrection, which is described as the restoration of a body to the soul. This tendency among conservative biblical scholars and theologians is not necessarily due to outright rejection of the textual studies mentioned above. Robert Gundry, for instance, has offered a point-by-point rebuttal to Bultmann's arguments in his book *Soma in Biblical Theology*.[38]

A second complication is Roman Catholic thought. Here there appears little difference between Catholic and Protestant biblical scholarship, but considerable difference between (official) Catholic theology and that of Protestant thinkers. In his *Dictionary of the Bible* John A. McKenzie discusses both *nephesh* and *psyche* under the heading of "soul," but emphasizes that in neither case is meant either a Platonic conception of soul or what it means "in common speech." The closest we can come to an adequate English translation of *nephesh* in the Old Testament is "life" or perhaps "self." In the New Testament, he says, the *psyche* is the totality of the self as a living and conscious subject, and "it is the totality of the self which is saved for eternal life."[39] In a *Theological Dictionary* published in the same year, however, the authors distinguish the Christian conception of the soul from a Platonic view—the Platonic soul is a being, whereas the Christian soul is a "real principle of being." This "personal spirituality cannot be derived from matter." Because it "stands over against and independent of mere natural being" it does not cease to exist at death.[40] This theological account is clearly indebted to a Thomistic metaphysic.

A third complication has been brought to light by Paul Badham. He claims that while biblical scholars generally understand resurrection as transformation of our physical bodies, those theologians who have any conception at all of life after death generally conceive of resurrection as "[being] clothed with new bodies in heaven."[41] What, then, constitutes the person *to which* the new body will be given? Theologians, he says, speak of "personality" (Hugh Montefiore, Russell Aldwinckle, David Winter), "personal identity" (Alec Vidler), "the persons we have become" (Peter Hodgson), "the full integrity of our humanity" (Aldwinckle), "the vital principle of what we are" (Charles Gore), "the law or ration of our constitution" (A. M. Ramsey), "our formal identity" (John Baillie), "our intelligence" (Hugh Burnaby), "our memory traces and dispositions" (Michael Paternoster), and "our soul or spirit" (Aldwinckle).

38. Robert H. Gundry, *Soma in Biblical Theology: With Emphasis on Pauline Anthropology* (Grand Rapids: Zondervan, 1987).
39. John L. McKenzie, S. J., *Dictionary of the Bible* (New York: Macmillan, 1965), 839.
40. Karl Rahner and Herbert Vorgrimler, *Theological Dictionary* (New York: Herder and Herder, 1965), 442–443.
41. Paul Badham, *Christian Beliefs about Life after Death* (London: Macmillan, 1976), 88.

In short, Badham says, "the eighteen writers I have mentioned above all share the view that there is an important sense in which I shall still be 'I,' although destined to live in a totally new embodiment in a new kind of existence" (87). Badham goes on to argue that this concept of re-embodiment requires a concept of the soul as its necessary condition (93).

So it is clear that recent theological and biblical scholarship has not conclusively settled the issue. Biblical scholars are closer to consensus than theologians, but the dichotomy "Greek dualism versus Hebraic holism" is an oversimplification, and the typical method used to address this issue—studies of word usage—is now recognized to be inadequate.[42]

Perhaps it should not be a surprise that there is lack of theological consensus when we consider the wide number of theological issues that need to be addressed if a physicalist account of the person is substituted for body-soul dualism. The preceding historical survey shows the close tie to eschatological issues. Resurrection of the body has been a mere adjunct to a doctrine of the immortality of the soul for centuries. If there is no substantial soul to survive bodily death then what is to be made of doctrines, formalized at the time of the Reformation specifying that the dead enjoy conscious relation to God prior to the general resurrection?[43] There are at least two options here. Some consider the biblical evidence for an intermediate state to be both scanty and ambiguous, and claim that the entire person simply disintegrates at death to be recreated by God at the general resurrection. Another approach is to question the meaningfulness of a time-line in discussing eschatological issues. That is, we presume that God is, in some sense, "outside" of time. If those who have died are "with God" we cannot meaningfully relate their experience to our creaturely history.

The metaphysical makeup of the person is but one aspect of a much broader topic of theological concern, now designated "Christian anthropology"; one theological task is to trace the consequences of a physicalist account of the person for a variety of issues, such as the place of humankind in the rest of nature, the source and nature of human sinfulness, the claim that humans are made in the image of God.[44]

The doctrine of the intermediate state is but a minor issue in comparison to the central Christian doctrines of Christology, salvation, and eschatology. A revised concept of the person has implications for thinking about the person of Christ. Recognition of the centrality of resurrection to Christian teaching, combined with recognition of the continuity of humans with the whole of nature, calls for reconsideration of the scope of God's final transformative act.

42. See Green, chapter 7 of this volume.
43. This teaching was made official for Catholicism by the Fifth Lateran Council in 1513. Calvin's statement in 1542 has settled the issue for many Protestants.
44. See Green, chapter 7 of this volume, and R. Anderson, chapter 8 of this volume.

There is increased motive to agree with such theologians as Wolfhart Pannenberg who argue that the resurrection of Jesus is a foretaste of the transformation awaiting the entire cosmos.[45] Paul hints at this in Romans: "For the creation waits with eager longing for the revealing of the children of God; for the creation was subjected to futility, not of its own will but by the will of the one who subjected it, in hope that the creation itself will be set free from its bondage to decay and will obtain the freedom of the glory of the children of God" (Rom. 8:19-21).

There are equally important issues to be re-examined in related areas of Christian thought. The concept of the soul has played a major role in the history of Christian ethics for centuries, for example, as justification for prohibition of abortion and euthanasia, and for differential treatment of animals and humans.[46] Where do these arguments stand with a revised concept of the nature of the person? The soul has also long been the focus of spiritual direction and pastoral counseling. There have been reactions in recent years against the asceticism fostered by Platonic dualism as well as against the tendency to distinguish between saving souls and caring for people's physical needs. There is much room for development of more holistic approaches to these issues.

WHERE DO WE STAND?

It is undeniable that a serious theological problem awaits solution. Philosophers see dualism as no longer tenable; the neurosciences have completed the Darwinian revolution, bringing the entire human being under the purview of the natural sciences. Scientists and philosophers alike associate dualism with Christianity, and the "evangelical atheists" among them (such as Daniel Dennett) use these scientific and philosophical developments as potent apologetic tools.

If the only options were dualism or the reductive materialism so often promoted in the secular academy, Christians would face a major intellectual crisis. Our claim, however, is that these are not the only options; a third position exists that is not only theologically and biblically sound but consistent with current philosophy and science as well.

It may be helpful to summarize current options for accounts of the nature of the person as follows:

1. *Radical dualism:* the soul (or mind) is separable from the body, and the person is identified with the former.
2. *Holistic dualism:* the person is a composite of separable "parts" but is to be identified with the whole, whose normal functioning is as a unity.

45. Wolfhart Pannenberg, *Jesus: God and Man* (Philadelphia: Westminster, 1968).
46. See Post, chapter 9 this volume.

3. *Nonreductive physicalism:* the person is a physical organism whose complex functioning, both in society and in relation to God, gives rise to "higher" human capacities such as morality and spirituality.
4. *Eliminative/reductive materialism:* the person is a physical organism, whose emotional, moral, and religious experiences will all ultimately be explained by the physical sciences.

It is clear that neither position 1 nor 4 is compatible with Christian teaching. While 2 is consistent with (much of) Christian teaching, we have judged it worthwhile to consider the plausibility of 3, nonreductive physicalism, in that it is clearly more compatible with developments in science and philosophy.

Nonreductive physicalism requires defense from two sorts of objections. Physicalism needs theological and exegetical defense in light of earlier arguments (or assumptions) in favor of dualism. Such defense need not focus on arguments against dualism, but rather on the exploration of how a physicalist account of the person can be used theologically, ethically, and pastorally. This exploration must include a renewed examination of human distinctiveness: What is it about the *human* animal that matters to God? In what does human capacity to "image" God consist? But equally important are arguments for a real distinction between this nonreductive account and reductive materialism. The remaining chapters of the present volume contribute to this exploration and defense.

Chapter Two: In "Human Nature: One Evolutionist's View," Francisco J. Ayala recalls the biblical claim that humans are made in the image of God. How is this to be reconciled with an evolutionary history showing our continuity with the animal world? Ayala begins with a review of human evolutionary history. His account of continuity in the complex lineage leading to modern humans dispels the illusion that we can make a sharp distinction between ourselves and the other animals.

In what, then, does our distinctiveness lie? Ayala emphasizes that relatively small anatomical differences have enabled the process of cultural evolution, which transcends biological evolution in shaping the human species. A clear example of this transcendence is human morality. Ayala argues that the proclivity to make moral judgments evolved, not because it was itself adaptive, but rather because it is a consequence of three other developments with high survival value: the ability to anticipate the consequences of one's actions, to make value judgments, and to choose among alternative courses of action. Thus, we are ethical beings by biological nature. However, the fact that the proclivity to make moral judgments can be explained in evolutionary terms does not entail that *moral norms* are a product of biological evolution. Moral norms are instead products of cultural evolution, including the development of religious traditions. Ayala thus provides a powerful argument against evolutionists who attempt to reduce the content of morality to that which is necessary for survival of the species.

Chapter Three: In "A Genetic View of Human Nature," V. Elving Anderson points out that recent developments in genetics—mapping of the human genome, cloning, the discovery of the "obesity gene"—raise the question whether genes determine human nature. Anderson replies that while "the gene story" is, in some ways, surprisingly simple—a genetic code involving only four nucleotides—this story must be interpreted with care: Genes never act alone but always in interaction with other biological and environmental factors. The effect of genes on behavior, especially human behavior, is always indirect. Studies comparing various characteristics of twins, including personality variables and even church attendance, show varying degrees of genetic influence. However, even identical genetic endowment combined with essentially identical early environments do not produce identical characteristics.

Anderson concludes that while genes are ontologically necessary for human existence and for possession of the qualities that are considered essential components of human nature, they are by no means sufficient determinants. "Our capacities for moral and spiritual activity are genetically conditioned, but our use of them remains a matter of personal choice." Thus, Anderson shows that scientific understanding of the role of genetics in human behavior no more entails reductive materialism than does the evolutionary account of the development of those capacities.

Chapter Four: In "Brain, Mind, and Behavior," Malcolm Jeeves states that in light of advances in cognitive neuroscience the relation between mind and brain can best be described by speaking of *one set of events,* studied and analyzed from two aspects, physical and mental; there are no "mental" events that are without a physical realization in the brain, yet neurophysiological analysis will never give an adequate account of those events.

Jeeves reports some of the history leading up to the recognition of the role of the brain in cognitive and emotional life, and he provides a survey of some of the localization research tying cognitive processes and social behavior to specific regions of the brain. While recognizing that these results are open to a variety of interpretations, including the dualism of Sir John Eccles, Jeeves argues for a nonreductive physicalist account, and considers some of the theological and philosophical issues this interpretation entails. He concludes that such a view does not rule out free will and personal responsibility and is consistent with Christian belief so long as the results of the past 100 years of biblical criticism are taken into account. Furthermore, recognition of the neurobiological substrate of our spiritual capacities contributes significantly to our self-understanding.

Chapter Five: In "Cognitive Contributions to the Soul," Warren S. Brown begins with a rejection of body-soul dualism, but raises the question: if there is no substantial soul, then what accounts for the human capacities once attributed to the soul in the Christian tradition? He claims that the most important functions of the soul involve personal relations: the capacity for self-relatedness, relations with other humans, and relation with God. Next he asks: what cognitive capacities do humans have (in distinction from the other higher primates) that make such personal relations possible? The capacities he recognizes are language, a theory of other minds, episodic memory, conscious top-down agency, future orientation, and emotional modulation of social behavior.

These cognitive capacities are *emergent* in the human species. Emergent properties appear as a result of a significant increase in some set of lower-level abilities. While emergent properties (such as full-scale language) are dependent on lower-level abilities, they cannot be totally accounted for in terms of the lower-level abilities. Thus, Brown suggests that we use "soul" to designate not a separable part of the person but rather the person's *emergent* property of capacity for personal relatedness. This capacity, then, is dependent on but not reducible to the neurological features enabling higher forms of cognition.

Chapter Six: In "Nonreductive Physicalism: Philosophical Issues," Nancey Murphy addresses three problems facing a physicalist account of the person. First, how can a physicalist account of the person fail to be reductive? That is, we assume that neurobiological processes are governed by natural laws. If mental events such as intending to do a good act or believing that a theory is true are also neurological events, as Jeeves has argued, then how can it not be the case that actions and beliefs are merely the product of blind biological processes. To answer this question, Murphy pursues the issues of emergence and top-down causation raised by Brown.

Second, Jeeves has pointed out that nothing in science can prove dualism false or physicalism true. What, then, is the epistemological status of nonreductive physicalism? Murphy uses recent developments in philosophy of science to argue that while the scientific evidence presented in previous chapters does not provide proof, it does provide reasonable scientific evidence for physicalism.

Third, a number of authors in this book emphasize the centrality in Christian conceptions of the person of our ability to be in relationship with God (Brown, Green, Anderson). The soul has traditionally been seen as that which enables us to relate to God. What accounts for this capacity in a physicalist theory of the person? Brown has already discussed the cognitive abilities that enable personal relatedness. In this chapter Murphy surveys types of religious experience and argues that the same faculties that enable our higher cognitive and emotional experience also account for our capacity for religious experience.

Chapter Seven: In " 'Bodies—That Is, Human Lives': A Re-Examination of Human Nature in the Bible," Joel B. Green points out the difficulties involved in an attempt to reconstruct biblical views of the composition of the person. New Testament writers worked against the background of a variety of conflicting accounts, and the questions we raise from our particular historical location are not the questions with which the writers of either the Hebrew or New Testament Scriptures were concerned.

Green explores texts from Luke and Paul and concludes that the New Testament is not as dualistic as the traditions of Christian theology and biblical interpretation have taught us to think. In fact, the dominant view of the human person in the New Testament is that of ontological monism, with such notions as "escape from the body" or "disembodied soul" falling outside the parameters of New Testament thought. The central concern of these New Testament writers is the concept of soteriological wholism; in their portraits of human nature they place a premium on the person's relatedness to God and to others. Furthermore, the emphasis on anthropological monism in the New Testament underscores the cosmic repercussions of reconciliation; the fate of the human family cannot be dissociated from that of the cosmos.

Chapter Eight: In "On Being Human: The Spiritual Saga of a Creaturely Soul," Ray S. Anderson argues that the term "soul" can be rescued from dualistic understandings and employed as a meaningful theological term designating a distinctive *aspect* of the person. Current use of "soul" in our culture reflects a concern for the deeper aspects of human life such as the ethical and spiritual dimensions.

This chapter presents a theology of human nature that views human life as emerging from the physical elements of the created world, engaged in social interactions with other humans, and destined to share in the Creator's own eternal life. This threefold orientation does not divide humans into two or three discrete entities, nor does it mean that there are three successive stages to human life. Anderson concurs with Green that biblical texts do not support a dualist view of body and soul. While there are different emphases intended when the Bible speaks of the soul, spirit, and body, these terms do not denote entities within the person but the whole person.

Anderson proposes that we use the word "soul" to describe the core unity of the person. This life/soul is dependent upon God for continued existence; apart from divine intervention death ends human life. The resurrection of Jesus is the basis for Christian hope for continuing survival.

Chapter Nine: In "A Moral Case for Nonreductive Physicalism," Stephen G. Post asks: what might be the practical moral considerations raised by an anthropology that denies the existence of a substantial, immortal soul? Undoubtedly body-soul dualism has played an important and often positive role in the history of Christian ethics and Western ethics generally. It has served as the basis for arguments for the value of all human life, including those with diminished capacities. However, Post argues, certain forms of body-soul dualism have also been implicated in justifications for slavery, an inferior status for women, and degradation of marriage.

Post suggests that an ethical approach based on the Christian story better provides for the inclusion of all human beings within the sphere of ethical concern. Thus, the shift from a dualist to a nonreductive physicalist account of the person entails no significant loss of resources for Christian ethics and in fact this "agapic inclusivist tradition" may well be enhanced by a physical- ist anthropology.

Chapter Two

Human Nature: One Evolutionist's View

Francisco J. Ayala

It is a disgraceful and dangerous thing for an infidel to hear a Christian, while presumably giving the meaning of Holy Scripture, talking nonsense. We should take all means to prevent such an embarrassing situation, in which people show up vast ignorance in a Christian and laugh it to scorn. . . . If they find a Christian mistaken in a field which they themselves know well, and hear him maintaining his foolish opinions about the Scriptures, how then are they going to believe those Scriptures in matters concerning the resurrection of the dead, the hope of eternal life, and the kingdom of heaven?

—St. Augustine, *The Literal Meaning of Genesis,* Book 1, Chapter 19.

"IN THE IMAGE OF GOD"

The Book of Genesis dramatically sets forth humans' lofty uniqueness within the natural world: "So God created humankind in his image, in the image of God he created them; male and female he created them" (Gen. 1:27).

It does not take a great deal of biological expertise to realize that humans have organs and limbs similar to those of other animals; that we bear our young like other mammals; that, bone by bone, there is a precise correspondence between the skeletons of a chimpanzee and a human. But it does not take much reflection to notice the unique distinctiveness of our species. There is the bipedal gait and the enlarged brain. Much more conspicuous than the anatomical differences are the distinct behaviors and their outcomes. Humans have elaborate social and political institutions, codes of law, literature and art, ethics and religion; humans build roads and cities, travel by motorcars, ships, and airplanes, and communicate by means of telephones, computers, and televisions.

I will first, in the pages that follow, set forth the biological continuity between humans and animals. I will outline what we currently know about the evolutionary history of humans for the last four million years, from bipedal but small-brained *Australopithecus* to modern *Homo sapiens,* our species, through the prolific toolmaker *Homo habilis* and the continent-wanderer *Homo erectus.* The genes of living humans manifest that our ancestors were no fewer than several thousand individuals at any one time in the history of these hominid species.

I will then identify anatomical traits that distinguish us from other animals and point out our two kinds of heredity, the biological and the cultural. Biological inheritance is based on the transmission of genetic information, very much the same in humans as in other sexually reproducing organisms. But cultural inheritance is distinctively human, based on transmission of information by a teaching and learning process, which is, in principle, independent of biological parentage. Cultural inheritance makes possible the cumulative transmission of experience from generation to generation. Cultural heredity is a swifter and more effective mode of adaptation to the environment than the biological mode because it can be designed. The advent of cultural heredity ushered in cultural evolution, which transcends biological evolution.

In the latter part of this essay I will explore ethical behavior as a model case of a distinctive human trait and seek to ascertain the causal connections between human ethics and human biology. My conclusions are that (1) the proclivity to make ethical judgments, that is, to evaluate actions as either good or evil, is rooted in our (biological) nature, a necessary outcome of our exalted intelligence; but (2) the moral codes that guide our decisions as to which actions are good and which ones are evil are products of culture, including social and religious traditions. This second conclusion contradicts evolutionists and sociobiologists who claim that the morally good is simply that which is promoted by the process of biological evolution.

The biological mechanisms that have brought about the evolution of the human species are essentially the same as those involved in the evolution of other animal species. But with the advent of *Homo sapiens* biological evolution transcended itself and ushered in culture, the life of the mind and its products. In the text that follows, I seek to provide what I see as a necessary dimension, the biological, of any view of human nature that seeks to be relevant and complete. But in order to understand ourselves and our place in the economy of things, we need much more than biological knowledge. We need psychology and sociology, as well as history, aesthetics, and philosophy; and if we seek religious understanding, we will profit from theology.

HUMANKIND'S BIOLOGICAL ORIGINS

Humankind is a biological species that has evolved from other nonhuman species. In order to understand human nature, we must know our biological makeup and whence we come, the story of our humbler beginnings. For a century after the publication of Charles Darwin's *On the Origin of Species* (1859), the story of evolution was reconstructed with evidence from paleontology (the study of fossils), biogeography (the study of the geographical distribution of organisms), and from the comparative study of living organisms: their morphology, development, physiology, and the like. Since mid-twentieth century we have, in addition, molecular biology, the most informative and precise discipline for reconstructing the ancestral relationships of living species.

Our closest biological relatives are the great apes and, among them, the chimpanzees, who are more closely related to us than they are to the gorillas, and much more closely than to the orangutans. The hominid lineage diverged from the chimpanzee lineage 5 to 7 million years ago (Mya) and it evolved exclusively in the African continent until the emergence of *Homo erectus*, somewhat before 1.8 Mya. The first known hominid, *Ardipithecus ramidus*, lived 4.4 Mya, but it is not certain that it was bipedal or in the direct line of descent to modern humans, *Homo sapiens*. The recently described *Australopithecus anamensis*, dated 3.9 to 4.2 Mya, was bipedal and has been placed in the line of descent to *Australopithecus afarensis*, *Homo habilis*, *H. erectus*, and *H. sapiens*. Other hominids, not in the direct line of descent to modern humans, are *Australopithecus africanus*, *Paranthropus aethiopicus*, *P. boisei*, and *P. robustus*, who lived in Africa at various times between 3 and 1 Mya, a period when three or four hominid species lived contemporaneously in the African continent.

Shortly after its emergence in tropical or subtropical eastern Africa, *H. erectus* spread to other continents. Fossil remains of *H. erectus* are known from Africa, Indonesia (Java), China, the Middle East, and Europe. *H. erectus* fossils from Java have been dated $1.81+0.04$ and $1.66+0.04$ Mya, and from Georgia between 1.6 and 1.8 Mya. Anatomically distinctive *H. erectus* fossils have been found in Spain, deposited before 780,000 years ago, the oldest in southern Europe.

The transition from *H. erectus* to *H. sapiens* occurred around 400,000 years ago, although this date is not well determined owing to uncertainty as to whether some fossils are *erectus* or "archaic" forms of *sapiens*. *H. erectus* persisted for some time in Asia, until 250,000 years ago in China, and perhaps until 100,000 ago in Java, and thus was coetaneous with early members of its descendant species, *H. sapiens*. Fossil remains of Neanderthal hominids (*Homo neanderthalensis*), with brains as large as those of *H. sapiens*, appeared in Europe around 200,000 years ago and persisted until 30,000 or 40,000 years ago. The

Neanderthals were thought to be ancestral to anatomically modern humans, but now we know that modern humans appeared at least 100,000 years ago, much before the disappearance of the Neanderthals. Moreover, in caves in the Middle East, fossils of modern humans have been found dated 120,000 to 100,000 years ago, as well as Neanderthals dated at 60,000 and 70,000 years ago, followed again by modern humans dated at 40,000 years ago. It is unclear whether the two forms repeatedly replaced one another by migration from other regions, or whether they coexisted in the same areas. Recent genetic evidence indicates that interbreeding between *sapiens* and *neanderthalensis* never occurred.

There is considerable controversy about the origin of modern humans. Some anthropologists argue that the transition from *H. erectus* to archaic *H. sapiens* and later to anatomically modern humans occurred consonantly in various parts of the Old World. Proponents of this "multiregional model" emphasize fossil evidence showing regional continuity in the transition from *H. erectus* to archaic and then modern *H. sapiens*. In order to account for the transition from one to another species (something that cannot happen independently in several places), they postulate that genetic exchange occurred from time to time between populations, so that the species evolved as a single gene pool, even though geographic differentiation occurred and persisted, just as geographically differentiated populations exist in other animal species, as well as in living humans. This explanation depends on the occurrence of persistent migrations and interbreeding between populations from different continents, of which no direct evidence exists. Moreover, it is difficult to reconcile the multiregional model with the contemporary existence of different species or forms in different regions, such as the persistence of *H. erectus* in China and Java for more than 100,000 years after the emergence of *H. sapiens*.

Other scientists argue instead that modern humans first arose in Africa or in the Middle East somewhat prior to 100,000 years ago and from there spread throughout the world, replacing elsewhere the preexisting populations of *H. erectus* or archaic *H. sapiens*. Some proponents of this "African replacement" model claim further that the transition from archaic to modern *H. sapiens* was associated with a very narrow bottleneck, consisting of only two or very few individuals who are the ancestors of all modern humans. This particular claim of a narrow bottleneck is supported, erroneously as I will soon show, by the investigation of a peculiar small fraction of our genetic inheritance, the mitochondrial DNA (mtDNA). The African (or Middle East) origin of modern humans is, however, supported by a wealth of recent genetic evidence and is, therefore, favored by many evolutionists.

The Myth of the Mitochondrial Eve

The genetic information we inherit from our parents is encoded in the linear sequence of the DNA's four nucleotide components (represented by A, C, G, T) in the same fashion as semantic information is encoded in the sequence of letters of a written text. Most of the DNA is contained in the chromosomes inside the cell nucleus. The total amount of DNA in a human cell nucleus consists of six-thousand million nucleotides, half in each set of 23 chromosomes inherited from each parent. A relatively small amount of DNA, about 16,000 nucleotides, exists in the mitochondria, cell organelles outside the nucleus. The mtDNA is inherited in a peculiar manner, that is, exclusively along the maternal line. The inheritance of the mtDNA is a gender mirror image of the inheritance of the family name. Sons and daughters inherit their mtDNA from their mother but only the daughters transmit it to their progeny, just as sons and daughters receive the family name of the father, but only the sons transmit it to their children.

Analysis of the mtDNA from ethnically diverse individuals has shown that the mtDNA sequences of modern humans coalesce to one ancestral sequence, the "mitochondrial Eve" that existed in Africa about 200,000 years ago.[1] This Eve, however, is not the one mother from whom all humans descend, but an mtDNA molecule (or the woman carrier of that molecule) from whom all modern mtDNA *molecules* descend.

Some science writers have drawn the inference that all humans descend from only one, or very few women, but this is based on a confusion between gene genealogies and individual genealogies. Gene genealogies gradually coalesce toward a unique DNA ancestral sequence (in a similar fashion as living species, such as humans, chimpanzees, and gorillas, coalesce into one ancestral species). Individual genealogies, on the contrary, increase by a factor of two in each ancestral generation: an individual has two parents, four grandparents, and so on.[2] Coalescence of a gene genealogy into one ancestral gene, originally present in one individual, does not disallow the contemporary existence of many other individuals, who are also our ancestors, and from whom we have inherited the other genes.

This conclusion can be illustrated with an analogy. My family name is shared by many people who live in Spain, Mexico, the Philippines, and other countries. A historian of our family name has concluded that all Ayalas descend

1. A. C. Wilson and R. L. Cann, "The Recent African Genesis of Humans," *Scientific American* (April 1992): 68-73.
2. The theoretical number of ancestors for any one individual becomes enormous after some tens of generations, but "inbreeding" occurs: after some generations, ancestors appear more than once in the genealogy.

from Don Lope Sánchez de Ayala, grandson of Don Vela, vassal of King Alfonso VI, who established the domain *señorío* de Ayala in the year 1085, in the now Spanish Basque province of Alava. Don Lope is the Adam from whom we all descend on the paternal line, but we also descend from many other men and women who lived in the eleventh century, as well as earlier and later.

The inference warranted by the mtDNA analysis is that the mitochondrial Eve is the ancestor of modern humans in the *maternal line*. Any person has a single ancestor in the maternal line in any given generation. Thus, a person inherits the mtDNA from the mother, from the maternal grandmother, from the great-grandmother on the maternal line, and so on. But the person also inherits other genes from other ancestors. The mtDNA that we have inherited from the mitochondrial Eve represents .400 of the DNA present in any modern human (16,000 out of 6 billion nucleotides). The rest of the DNA, 400,000 times more than the mtDNA, we have inherited from other contemporaries of the mitochondrial Eve.

From how many contemporaries? The issue of how many human ancestors we had in the past has been elucidated by investigating the genes of the human immune system.[3] The genes of the human leucocyte antigen (HLA) complex exist in multiple versions, which provide people with the diversity necessary to confront bacteria and other pathogens that invade the body. The evolutionary history of some of these genes shows that they coalesce into one ancestral gene 30 to 60 Mya, that is, much before the divergence of humans and apes. (Indeed, humans and apes share many of these genes.) The mathematical theory of gene coalescence makes it possible to estimate the number of ancestors that must have lived in any one generation in order to account for the preservation of so many diverse genes through hundreds of thousands of generations. The estimated *effective* number is about 100,000 individuals per generation. This "effective" number of individuals is an average rather than a constant number, but it is a peculiar kind of average (a "harmonic mean"), compatible with much larger but not much smaller numbers of individuals in different generations. Thus, through millions of years our ancestors existed in populations that were 100,000 individuals strong, or larger. Population bottlenecks may have occurred in rare occasions. But the genetic evidence indicates that human populations never consisted of fewer than several thousand individuals.[4]

Human Uniqueness
The most distinctive human anatomical traits are erect posture and large brain. We are the only vertebrate species with a bipedal gait and erect posture; birds

3. F. J. Ayala, "The Myth of Eve: Molecular Biology and Human Origins," *Science* 270 (1995): 1930-1936.
4. Ibid.

are bipedal, but their backbone stands horizontal rather than vertical. Brain size is generally proportional to body size; relative to body mass, humans have the largest (and most complex) brain. The chimpanzee's brain weighs less than a pound; a gorilla's slightly more. The human male adult brain is 1,400 cubic centimeters (cc), about three pounds in weight.

Evolutionists used to raise the question whether bipedal gait or large brain came first, or whether they evolved consonantly. The issue is now resolved. Our *Australopithecus* ancestors had, since four million years ago, a bipedal gait, but a small brain, about 450 cc, a pound in weight. Brain size starts to increase notably with our *Homo habilis* ancestors, about 2.5 Mya, who had a brain about 650 cc and also were prolific tool-makers (hence the name *habilis*). Between one and two million years afterwards, there lived *Homo erectus*, with adult brains about 1,200 cc. Our species, *Homo sapiens*, has a brain about three times as large as that of *Australopithecus*, 1,300-1,400 cc, or some three pounds of gray matter. Our brain is not only much larger than that of chimpanzees or gorillas, but also much more complex. The cerebral cortex, where the higher cognitive functions are processed, is in humans disproportionately much greater than the rest of the brain when compared to apes.

Erect posture and large brain are not the only anatomical traits that distinguish us from nonhuman primates, even if they may be the most obvious. A list of our most distinctive anatomical features includes the following (of which the last five items are not detectable in fossils):

1. Erect posture and bipedal gait (entail changes of the backbone, hipbone, and feet)
2. Opposing thumbs and arm and hand changes (make possible precise manipulation)
3. Large brain
4. Reduction of jaws and remodeling of face
5. Changes in skin and skin glands
6. Reduction in body hair
7. Cryptic ovulation (and extended female sexual receptivity)
8. Slow development
9. Modification of vocal tract and larynx
10. Reorganization of the brain

Humans are notably different from other animals not only in anatomy, but also and no less importantly in their behavior, both as individuals and socially. A list of distinctive human behavioral traits includes the following:[5]

5. A discussion of some of these traits can be found in Brown, chapter 5 of this volume..

1. Subtle expression of emotions
2. Intelligence: abstract thinking, categorizing, and reasoning
3. Symbolic (creative) language
4. Self-awareness and death-awareness
5. Tool-making and technology
6. Science, literature, and art
7. Ethics and religion
8. Social organization and cooperation (division of labor)
9. Legal codes and political institutions

Biological Evolution and Cultural Evolution

Humans live in groups that are socially organized, and so do other primates. But primate societies do not approach the complexity of human social organization. A distinctive human social trait is culture, which may be understood as the set of nonstrictly biological human activities and creations. Culture includes social and political institutions, ways of doing things, religious and ethical traditions, language, common sense and scientific knowledge, art and literature, technology, and in general all the creations of the human mind. The advent of culture has brought with it cultural evolution, a superorganic mode of evolution superimposed on the organic mode, which has in the last few millennia become the dominant mode of human evolution. Cultural evolution has come about because of cultural change and inheritance, a distinctively human mode of achieving adaptation to the environment and transmitting it through the generations.

There are in humankind two kinds of heredity—the biological and the cultural, which may also be called organic and superorganic, or *endosomatic* and *exosomatic* systems of heredity. Biological inheritance in humans is very much like that in any other sexually reproducing organism; it is based on the transmission of genetic information encoded in DNA from one generation to the next by means of the sex cells. Cultural inheritance, in contrast, is based on transmission of information by a teaching-learning process, which is in principle independent of biological parentage. Culture is transmitted by instruction and learning, by example and imitation, through books, newspapers and radio, television and motion pictures, through works of art, and by any other means of communication. Culture is acquired by every person from parents, relatives and neighbors, and from the whole human environment.

Cultural inheritance makes possible for humans what no other organism can accomplish—the cumulative transmission of experience from generation to generation. Animals can learn from experience, but they do not transmit their experiences, their "discoveries" (at least not to any large extent) to the following generations. Animals have individual memory, but they do not have a "social memory." Humans, on the other hand, have developed a culture because they can transmit cumulatively their experiences from generation to generation.

Cultural inheritance makes possible cultural evolution, that is, the evolution of knowledge, social structures, ethics, and all other components that make up human culture. Cultural inheritance makes possible a new mode of adaptation to the environment that is not available to nonhuman organisms—adaptation by means of culture. Organisms in general adapt to the environment by means of natural selection, by changing over generations their genetic constitution to suit the demands of the environment. But humans, and humans alone, can also adapt by changing the environment to suit the needs of their genes. (Animals build nests and modify their environment also in other ways, but the manipulation of the environment by any nonhuman species is trivial compared to humankind's.) For the last few millennia humans have been adapting the environments to their genes more often than their genes to the environments.

In order to extend its geographical habitat, or to survive in a changing environment, a population of organisms must become adapted, through slow accumulation of genetic variants sorted out by natural selection, to the new climatic conditions, different sources of food, different competitors, and so on. The discovery of fire and the use of shelter and clothing allowed humans to spread from the warm tropical and subtropical regions of the Old World to the whole earth, except for the frozen wastes of Antarctica, without the anatomical development of fur or hair. Humans did not wait for genetic mutants promoting wing development; they have conquered the air in a somewhat more efficient and versatile way by building flying machines. People travel the rivers and the seas without gills or fins. The exploration of outer space has started without waiting for mutations providing humans with the ability to breathe with low oxygen pressures or to function in the absence of gravity; astronauts carry their own oxygen and specially equipped pressure suits. From their obscure beginnings in Africa, humans have become the most widespread and abundant species of mammal on earth. It was the appearance of culture as a superorganic form of adaptation that made humankind the most successful animal species.

Cultural adaptation has prevailed in humankind over biological adaptation because it is a more rapid mode of adaptation and because it can be directed. A favorable genetic mutation newly arisen in an individual can be transmitted to a sizable part of the human species only through innumerable generations. However, a new scientific discovery or technical achievement can be transmitted to the whole of humankind, potentially at least, in less than one generation. Moreover, whenever a need arises, culture can directly pursue the appropriate changes to meet the challenge. On the contrary, biological adaptation depends on the accidental availability of a favorable mutation, or of a combination of several mutations, at the time and place where the need arises.

AN EVOLUTIONARY ACCOUNT OF ETHICS

Erect posture and large brain are distinctive anatomical features of modern humans. High intelligence, symbolic language, religion, and ethics are some of the behavioral traits that distinguish us from other animals. The account of human origins that I have sketched above implies a continuity in the evolutionary process that goes from our nonhuman ancestors of eight million years ago through primitive hominids to modern humans. A scientific explanation of that evolutionary sequence must account for the emergence of human anatomical and behavioral traits in terms of natural selection together with other distinctive biological causes and processes. One explanatory strategy is to focus on a particular human feature and seek to identify the conditions under which this feature may have been favored by natural selection. Such a strategy may lead to erroneous conclusions as a consequence of the fallacy of selective attention: some traits may have come about not because they are themselves adaptive, but rather because they are associated with traits that are favored by natural selection.

Geneticists have long recognized the phenomenon of "pleiotropy," the expression of a gene in different organs or anatomical traits. It follows that a gene that becomes changed owing to its effects on a certain trait will result in the modification of other traits as well. The changes of these other traits are epigenetic consequences of the changes directly promoted by natural selection. The cascade of consequences may be, particularly in the case of humans, very long and far from obvious in some cases. Literature, art, science, and technology are among the behavioral features that may have come about not because they were adaptively favored in human evolution but because they are expressions of the high intellectual abilities present in modern humans: what may have been favored by natural selection (its "target") was an increase in intellectual ability rather than each one of those particular activities.

I now will briefly explore ethics and ethical behavior as a model case of how we may seek the evolutionary explanation of a distinctively human trait. I select ethical behavior because morality is a human trait that seems remote from biological processes. My goal is to ascertain whether an account can be advanced of ethical behavior as an outcome of biological evolution and, if such is the case, whether ethical behavior was directly promoted by natural selection, or has rather come about as an epigenetic manifestation of some other trait that was the target of natural selection.

I will argue that ethical behavior (the proclivity to judge human actions as either good or evil) has evolved as a consequence of natural selection, not because it was adaptive in itself, but rather as a pleiotropic consequence of the high intelligence characteristic of humans. The question whether ethical behavior is biologically determined may refer either to (1) the *capacity* for ethics (i.e., the proclivity to judge human actions as either right or wrong) and which I will refer to as "ethical behavior," or (2) the moral *norms* or moral codes accepted by human beings for guiding their actions. My theses are first that the capacity for ethics is a necessary attribute of human nature, and thus a product of biological evolution and, second, that moral norms are products of cultural evolution, not of biological evolution.

My first thesis is grounded on the argument that humans exhibit ethical behavior because their biological makeup determines the presence of the three necessary, and jointly sufficient, conditions for ethical behavior; namely, the ability to anticipate the consequences of one's own actions, to make value judgments, and to choose between alternative courses of action. I thus maintain that ethical behavior came about in evolution not because it is adaptive in itself but as a necessary consequence of our species' eminent intellectual abilities, which are an attribute directly promoted by natural selection.

My second thesis contradicts the proposal of many distinguished evolutionists who, since Darwin's time, have argued that the norms of morality are derived from biological evolution. It also contradicts the sociobiologists, who have recently developed a subtle version of that proposal. The sociobiologists' argument is that human ethical norms are sociocultural correlates of behaviors fostered by biological evolution. I argue that such proposals are misguided and do not escape the naturalistic fallacy. It is true that both natural selection and moral norms sometimes coincide on the same behavior; that is, the two are consistent. But this isomorphism between the behaviors promoted by natural selection and those sanctioned by moral norms exists only with respect to the consequences of the behaviors; the underlying causations are completely disparate.

Ethics and Language: A Parallel Distinction

I have just noted that the question of whether ethical behavior is biologically determined may refer to either one of the following issues: (1) Is the capacity for ethics—the proclivity to judge human actions as either right or wrong—determined by the biological nature of human beings? (2) Are the systems or codes of ethical norms accepted by human beings biologically determined? A similar distinction can be made with respect to language. The issue whether the capacity for symbolic language is determined by our biological nature is different from the question of whether the particular language we speak (English, Spanish, or Japanese) is biologically necessary.

The first question posed is more fundamental; it asks whether or not the biological nature of *Homo sapiens* is such that humans are necessarily inclined to make moral judgments and to accept ethical values, to identify certain actions as either right or wrong. Affirmative answers to this first question do not necessarily determine what the answer to the second question should be. Independently of whether or not humans are necessarily ethical, it remains to be determined whether particular moral prescriptions are in fact determined by our biological nature, or whether they are chosen by society, or by individuals. Even if we were to conclude that people cannot avoid having moral standards of conduct, it might be that the choice of the particular standards used for judgment would be arbitrary or that it depended on some other, nonbiological criteria. The need for having moral values does not necessarily tell us what these moral values should be, just as the capacity for language does not determine which language we shall speak.

I propose that humans are ethical beings by their biological nature. Humans evaluate their behavior as either right or wrong, moral or immoral, as a consequence of their eminent intellectual capacities, which include self-awareness and abstract thinking. These intellectual capacities are products of the evolutionary process, but they are distinctively human. Thus, I maintain that ethical behavior is not causally related to the social behavior of animals, including kin and reciprocal "altruism."

My second thesis is that the moral norms according to which we evaluate particular actions as morally either good or bad (as well as the grounds that may be used to justify the moral norms) are products of cultural evolution, not of biological evolution. The norms of morality belong, in this respect, to the same category of phenomena as the languages spoken by different peoples, their political and religious institutions, and the arts, sciences, and technology. The moral codes, like these other products of human culture, are often consistent with the biological predispositions of the human species, dispositions we may to some extent share with other animals. But this consistency between ethical norms and biological tendencies is not necessary or universal: it does not apply to all ethical norms in a given society, much less in all human societies.

Moral codes, like any other dimensions of cultural systems, depend on the existence of human biological nature and must be consistent with it in the sense that they could not counteract it without promoting their own demise. Moreover, the acceptance and persistence of moral norms is facilitated whenever they are consistent with biologically conditioned human behaviors. But the moral norms are independent of such behaviors in the sense that some norms may not favor, and may hinder, the survival and reproduction of the individual and its genes, which are the targets of biological evolution.

Discrepancies between accepted moral rules and biological survival are, however, necessarily limited in scope or would otherwise lead to the extinction of the groups accepting such discrepant rules.

The Necessary Conditions for Ethical Behavior

The question whether ethical behavior is determined by our biological nature must be answered in the affirmative. By "ethical behavior" I mean here to refer to the *judging* of human actions as either good or bad, which is not the same as "good behavior" (i.e., *doing* what is perceived as good instead of what is perceived as evil). Humans exhibit ethical behavior by nature because their biological constitution determines the presence of the three necessary, and jointly sufficient, conditions for ethical behavior. These conditions are: (1) the ability to anticipate the consequences of one's own actions; (2) the ability to make value judgments; and (3) the ability to choose between alternative courses of action. I shall briefly examine each of these abilities and show that they are consequences of the eminent intellectual capacity of human beings.

The ability to anticipate the consequences of one's own actions is the most fundamental of the three conditions required for ethical behavior. Only if I can anticipate that pulling the trigger will shoot the bullet, which in turn will strike and kill my enemy, can the action of pulling the trigger be evaluated as nefarious. Pulling a trigger is not in itself a moral act; it becomes so by virtue of its relevant consequences. My action has an ethical dimension only if I do anticipate these consequences.

The ability to anticipate the consequences of one's actions is closely related to the ability to establish the connection between means and ends; that is, of seeing a means precisely as means, as something that serves a particular end or purpose. This ability to establish the connection between means and their ends requires the ability to anticipate the future and to form mental images of realities not present or not yet in existence.

The ability to establish the connection between means and ends happens to be the fundamental intellectual capacity that has made possible the development of human culture and technology. The evolutionary roots of this capacity may be found in the evolution of bipedal gait, which transformed the anterior limbs of our ancestors from organs of locomotion into organs of manipulation. The hands thereby gradually became organs adept for the construction and use of objects for hunting and other activities that improved survival and reproduction, that is, that increased the reproductive fitness of their carriers.

The construction of tools, however, depends not only on manual dexterity but on perceiving them precisely as tools, as objects that help to perform certain actions, that is, as means that serve certain ends or purposes: a knife for cutting, an arrow for hunting, an animal skin for protecting the body from the cold. The hypothesis I am propounding is that natural selection promoted the intellectual capacity of our biped ancestors because increased intelligence facilitated the perception of tools as tools, and therefore their construction and use, with the ensuing amelioration of biological survival and reproduction.

The development of the intellectual abilities of our ancestors took place over two million years or longer, gradually increasing the ability to connect means with their ends and, hence, the possibility of making ever more complex tools serving remote purposes. The ability to anticipate the future, essential for ethical behavior, is therefore closely associated with the development of the ability to construct tools, an ability that has produced the advanced technologies of modern societies and that is largely responsible for the success of humankind as a biological species.

The second condition for the existence of ethical behavior is the ability to make value judgments, to perceive certain objects or deeds as more desirable than others. Only if I can see the death of my enemy as preferable to his or her survival (or vice versa) can the action leading to his or her demise be thought of as within the moral sphere. If the alternative consequences of an action are neutral with respect to value, the action cannot be characterized as ethical. The ability to make value judgments depends on the capacity for abstraction, that is, on the capacity to perceive actions or objects as members of general classes. This makes it possible to compare objects or actions with one another and to perceive some as more desirable than others. The capacity for abstraction, necessary to perceive individual objects or actions as members of general classes, requires an advanced intelligence such as it exists in humans and apparently in them alone. Thus, I see the ability to make value judgments primarily as an implicit consequence of the enhanced intelligence favored by natural selection in human evolution. Nevertheless, valuing certain objects or actions and choosing them over their alternatives can be of biological consequence; doing this in terms of general categories can be beneficial in practice.

Moral judgments are a particular class of value judgments; namely, those where preference is not dictated by one's own interest or profit but by regard for others, which may cause benefits to particular individuals (altruism) or take into consideration the interests of a social group to which one belongs. Value judgments indicate preference for what is perceived as good and rejection of what is perceived as bad; good and bad may refer to monetary, aesthetic, or all sorts of other kinds of values. Moral judgments concern the values of right and wrong in human conduct.

The third condition necessary for ethical behavior is the ability to choose between alternative courses of action. Pulling the trigger can be a moral action only if I have the option not to pull it. A necessary action beyond our control is not a moral action: the circulation of the blood or the digestion of food are not moral actions.

Whether there is free will has been much discussed by philosophers,[6] and this is not the appropriate place to review the arguments. I will only advance two considerations based on our common-sense experience. One is our profound personal conviction that the possibility of choosing between alternatives is genuine rather than only apparent.[7] The second consideration is that when we confront a given situation that requires action on our part, we are able mentally to explore alternative courses of action, thereby extending the field within which we can exercise our free will. In any case, if there were no free will, there would be no ethical behavior; morality would only be an illusion. The point that I wish to make here is, however, that free will is dependent on the existence of a well-developed intelligence, which makes it possible to explore alternative courses of action and to choose one or another in view of the anticipated consequences.

In summary, ethical behavior is an attribute of the biological makeup of humans and is, in that sense, a product of biological evolution. But I see no evidence that ethical behavior developed because it was adaptive in itself. I find it hard to see how *evaluating* certain actions as either good or evil (not just choosing some actions rather than others, or evaluating them with respect to their practical consequences) would promote the reproductive fitness of the evaluators. Nor do I see how there might be some form of "incipient" ethical behavior that would then be further promoted by natural selection. The three necessary conditions for there being ethical behavior are manifestations of advanced intellectual abilities.

It seems rather that the likely target of natural selection was the development of these advanced intellectual capacities. This development was favored by natural selection because the construction and use of tools improved the strategic position of our biped ancestors. Once bipedalism evolved and tool-using and tool-making became possible, those individuals more effective in these functions had a greater probability of biological success. The biological advantage provided by the design and use of tools persisted long enough so that intellectual abilities continued to increase, eventually yielding the eminent development of intelligence that is characteristic of *Homo sapiens.*

6. See Jeeves, chapter 4 of this volume, and Murphy, chapter 6 of this volume.
7. That free will is a universal and inalienable human attribute was thus conveyed by Confucius: "One may rob an army of its commander-in-chief; one cannot deprive the humblest man of his free will" (*The Analects of Confucius,* translation and notes by Simon Leys Norton [New York: Norton, 1996]).

Evolutionary Theories of Morality

There are many theories concerned with the rational grounds for morality, such as deductive theories that seek to discover the axioms or fundamental principles that determine what is morally correct on the basis of direct moral intuition. There also are theories, like logical positivism or existentialism, which negate rational foundations for morality, reducing moral principles to emotional decisions or to other irrational grounds. Since the publication of Darwin's theory of evolution by natural selection, philosophers as well as biologists have attempted to find in the evolutionary process the justification for moral norms. The common ground of all such proposals is that evolution is a natural process that achieves goals that are desirable and thereby morally good; indeed it has produced humans. Proponents of these ideas claim that only the evolutionary goals can give moral value to human action: whether a human deed is morally right depends on whether it directly or indirectly promotes the evolutionary process and its natural objectives.

Herbert Spencer[8] was perhaps the first philosopher seeking to find the grounds of morality in biological evolution. More recent attempts include those of the distinguished evolutionists J. S. Huxley[9] and C. H. Waddington[10] and of Edward O. Wilson[11] founder of sociobiology as an independent discipline engaged in discovering the biological foundations of social behavior. I have argued elsewhere[12] that the moral theories proposed by Spencer, Huxley, and Waddington are mistaken and fail to avoid the naturalistic fallacy.[13] These

8. Herbert Spencer, *The Principles of Ethics* (London, 1893).

9. T. H. Huxley and J. S. Huxley, *Touchstone for Ethics* (New York: Harper, 1947), and J. S. Huxley, *Evolution in Action* (New York: Harper, 1953).

10. C. H. Waddington, *The Ethical Animal* (London: Allen & Unwin, 1960).

11. E. O. Wilson, *Sociobiology: The New Synthesis* (Cambridge, Mass.: Harvard University Press, 1975); and E. O. Wilson, *On Human Nature* (Cambridge, Mass.: Harvard University Press, 1978).

12. F. J. Ayala, "The Biological Roots of Morality," *Biology and Philosophy* 2 (1987): 235–252.

13. The "naturalistic fallacy" consists in identifying what "is" with what "ought" to be. (See G. E. Moore, *Principia Ethica* [Cambridge: Cambridge University Press, 1903].) This error was already pointed out by David Hume: "In every system of morality which I have hitherto met with I have always remarked that the author proceeds for some time in the ordinary way of reasoning . . . when of a sudden I am surprised to find, that instead of the usual copulations of propositions, *is* and *is not*, I meet with no proposition that is not connected with an *ought* or *ought not*. This change is imperceptible; but is, however, of the last consequence. For as this *ought* or *ought not* expresses some new relation or affirmation, it is necessary that it should be observed and explained; and at the same time a reason should be given, for what seems altogether inconceivable, how this new relation can be a deduction from others, which are entirely different from it"

authors argue, in one or another fashion, that the standard by which human actions are judged good or evil derives from the contribution the actions make to evolutionary advancement or progress. A blunder in this argumentation is that it is based on value judgments about what is or is not progressive in (particularly human) evolution.[14] There is nothing objective in the evolutionary process itself that makes the success of bacteria, which have persisted for more than three billion years and in enormous diversity and numbers, less "progressive" than that of the vertebrates, even though the latter are more complex.[15] Nor are the insects, of which more than one million species exist, less successful or less progressive from a purely biological perspective than humans or any other mammal species. Moreover, the proponents of evolution-grounded moral codes fail to demonstrate why the promotion of biological evolution by itself should be the standard to measure what is morally good.

The most recent and most subtle attempt to ground moral codes on the evolutionary process is that of the sociobiologists, particularly E. O. Wilson, who starts by proposing that "scientists and humanists should consider together the possibility that the time has come for ethics to be removed temporarily from the hands of the philosophers and biologicized."[16] The sociobiologists' argue that the perception that morality exists is an epigenetic manifestation of our genes, which so manipulate humans as to make them believe that some behaviors are morally "good" so that people behave in ways that are good for their genes. Humans might not otherwise pursue these behaviors (altruism, for example) because their genetic benefit is not apparent (except to sociobiologists after the development of their discipline).[17]

As I have argued elsewhere, the sociobiologists' account of the evolution of the moral sense is misguided.[18] I argued above that we make moral judgments

---

(David Hume, *Treatise of Human Nature* [Oxford: Oxford University Press, (1740) 1978]).

14. F. J. Ayala, "The Evolutionary Concept of Progress," in *Progress and Its Discontents*, ed. G. A. Almond et al. (Berkeley: University of California Press, 1982), 106-124.

15. See Stephen Gould, *Full House: The Spread of Excellence from Plato to Darwin* (New York: Harmony Books, 1996).

16. Wilson, *Sociobiology,* 562.

17. M. Ruse, *Taking Darwin Seriously: A Naturalistic Approach to Philosophy* (Oxford: Basil Blackwell, 1986); M. Ruse, "Evolutionary Ethics: A Phoenix Arisen," *Zygon* 21 (1986): 95-112; Michael Ruse and E. O. Wilson, "Moral Philosophy as Applied Science," *Philosophy: Journal of the Royal Institute of Philosophy* 61 (1986): 173-192.

18. F. J. Ayala, "The Difference of Being Human: Ethical Behavior as an Evolutionary Byproduct," in *Biology, Ethics and the Origin of Life,* ed. H. Rolston III (Boston and London: Jones and Bartlett, 1995), 113-135; and Ayala, "The Biological Roots of Morality."

as a consequence of our eminent intellectual abilities, not as an innate way for achieving biological gain. Moreover, the sociobiologists' position may be interpreted as calling for the supposition that those *norms* of morality should be considered supreme that achieve the most biological (genetic) gain (because that is, in their view, why the moral sense evolved at all). This, in turn, would justify social preferences, including racism and even genocide, that many of us (sociobiologists included) judge morally obtuse and even heinous.

The evaluation of moral codes or human actions must take into account biological knowledge, but biology is insufficient for determining which moral codes are, or should be, accepted. This may be reiterated by returning to the analogy with human languages. Our biological nature determines the sounds that we can or cannot utter and also constrains human language in other ways. But a language's syntax and vocabulary are not determined by our biological nature (otherwise, there could not be a multitude of tongues), but are products of human culture. Likewise, moral norms are not determined by biological processes, but by cultural traditions and principles including religious beliefs, that are products of human history.

THE ROAD TRAVERSED

The portrait of human nature that I have presented here abides by Augustine's injunction against "talking nonsense" and "maintaining foolish opinions about the Scriptures." It is cognizant of science's achievements, particularly the discoveries of evolutionary biology and the continuity of descent between humans and other animals. Further, it is an image that acknowledges that human nature transcends biology.

I started this essay summoning evidence for the evolutionary continuity between humans and our primate ancestors. Human nature, I argued, is biological nature, but is also much more. In humankind, biological evolution has transcended itself and has ushered in a new mode, cultural evolution, more rapid and effective than the biological mode. A complete portrait of human nature must integrate humankind's two dimensions, the biological and the cultural, its biological continuity with the living world and its radical distinctness. Humankind's uniqueness is embodied in a suite of features that include ethical behavior and religious beliefs. These distinctly human characteristics (and surely others, like art, science, technology, and sociopolitical institutions) emanate as epigenetic outcomes of humankind's enhanced intelligence, which may very well be the fundamental and most distinctive trait targeted by natural selection in the process that brought about *Homo sapiens*.

Chapter Three

*A Genetic View of Human Nature**

V. Elving Anderson

THE IMPORTANCE OF A GENETIC VIEW

The recent cloning of Dolly has sharply intensified public interest and concern about the impact of genetics. To be sure, there were earlier efforts to stimulate such discussion,[1] but the birth of Dolly moved us from speculation to reality. Much of the ensuing conversation has centered on the question: "Do genes make us who we are?" If we knew all the factors completely, would we find that our actions are fully *determined?*

In a similar vein, when the media report the discovery of a new "obesity" gene, "criminal" gene, or "novelty seeking" gene, readers may wonder if they are truly persons or merely the embodiment of their genes. [2] As the Human Genome Project continues toward its goal of mapping and sequencing all human genes, will we finally "understand" human nature? When the details are worked out for the thousands of genes that are expressed in the brain, will we have mastered human behavior? Will our human nature be *reduced* to DNA?

W. French Anderson, a leading proponent of gene therapy, carried the argument one step further by asking if we could alter our humanness itself by

---

*Helpful comments from R. J. Berry, Bruce Reichenbach, and the editors of this volume are gratefully acknowledged, although responsibility for the opinions expressed remain with the author.

1. See, for example, Nancy Freedman, *Joshua: Son of None* (New York: Dell Publishing Company, 1973); and David Rorvik, *In His Image: The Cloning of a Man* (Philadelphia: J. B. Lippincott, 1978). For the broader ethical and theological implications, see Ronald Cole-Turner, ed., *Human Cloning: Religious Responses* (Louisville: Westminster/John Knox Press, 1997).

2. *Are Genes Us? The Social Consequences of the New Genetics* (New Brunswick, N.J.: Rutgers University Press, 1994).

genetic engineering. He concluded: "If what is uniquely human about us is something beyond our physical structure—if it is not our body, or our mind, or any collection of measurable traits, but rather something profound and unmeasurable—then, since genetic engineering can only alter our physical structure, we cannot alter that which is uniquely human, i.e., our soul, by scientific technology. . . . My tentative conclusion is this: We cannot alter our humanness by genetic engineering except in ways that can be measured and, therefore, potentially controlled."[3]

When I entered the field of human genetics, there was a sense of fatalism. "If it's genetic, what can you do about it?" Now that the genetic code can be altered, gene therapy has become a present reality. In this context James M. Gustafson pointed out that "what a biologist believes about the very essence of humanity, and what he or she posits as the distinctive values of that essence, will affect what experimentation and therapy would be supported. The regulative idea of the nature of the human, a background belief not derived from science alone, is a critical factor for theologians and for geneticists."[4]

THE FORMATION OF A GENETIC VIEW

It seems likely that many people live with some idea about heredity, even though it might not have been made explicit. What, then, can serve as the basis for a more detailed genetic view of human nature?[5] We can begin with two assumptions—that human genes are an absolute requirement for human existence, and that humans differ, in some ways, from other forms of life. The mere presence of genes, of course, does not establish human distinctiveness since essentially all forms of life possess DNA. If genes are indeed connected with uniqueness, it must be in some other way.

One possibility is that humans possess a unique gene or set of genes. If there were such genes, we then could ask whether they have a significant effect upon characteristics that are considered essential for humanness. The research needed to show that *no other species* has an equivalent, however, would have to be truly exhaustive. Based on evidence to date one can provisionally conclude that no such gene or set of genes exists.

3. W. French Anderson, "Genetic Engineering and Our Humanness," *Human Gene Therapy* 5 (1994): 758-759.
4. James M. Gustafson, "Where Theologians and Geneticists Meet," *Dialog* 33, no. 1 (Winter 1994): 11. See also LeRoy Walters and Julie Gage Palmer, *The Ethics of Human Gene Therapy* (New York: Oxford University Press, 1997).
5. For a more extensive treatment of the meaning of "human nature" see Mary Midgley, *Beast and Man: The Roots of Human Nature* (New York: New American Library, 1978). Also Gustafson, "Where Theologians and Geneticists Meet," 7-16.

Even if we limit the comparison to primates, there is no evidence for such unique genes. We already know that the total amount of DNA is very similar for humans and higher primates. Humans do have 23 pairs of chromosomes while chimpanzees have 24, but two of the shorter primate chromosomes placed end to end strongly resemble one human chromosome. (Comparisons at the DNA level indicate a similarity of about 98.4 percent.)

A second possibility is that similar genes may have a different effect on the phenotype (the observable effects of gene action) in different species. Some genes from different species are known to have long portions that are almost identical; yet the related genes may carry out quite different functions.

Finally, we must consider the developmental regulation of genes. Clefts of the palate and lip, for example, can result from slight delays in the movement of tissues that normally close a gap. Changes in the timing of gene expression can cause significant differences in the subsequent structure and function of parts of the body.

Human uniqueness may, in fact, involve several of these options and arise from a particular *combination* of genes having specific functions, together with a unique pattern for their developmental timing. This may seem to be a modest answer to a very large question, but Gustafson has suggested that "our biological distinctiveness is both small and decisive."[6]

In this chapter I use an alternative approach. Instead of beginning with genes themselves, we can first identify abilities that are considered essential for human nature and then ask what role genes play in their development. Other chapters in this book provide an excellent selection of such abilities for this purpose. Ayala, for example, outlines such characteristics as self-awareness and death-awareness, tool-making and technology, symbolic (creative) language, subtle expression of emotions, and intelligence. He then proposes that human *ethical behavior* has come about as an indirect consequence of natural selection for human intellectual capacity, and that the latter now involves three abilities: (1) the ability to anticipate the consequences of one's behavior, (2) the ability to make value judgments, and (3) the ability to choose alternative courses of action (chapter 2). Brown stresses *personal relatedness* as a central theme of human nature and identified the cognitive traits that make this relatedness possible: language, a theory of mind, episodic memory, conscious top-down agency, and future orientation (chapter 5). Murphy identifies four major aspects of behavior—consciousness, intelligence, emotion, and volition. Under intelligence she lists memory (short and long), categorization, imagination, judgment (including moral and aesthetic), reasoning (including intuitive leaps and

6. James M. Gustafson, "A Christian Perspective on Genetic Engineering," *Human Gene Therapy* 5 (1994): 750.

discursive reasoning), and practical reasoning (chapter 6). Finally, Jeeves reviews the brain's links that the brain has with language, intellectual function, and personality, including social and ethical behavior (chapter 4).

It is clear that all the traits outlined above are behavioral in nature. The task in the sections that follow will be to examine the present evidence that genes are involved in the development of such specific behavioral traits. It may be helpful, however, to set the stage with some general comments about behavior genetics and about the pathways between genes and behavior.

At the outset, it is important to recognize that variability is required before any genetic study of behavior can begin. It would be difficult, if not impossible, to study the genetics of traits which all humans possess to essentially the same degree. Fortunately, for these purposes, both intelligence and personality show a wide variation that can be assessed on a quantitative scale, of which the IQ score is one example. When the scores for a population sample are tabulated they often take the form of a statistically normal distribution, or "bell-shaped curve." The majority of individuals form a bulge in the middle of the curve, which is the net result of a number of genetic and environmental factors. Individuals at the tails of the curve are likely to show more extreme problems, which result from single mutations or major environmental causes.

Studies of human behavior should consider both genetic and environmental factors, since misleading interpretations can be expected from environmental research that disregards genetics, or vice versa. As a general rule, however, the genetic contribution to variation can be quantified more readily than that of the environment. For example, the degree of relationship (the proportion of genes that are shared) is 1.0 for monozygotic (MZ) twin pairs and 0.5 for comparisons of parents with offspring and within pairs of siblings. The trait-relevant factors of the environment (those that actually have an effect on the trait under investigation) are more difficult to identify and measure.

There is a continuous and inevitable interaction between organism and environment throughout life. Furthermore, the process of human development does not follow a steady progression, but proceeds in spurts and lags. As a result, the relative contribution of genes may vary from one age period to another.

In addition, the relationships between the genotype and the environment in their contributions to individual variability may be quite complex.[7] Genotype-environment *correlation* refers to situations in which genotypes are *exposed* to environments differentially. Some children may receive from their parents favorable genes together with a supportive environment, while other

7. John C. Loehlin, *Genes and Environment in Personality Development* (Newbury Park, Calif.: SAGE Publications, 1992): 105-111.

children may possess a less favorable genetic endowment together with a neutral or unfavorable environmental setting. Thus it may be hard to separate the roles of genetic and environmental factors. On the other hand, genetic-environment *interaction* involves different *responses* to environments. Two individuals, for example, might show very similar behaviors in normal situations, but differ greatly in their response to a stressful environment.

There are two aspects of behavior that will have considerable importance for discussions that follow. (1) A given individual may have the potential to develop different behavioral phenotypes in response to different situations, a condition described as *plasticity*. (In contrast, some species of birds and fish display stereotyped patterns of behavior that cannot be altered, as in mating responses.) This plasticity is a significant feature of human behavior and has a very important survival value. (2) Each individual starts life with genetic arrays of potential for various behaviors. Environment and experience will help to determine the level of actual functioning within each *reaction range,* but behaviors at either extreme will not be seen unless there are extreme circumstances.

At a practical level the simplest approach to genetic influence comes from studies of identical twins. Co-twins start out with identical sets of genes, although over time they may accumulate different mutations. The common experiences of life may affect the twins differently and may even change permanently the expression of some genes. Individuality in personal choices leads to further divergence. The information about identical twins thus can provide a first approximation on which to base expectations and predictions about the degree of genetic control.

The data in Table 1 are in the form of correlations, which provide a measure of similarity between twins in pairs, from the most (1.00) to the least (0.00) similar. The variables are arranged from greater similarity at the top to less similarity at the bottom. In most, but not all, cases the correlations are higher for pairs of identical twins reared together (MZT) than for identical twins reared apart (MZA), and the MZT-MZA differences give some estimate of the effect of being raised apart.

In general, the correlations are highest for structural and physiological variables, in the mid-range but somewhat higher for mental ability than for personality, and fairly low for interests. The highest values are for fingerprint ridge count, which is measured by drawing lines between landmarks on the print for each finger and counting the number of ridges crossed by the lines. Here the genetic effect is so strong that the matching hands of MZ twin pairs are as much alike as the right and left hands of individuals. The background wave pattern on the electroencephalogram (EEG) is known to be one of the most heritable human traits, and it is not affected at all by rearing. Toward the bottom of the table you will find some traits that show a genetic effect even

TABLE 1

Interclass Correlations for Monozygotic Twins Reared Together (MZT)
and Apart (MZA) from the Minnesota Study of Twins Reared Apart

VARIABLES	MZA	MZT
Fingerprint ridge count	0.97	0.96
Height	0.86	0.93
Weight	0.73	0.83
EEG: amount of alpha activity (8–12 per second)	0.80	0.81
Systolic blood pressure	0.64	0.70
Heart rate	0.49	0.54
Information processing (speed of response)	0.56	0.73
Mental ability (WAIS IQ—full scale)	0.69	0.88
Personality (mean of 11 MPQ* scales)	0.50	0.49
Interests (mean of 23 Strong Campbell scales)	0.39	0.48
Social attitudes		
Mean of 2 religiosity scales	0.49	0.51
Mean of 14 nonreligious items	0.34	0.28
MPQ* traditionalism scale	0.53	0.50

*Multidimensional Personality Questionnaire
Source: Thomas J. Bouchard Jr., David T. Lykken, Matthew McGue, Nancy L. Segal and Auke Tellegen, "Sources of Human Psychological Differences: The Minnesota Study of Twins Reared Apart," *Science* 250 (1990): 250.

though some might have assumed that such traits are completely the result of culture and personal choice.

PATHWAYS FROM GENES TO BEHAVIORS

In some ways the gene story is surprisingly simple. The double-helix structure of the DNA molecule is essentially the same in all organisms, although the gene sequences may be quite different. The genetic code involves four nucleotides (abbreviated as A, C, G, and T), and these form pairs across the helix (A-T and C-G). However, the gene story must not be interpreted simplistically. The pathways from genes to behavior are not direct and are not readily predictable. Furthermore, behavior is biopsychosocial in nature. The following discussion moves up the levels of analysis from molecules to populations and, in so doing, traces the broadening circles of context for gene action. [8]

8. The discussion that follows is based, in part, on my chapter, "Resisting Reductionism by Restoring the Context," in *Genetic Ethics: Do the Ends Justify the Genes?* ed. John F.

Genes Never Act Alone

Human development starts as a single cell formed by the joining of an ovum and a sperm cell. Both the ovum and the sperm cell carry DNA, but the ovum also brings an initial pool of energy together with numerous mitochondria which can generate more energy. Then there are the enzymes and other factors that are needed for replication of the DNA, for initiating and controlling the early cell divisions, and for making gene products.

The growing embryo soon implants in the uterine wall and continues to be dependent on the nutrition provided by the mother. Throughout development the function of a given gene can be influenced by external factors or by the action of other genes. Thus many human traits are best described as *multifactorial*, representing the combined effect of a number of these genes together with internal and external environmental factors.

Gene Action on Behavior Is Indirect

The analogy of genes as a "blueprint" is quite appropriate in a strict sense. A blueprint does indeed contain essential information about the design of a specific building, but it has no power to complete its construction. Someone must interpret the plans and establish a sequence for steps in the process. Materials and energy (in the form of machines and manpower) must be available. An architect continually checks the progress and even alters the plans if necessary to meet unexpected circumstances.

A simplified view of gene action would look like the following:

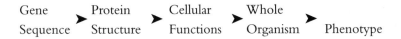

Gene Sequence → Protein Structure → Cellular Functions → Whole Organism → Phenotype

The primary function of the DNA sequence is to provide the information for arranging amino acids into a one-dimensional strand. This strand then folds into a three-dimensional protein, with the assistance of molecular "chaperones" (produced by other genes). Some proteins are used as structural components, some form enzymes, and yet others have many different functions. The chain of events finally leads to the expressed phenotype—the features that can be observed and measured, directly or indirectly. Each of the steps in the diagram is subject to internal or external environmental factors. Without the genes nothing would happen, but the final phenotypic effects are modifiable in transit.

Kilner, Rebecca D. Pentz, and Frank E. Young (Grand Rapids: Wm. B. Eerdmans, 1997): 84–92. See also Craig Holdrege, *Genetics and the Manipulation of Life: The Forgotten Factor of Context* (Hudson, N.Y.: Lindisfarne Press, 1996).

Genes Are Turned On and Off

There may be as many as 80,000 genes in the human genome (a full set of genes), and about half of these are expressed mainly in the brain. In any given cell, however, only a small number of the genes present (perhaps 5 to 10 percent) are functioning. Thus, gene action must be regulated, often by promoters or enhancers in the DNA sequence at either end of the gene itself or by circulating hormones or transcription factors. Many genes are active only in particular tissues, such as the liver or the brain. Furthermore, even though all cells in the brain have the same genetic information, a given gene may be restricted even further and be expressed only in a specific brain area or in a specific cell type, and then only within a limited time during development.

At the biochemical level it has become clear that the pathway between genes and behavior is not in one direction only. Genes may indeed influence certain behaviors, but experience may also affect how genes are expressed. Seizures, for example, can induce the selective expression of "immediate early" genes, which in turn may have a critical role in long-term synaptic plasticity. Also, hormones released during stress can change the relative expression of a number of genes. Although identical twins start out with the same sets of genes, as adults their functioning genes may no longer be completely identical. The importance of this gene regulation is further demonstrated by those medical treatments that act by turning up the expression of some genes or turning down others.

Genes Act at Different Times during Development

Genes guide the development of an organ, but not in a fully pre-programmed manner. For example, genes lay out the basic segmentation of the early brain. This is followed by considerable movement or migration of cells as the neurons elongate and follow cues, both structural and biochemical, which are themselves partly under genetic control. Some areas generate too many neurons, but those that fail to form synaptic connections are removed by cell death, which again is genetically programmed. The final differentiation of neurons relies mainly on signals from their immediate environment.

Genes and Environment Continue to Interact throughout Life

Within the brain, cell to cell communication occurs through chemical messengers (neurotransmitters) that interact with channels and receptors on the surface of neurons. Some receptors contain channels that open or close to control the flow of specific ions (calcium, sodium, potassium, or chloride), while others trigger secondary biochemical changes within the cell. Taken together, the neurotransmitters, receptors, and channels control the excitation and inhibition of neuronal activity. The overall process thus provides a fine-tuning control that has been likened to the balancing effect of accelerator and brake in a car.

Furthermore, some receptors are constructed from subunits that are produced by different genes. This mix can be altered in response to changes in the local cellular environment. The various combinations of subunits permit an amazing diversity in receptor function, thus providing a major mechanism for brain plasticity.[9]

The major concern in this chapter, of course, is not with the brain per se, but with the effect of genes on the behaviors that reflect the brain's activity. The pathways from genes to behavior (as with any other phenotype) are necessarily indirect, since they involve complex physiological systems and are affected by experience throughout development. For some traits the analysis may be relatively simple, whenever significant alterations in a single biochemical process account for the main behavioral consequences. Most behaviors, on the other hand, appear to involve many genes, each with a small effect.

Development is as important for behavior as for the brain itself, since later stages are conditioned by prior experience. Furthermore, there may be critical time windows during which specific genetic and environmental factors may be particularly influential.

In summary, genes are now known to be less stable and more subject to regulatory factors than we used to think, and the pathways from genes to expressed traits are more complex and less predictable. The history of an organism becomes important for its later behavior, with each developmental step dependent on prior events that continually alter the internal environment. Thus, the effect of individual genes must be described in terms of probabilities rather than rigorously determined outcomes:

> In ontogenesis, genetic and nongenetic factors interact in producing successive stages, each of which is the prerequisite, and determines the conditions, for the next one to follow. In this interplay, genes are a *necessary, but not sufficient,* component. The structures already present, gradients, threshold values, positional relationships, and conditions of the internal milieu, are equally essential.[10]

With this general background we can explore two major categories of human behavior: intelligence (or cognitive ability) and personality. In each case a discussion of the broad category will be followed by several specific

9. For a concise description of brain development, see Martin Raff, "Neural Development: Mysterious No More?" *Science* 274 (1996): 1063.
10. U. Wolf, "The Genetic Contribution to the Phenotype," *Human Genetics* 95 (1995): 127-148. Emphasis added.

examples which illustrate three goals in the study of any behavior—to determine whether the behavior is heritable, to map or identify genes for the behavior, and to determine the mechanisms for the effect of genes on the behavior.[11]

GENES AND COGNITIVE ABILITIES

Many studies have treated intelligence as a single (complex) trait measurable by standardized tests. The resulting scores are standardized for age and are conventionally reported as a ratio of tested ability to chronological age (an IQ). The degree of familial resemblance in IQ is expressed as a *correlation coefficient* indicating the strength of resemblance between members of twin pairs (or other pair-wise combinations of relatives). A correlation of 1.00 would mean complete identity, while a correlation of zero would indicate that members of a twin pair are neither more nor less alike than pairs of individuals taken at random from the general population.

   In order to estimate the contribution from genetic and environmental factors, information is used from many types of biological relationships. The correlations for IQ can be compared with those for body weight, between monozygotic (identical) twins reared together (MZT); monozygotic twins reared apart (MZA); dizygotic (fraternal) twins reared together (DZT); and non-twin siblings:

	IQ	WT
MZT	0.86	0.80
MZA	0.73	0.72
DZT	0.60	0.43
Single-born pairs	0.47	0.34

The MZ pairs are more alike than the DZ pairs (mainly a genetic effect) while DZ pairs are more alike than ordinary siblings (probably from being reared together). The small difference between MZA and MZT pairs suggests some modest effect of the environment of rearing. Finally, among pairs that are biologically unrelated but reared together, the IQ correlations are 0.25 in childhood, but fall to zero in adulthood. [12]

11. For a current description of work in the field, see Stephanie L. Sherman, John C. DeFries, Irving I. Gottesman, John C. Loehlin, et al., "Recent Developments in Human Behavioral Genetics: Past Accomplishments and Future Directions," *American Journal of Human Genetics* 60 (1997): 1265-1275.

12. For a discussion of the IQ data, see Matt McGue, Thomas J. Bouchard Jr., William B. Iacono, and David T. Lykken, "Behavioral Genetics of Cognitive Ability: A Life-Span

The environmental contribution to IQ can be divided further into two parts. The proportion attributable to non-shared environment (those experiences of one person in the pair but not the other) remains relatively constant at 0.15 throughout life. The shared environmental variance is estimated at 0.30 from 4-20 years of life but falls to zero among adults. The genetic component is 0.51 from 4–20 years but rises to .80 for adults, mainly because the shared environmental fraction has disappeared.[13] These results suggest that the effect of genes on cognitive abilities involves a continuing interaction between the genes and the changing factors in environment and experience.

Such observations are interesting, but they do not go far enough for our present discussion. Matt McGue has argued that "the day has come when showing that some trait is under partial genetic or environmental control without accounting for, or hypothesizing about, the mechanism of that influence simply will not do."[14] In like vein, Rutter commented: "The real interest, and value, of genetic findings does *not* lie in quantification of the genetic component but rather in understanding *how* the risk is mediated and *how* genetic factors combine with environmental influences to predispose to antisocial behaviour."[15] The most direct way to reach these goals is to design tests for specific aspects of behavior, carry out family studies, map a gene for this trait to a specific chromosome, identify the gene and its product, and finally determine the mechanism whereby the gene product can lead to this behavior. This is an example of methodological reductionism, taking a developmental pathway apart to explore the single steps that are involved.

The section that follows will review briefly the current status of three research studies on different aspects of cognitive ability, while illustrating research strategies that have become possible only in recent years. All represent work in progress, and conclusions from them are inevitably tentative.

(1) Five components of memory have been identified. *Episodic memory* is the ability to remember events and episodes from one's personal experience, and is mentioned by Brown as essential for the development of personal relatedness. A second component, *semantic memory*, enables people to acquire factual information and to use it when needed at a later time. The genetic analysis

Perspective," in *Nature, Nurture, and Psychology*, ed. Robert Plomin and Gerald E. McClearn (Washington, D.C.: American Psychological Association, 1993), 60. The data for weight are from David C. Rowe, "Genetic Perspectives on Personality," in *Nature, Nurture, and Psychology*, 185.

13. McGue et al., "Behavioral Genetics," 63-64.

14. Matt McGue, "Nature, Nurture, and Intelligence," *Nature* 340 (1989): 508.

15. Sir Michael Rutter, "Concluding Remarks," in *Genetics of Criminal and Antisocial Behaviour*, Ciba Foundation Symposium 194 (Chichester: Wiley, 1995): 266.

comes from an ongoing study of memory, health, and aging in a northern Swedish population.[16] A sample of adults was given 34 tests, including 26 that were designed specifically to measure *episodic memory*. Those persons with scores in the top and bottom 8 percent of the sample were analyzed for genetic markers in blood that are known to show variability in the population and to have a known position on a specific human chromosome. Significant differences between the top and bottom groups were found in four out of six markers in females, but in only one marker among males.

(2) Developmental *dyslexia* (specific reading disability) is a serious problem in children and adults who otherwise have normal cognitive skills. Since 1950 it has been known that certain forms of dyslexia are inherited, since 80 percent of the cases have affected parents. More recently, regions on chromosomes 6, 15, and 16 have been identified as possible sites for major genes that increase the risk for dyslexia. A 1997 study identified six families, each with at least four affected members, and a battery of tests was used to evaluate both the affected and unaffected relatives. These tests had been designed to distinguish five components of dyslexia and were selected on the basis of theories about the mechanisms involved in reading ability.[17]

In that study, genetic markers on chromosome 6 showed evidence of linkage to *phonological awareness*, the ability to distinguish individual phonemes (parts of words), to segment words into their phonemes, and to sequence the phonemes appropriately; but there was no linkage to scores of single-word reading. Markers on chromosome 15 showed evidence for linkage with *single-word reading* (orally, of printed real words), but not with phonological awareness. These results were a surprise, since the cognitive mechanisms involved in single-word reading were not thought to be separate from those in phoneme awareness. Clearly dyslexia is a complex trait.

In a review of the study described above, Pennington posed an important question that seems relevant for all areas of behavior genetics.[18] (1) Is the mind-brain "a collection of specific and separate components or modules, each evolved to serve a particular adaptive purpose? . . . Proponents of such a view have even proposed genes for particular aspects of grammar!" (2) Or is

16. The three other components in this classification system are primary memory, perceptual representation system, and procedural memory. The genetic analysis was carried out by L. G. Nilsson and others, "Genetic Markers Associated with High versus Low Performance on Episodic Memory Tasks," *Behavior Genetics* 26 (1996): 555-562.
17. E. L. Grigorenko et al., "Susceptibility Loci for Distinct Components of Developmental Dyslexia on Chromosomes 6 and 15," *American Journal of Human Genetics* 60 (1997): 27-39.
18. Bruce F. Pennington, "Using Genetics to Dissect Cognition," *American Journal of Human Genetics* 60 (1997): 13-16.

the brain "a highly interdependent dynamical system" that is specialized to perform many tasks, but that does not contain prespecified modules. On the first view there may be genes (on chromosomes 6 and 15) that *support* the development of two separate components of reading skill, and a mutation in either gene will lead to a *loss* of the specific skill. On the second view, the genes on 6 and 15 may *disrupt* normal development by some other mechanism.

(3) *Williams Syndrome* (WS) is a rare developmental disorder with varying combinations of congenital heart disease, hypertension, premature aging of skin, dysmorphic facial features, gregarious personality, and mental retardation (IQs from 20 to 106, with a mean of 58). [19] Language development is relatively spared and some elements may appear to be enhanced in the form of "cocktail speech" (strings of meaningless pleasantries). In fact, the expressive language abilities may disguise specific cognitive deficits. Many patients sing or play musical instruments with considerable expertise and they seldom forget a name. One common feature is a type of aortic stenosis, which results from a mutation in a gene (for elastin) on chromosome 7. That finding led to the suggestion that WS is a contiguous gene disorder, a type of condition that results from deletion of part of a chromosome. The clinical severity depends on how many, and which, genes have been lost.

Of particular interest for this present discussion is the fact that WS often includes a "visuospatial constructive cognitive deficit." This shows up as a marked difficulty in tasks involving the use of a pattern to assemble an object, such as copying a picture of a block design by using cubes of varying color and designs. Two families have been described in which the affected members have only this cognitive profile and the vascular disease but not the retardation or other WS features. DNA analysis showed that the deletions in the WS area in these families were quite small, removing only two known genes, *elastin* (*ELN*) and *LIM-kinase 1* (*LIMK1*). [20] Other evidence strongly suggests that it is a mutation in the latter gene that causes the cognitive defect.

These three studies relate directly (episodic memory) or indirectly (language and cognitive abilities) to the traits listed in other chapters as important for human nature. Furthermore, the studies used two recently developed research strategies: (1) the development of tests for a specific aspect of behavior, and (2) the use of genetic markers to identify specific chromosomal regions or genes.

19. Amanda K. Ewart et al., "Hemizygosity at the Elastin Locus in a Developmental Disorder, Williams Syndrome," *Nature Genetics* 5 (1993): 11-16.
20. John Ashkenas, "Williams Syndrome Starts Making Sense," *American Journal of Human Genetics* 59 (1996): 756-761.

GENES AND PERSONALITY

The data for personality (just as for cognitive ability) can be partitioned into (somewhat overlapping) traits that can be assessed on a quantitative scale. Although investigators have used different labels, there is general agreement on "the big five" as listed below:

1. Extraversion, dominance
2. Agreeableness, likability, friendliness
3. Conscientiousness, conformity, will to achieve
4. Emotional stability (with anxiety and neuroticism as opposites)
5. Culture, intellect, openness to experience

Data for extraversion are available from five large twin studies with sample sizes ranging from 475 to 12,777 pairs, an unusually large database.[21] The results of the analysis are expressed here (just as for cognitive abilities) in the form of correlation coefficients. The correlations for MZ pairs range from .46 to .65, and for DZ same-sex pairs from .13 to .28, with the MZ-DZ differences showing a clear genetic effect. When all the data from twins (reared together and apart) and from adoption studies are collated, genes account for 35 to 39 percent of the individual variation in extraversion. It had been assumed that shared environment accounts for much of the family resemblance in personality, but most of the studies showed the effect of shared environment to be close to zero.

Data for the other major trait domains are reasonably similar to those for extroversion, including the observation that the contributions from genetic factors and from shared environment tend to be lower for personality than for IQ.[22] Adoption studies for both extraversion and emotionality provide interesting examples of gene-environment interaction. When the children had a strong biological background for either emotionality or extraversion (based on data about the biological parents), the adoptive setting had little influence upon the children's behavior. On the other hand, with a weak biological background in emotionality or extraversion, the children's behavior tended to follow the adoptive environment.

Lindon Eaves collected data on nearly 4,000 pairs of twins concerning religion, education, and social attitudes (Table 2). [23] The columns show the data

21. These data sets are reviewed and analyzed critically by John C. Loehlin, *Genes and Environment in Personality Development,* 9-46.
22. Ibid., 47-68.
23. Lindon Eaves, "Behavioral Genetics, or What's Missing from Theological Anthropology?" in *Beginning with the End: God, Science, and Wolfhart Pannenberg,* ed. Carol Rausch Albright and Joel Haugen (Chicago: Open Court, 1997): 344-345.

TABLE 2
Correlations between Twins for Religion, Education, and Attitudes

TWIN TYPE	N	CHURCH	EDUC	SEX	ECON	MILIT	POLIT	REL RT
Monozygotic								
Male	643	0.51	0.81	0.57	0.53	0.59	0.48	0.51
Female	1338	0.62	0.79	0.65	0.52	0.50	0.47	0.47
Dizygotic								
Male	372	0.39	0.52	0.42	0.37	0.36	0.34	0.31
Female	671	0.45	0.61	0.50	0.31	0.32	0.28	0.40
Unlike-sex	997	0.33	0.48	0.36	0.26	0.33	0.29	0.28

Source: Lindon Eaves, "Behavioral Genetics, or What's Missing from Theological Anthropology?" in *Beginning with the End: God, Science, and Wolfhart Pannenberg,* ed. Carol Rausch Albright and Joel Haugen (Chicago: Open Court, 1997), 345.

for *church* attendance, years of *education,* and five clusters of social-attitude variables: *sexual permissiveness,* attitudes toward issues such as abortion, gay rights, and changing roles for women; *economic altruism,* such as taxation to benefit the underprivileged, and immigration; *militarism,* such as attitudes toward the draft, military drill, nuclear armaments, and pacifism; *political,* a preference for Democrats or Republicans, and *religious right,* covering the "moral majority," segregation, censorship, and school prayer. Eaves concluded that these data "are consistent with a significant contribution of genetic factors to variation in these dimensions of human variation which are often assumed, without proof, to be purely 'cultural' rather than biological."

Impulsive Aggressive Behavior
In 1993 a large family was identified in the Netherlands that had 14 males affected with aggressive behavior, often in response to anger, fear, or frustration.[24] Other manifestations included aggression toward family members and strangers, arson, attempted rape and murder, and exhibitionism. The aggressive behavior tended to cluster in periods of one to three days. The fact that all affected persons were related through unaffected females suggested X-linked

24. H. G. Brunner, M. R. Nelen, P. van Zandvoort, et al., "X-Linked Borderline Mental Retardation with Prominent Behavioral Disturbance: Phenotype, Genetic Localization, and Evidence for Disturbed Monoamine Metabolism," *American Journal of Human Genetics* 52 (1993): 1032-1039.

recessive inheritance, and genetic analysis showed this to be correct. Further studies revealed a complete deficiency of an enzyme (monoamine oxidase A, or MAOA) that breaks down and inactivates several neurotransmitters (serotonin, dopamine, and noradrenaline).[25]

A relationship between the enzyme deficiency and behavior also is seen in transgenic mice with a deficiency of the MAOA gene. Behavioral alterations included trembling and difficulty in righting, together with fearfulness in mouse pups and enhanced aggression in adult males. These effects were reversed in the mice by a drug that blocks the formation of serotonin, although no such effective treatment has yet been discovered for the human condition.[26]

The relationship between impulsive/aggressive behavior and the lack of MAOA activity in this family has not been firmly established, however. It is noteworthy that "all probands with this defect are capable to live in the community as long as the intensity of conflict situations is low, indicating that the degree of aggressive/impulsive behavior may be of a relatively mild nature. Much more prominent in the psychiatric profile are the disturbances in the ability to have intimate relationships or friends (autism-like features), problems with the handling of complex information and emotional vulnerability which leads to frequent feeling of being offended, episodes of paranoid ideation and thoughts of reference and affective instability with a greater stress reactivity."[27]

The Netherlands family raises three issues that are important for our present discussion. (1) Careful attention must be given to the terms used in the public media or in professional diagnosis to describe behavioral problems. Labels such as "mean" gene, "aggressive" gene, or "criminal" gene prejudge the situation and imply a level of understanding that usually is not present. In this family the severe episodes tended to be rare, were not alcohol-related, and became less severe with increasing adult age. It is not yet clear whether the underlying problem is enhanced stress reaction, a disorder of adaptive functioning, disruptive behavior, or impulsivity. It is easier to map a gene than to understand the pathogenesis of the associated disorder. (2) This is part of a much larger issue that has received intensive multidisciplinary analysis, the genetics of criminal and antisocial behavior. In particular, these problems involve social interactions that "occur in the space between organisms and

25. H. G. Brunner, M. Nelen, X. O. Breakefield, et al., "Abnormal Behavior Associated with a Point Mutation in the Structural Gene for Monoamine Oxidase A," *Science* 262 (1993): 578-580.
26. Olivier Cases et al., "Aggressive Behavior and Altered Amounts of Brain Serotonin and Norepinephrine in Mice Lacking MAOA," *Science* 268 (1995): 1763-1766.
27. S. Tuinier, W. M. A. Verhoeven, et al., "Neuropsychiatric and Biological Characteristics of X-linked MAO-A Deficiency Syndrome: A Single Case Intervention Study," *New Trends in Experimental and Clinical Psychiatry* 95 (1995): 105-106.

their environments. . . . Hence aggression cannot be reduced to the biology of either participant, or the context. It is an illusion to view aggressive behaviour as a static phenotype or the outcome of the internal processes (genetic or otherwise) of a single organism."[28] (3) Finally, Michael Rutter highlights the multiple facets of specific behaviors when he states that:

> Risks for antisocial behaviour may derive from characteristics that are not in themselves necessarily negative or harmful. A degree of risk-taking might be considered a useful element in creative research, and a diminished autonomic and behavioural response to stress may be protective against emotional disorders. Thus, if future research should succeed in identifying genes associated with an increased liability to antisocial behaviour, it does *not* follow that society would want to eliminate those genes. Rather, the need may be to develop better means of channelling the trait appropriately to foster adaptive, instead of antisocial, outcomes.[29]

Nurturing

Frequently a genetic component in the development of a behavioral pattern is detected first in experimental animals and is explored later in humans. Certain environmental stimuli lead rapidly to the expression of "immediate early" genes, one of which is termed *fosB*. The activity of these immediate early genes then induces the response of other genes a few hours later. This phenomenon was studied in a "knockout mouse" line in which activity of the *fosB* gene was eliminated.[30] An unexpected side result was that, although the affected female mice had normal pregnancies, most of their pups died in one to two days. After excluding other explanations, it was concluded that the "mothers" simply ignored the pups instead of crouching over them to keep them warm and nurse them. In normal non-pregnant (but not knockout) females, exposure to pups induces *fosB* in a part of the brain (the hypothalamus) that previously has been known to be involved in nurturing.

Nurturing is clearly a critical behavior for the survival of mammalian species, including the human. This new finding permits the design of studies to explore hypotheses about the physiological mechanisms that are involved in nurturing behavior in the mouse. Humans also have a *fosB* gene, but nothing is known of any mutations.

---

28. Robert S. Cairns, "Aggression from a Developmental Perspective: Genes, Environments and Interactions," in *Genetics of Criminal and Antisocial Behavior,* Ciba Foundation Symposium 194 (Chichester: Wiley, 1995), 49.
29. Sir Michael Rutter, "Concluding Remarks," 266.
30. Jon Cohen, "Does Nature Drive Nurture?" *Science* 273 (1996): 578-579.

Well-being

Most of our examples have been drawn from the pathological end of individual variability. In contrast, the Well-Being scale of the Multidimensional Personality Questionnaire (MPQ) appears to give a reliable and valid measure of the disposition to feel good about oneself and one's own corner of the world. Data from the MPQ were analyzed for 1,380 pairs of middle-aged twins who had been reared together. The intraclass correlation (a measure of similarity) was 0.44 for MZ pairs as compared with only 0.08 for DZ pairs. The self-reported well-being of one's identical twin was a far better predictor of one's self-related happiness than education attainment or socioeconomic scale, neither of which accounted for more than 2 percent of the variance.[31]

Some of the media called the report a discovery of the "happiness" gene, but this label misrepresents the complexity of the personality attribute and the indirect evidence for a genetic effect. It is more reasonable to interpret the data as indicating that day-to-day *variations* in sense of well-being are affected by immediate circumstances, whereas the average well-being (or *midpoint*) is strongly influenced by one's genes. Lykken concluded that the genetic effect is mainly indirect. "Our average levels of subjective well-being are determined largely by the things we *do* and the things we do are strongly influenced by our unique genetic makeup." [32]

Schizophrenia

Research on this category of psychopathology has produced pioneering work on other aspects of behavior genetics (taxonomy and classification, twin and population studies, linkage analysis). Research progress has been slow, however, and the reports often conflicting. The estimates of risk in the general population and among relatives of patients are essentially the same around the world:

General population	1%
Siblings	9%
Children	13%
DZ co-twins	17%
MZ co-twins	48%

About two-thirds of cases are assumed to have a multifactorial causation (a combination of genetic and environmental factors). The heritability of liabil-

---

31. David Lykken and Auke Tellegen, "Happiness Is a Stochastic Phenomenon," *Psychological Science* 7 (1996): 186–189.
32. David Lykken, personal communication.

ity is estimated at .63 and the contribution from shared environment at .29 (relatively high for a behavioral pattern).[33]

The generally accepted model for etiology of schizophrenia is genetic variation interacting with nongenetic variation to determine susceptibility to the disorder. There have been extensive studies of large families in an effort to identify linkage of markers on a specific chromosome to the schizophrenia phenotype, but thus far without clear success. For example, a Collaborative Group analysis of 1,899 affected individuals in 713 families produced suggestive (but not conclusive) evidence of linkage with markers on chromosomes 6 and 18, but with chromosome 3 being excluded.[34]

A different approach is to look for physiological indicators that may be closer to the primary action of genes and that produce a susceptibility to schizophrenia that is expressed only part of the time. One example is an eye tracking dysfunction that can be detected as a significant deviation from normal, smooth, pursuit eye movement. A preliminary study of eight families (each with at least two schizophrenic members)[35] produced evidence of linkage between eye tracking dysfunction and markers on chromosome 6.

The various cognitive abilities and personality traits presented up to this point represent a very small and somewhat arbitrary choice from the many traits and disorders that show a genetic effect. Further studies will confirm, change, and amplify our present understanding. Meanwhile, some general conclusions can be drawn.

(1) Genetic analysis requires some type of measurement or assessment. Two cautions should be noted, however. From time to time, new strategies are devised to analyze behaviors once thought to be unmeasurable. On the other hand, attributes that are not yet measurable may nevertheless be important and deserve some other form of recognition.

(2) For some behaviors the research path starts with assessment of individuals, then goes to evaluation of family members, and (perhaps) finally to DNA. In others the trail begins with DNA and, through a series of steps, eventually reaches families and the population. The use of both strategies gains the power of a reductionistic approach together with the recognition of behaviors as biopsychosociological phenomena.

33. Irving I. Gottesman, "Origins of Schizophrenia: Past as Prologue," in *Nature, Nurture, and Psychology,* 234, 238.
34. Kenneth K. Kidd, "Can We Find Genes for Schizophrenia?" *American Journal of Medical Genetics (Neuropsychiatric Genetics)* 74 (1997): 104-111.
35. Volker Arolt et al., "Eye Tracking Dysfunction Is a Putative Phenotypic Susceptibility Marker of Schizophrenia and Maps to a Locus on Chromosome 6p in Families with Multiple Occurrence of the Disease," *American Journal of Medical Genetics (Neuropsychiatric Genetics)* 67 (1996): 564-579.

(3) Each of these examples of data from behavior genetics has included some effort to understand the relative roles of genetic and environmental factors. This relationship can become fairly complex, since our genotypes affect the way that we perceive, modify, or respond to environment. Furthermore, a quantitative estimate of the fraction contributed by each component is only a first step toward a more complete understanding of the behavior.

(4) Finally, it seems reasonable to conclude with Eaves and Gross that "the highest measurable human functions, such as cognition, affect, and value, depend in part on the fundamental genetic structure of the individual as it exists in relationship to the environment."[36]

IMPLICATIONS OF THIS GENETIC VIEW

The final task is to consider how the above discussion of specific details relates to broader philosophical and practical questions. Much of the general framework that emerges can be described under three major headings.

Determinism and Free Will
The specter of genetic determinism is probably the source of more public concern than any other question about human nature. Are we merely the product of our genes, directly and indirectly? In what sense are we free to act and behave in ways that result from our own choices?

The answer must begin with our present understanding of the genetic material.[37] DNA designs proteins (such as enzymes and hormones), with a different gene for each protein. These proteins do not act independently of each other, but interact in complex networks that are an indirect result of gene action. Throughout a person's development the pattern of gene expression and repression is modified by environmental factors and other circumstances of life. (For this reason much of human development is described as epigenetic rather than genetic.)

The upshot of this is that genes are ontologically necessary for human existence and for our possession of the qualities that are considered to be essential components of human nature. Discussions of human nature that completely ignore genetics will be seriously incomplete, for no behavior is possible unless the genes provide the capability for that behavior.

36. Lindon Eaves and Lora Gross, "Exploring the Concept of Spirit as a Model for the God-World Relationship in the Age of Genetics," *Zygon* 27 (1992): 269. See also L. J. Eaves, H. J. Eysenck, and N. G. Martin, *Genes, Culture and Personality: An Empirical Approach* (New York: Academic Press, 1989).
37. See Section 3 above. See also R. David Cole, "The Molecular Biology of Transcending the Gene," in *Religion and Science: History, Method, Dialogue,* ed. W. Mark Richardson and Wesley J. Wildman (New York: Routledge, 1996): 343-350.

At the same time, while genes are necessary for human traits and behavior, they are by no means sufficient. Interactions with environment are crucial at every stage of development. While genes provide a range of possibilities for specific behaviors, the environment moderates and modulates genetic control, and thus softens what otherwise might be complete genetic determinism.

Discussion of the roles of genes and environment still leaves us with the need to understand human freedom. Is it possible that human behavior could, in principle, be explained fully by a combination of genes *and* circumstances (environment)? Here we confront a gap in our knowledge of ourselves. However, in our everyday experience we act as if, in varying degrees, we are major contributors to our actions. The more we see ourselves as meaningful contributors to our behavior, the more we call ourselves free. The less we feel we contribute, whether the restrictions are genetic or environmental or both, the less we see ourselves as free. Of course, our choices must in some way set in motion the physiological mechanisms required to implement the desired actions, but the exploration of the intervening steps has just begun in the detailed investigation of the brain and central nervous system.

Evidence suggesting the role of choice is found in the twin studies data. Even in monozygotic twins raised together, the correlations for behaviors never approach 1.00. So not even genes and environment together produce complete uniformity in behavior.

Several things follow from these considerations. Our actions lie on a continuum between complete freedom and complete determinism. Freedom is a matter of degree; it is an opportunity that must be seized and used. We create our freedom as we engage the world around us utilizing the resources of our genes and the environment at our disposal.

Reductionism

A second concern is the claim that all phenomena, including human behavior, are to be explained in terms of simpler and more basic or fundamental elements that are subject to deterministic, scientific laws. This form of reductionism has often been employed by scientific investigators as their standard methodological strategy. In complex conditions or traits (such as memory, dyslexia, visuospatial deficit, or nurturing) some effort to simplify seems essential. It is only by separating complex phenomena into smaller components and analyzing them in detail that the larger problems eventually can be resolved.

The more important question is whether the scientific use of methodological reductionism requires one to adopt an explanatory reductionism, the belief that all complex phenomena are reducible to basic elements in terms of which all proper explanation must be carried out. The answer lies partly in the

logic of the argument and partly in examination of the actual response by scientists. It seems likely that a reductionistic worldview may lead to research
designs that restrict the range of the questions that are asked and thus the
interpretation of the data produced.

The Netherlands family presents a relevant case history. Although the basic
problem is genetic and biochemical, the research reports also have drawn heavily on developmental, psychological, and sociological methods. Thus far, efforts
at biochemical intervention have not proved successful, but the broad range of
publications to date may help to decide if individual or group psychological
interventions might be considered. It is not yet clear how adequately the
affected men can handle choosing among options. Can they learn to choose
their environmental settings in order to reduce stress, or must they remain
dependent on family and friends to maintain protective situations? At another level, is it possible that counseling about ethical and religious implications
of aggressive behavior might help them to moderate their behavior?

Past experience in genetics does not show conclusively that explanatory
reductionism always follows from methodological reductionism. Prior to 1953
the chemical composition and the helical structure of the DNA molecule had
been worked out using the fundamental methods of physics and chemistry (a
bottom-up approach), but those methods did not help to resolve the arrangement of the component parts. The breakthrough came through a top-down
approach to explanation, by asking a biological question about the function of
genes. Watson and Crick reasoned that the structure of DNA must be such that
genes can be copied and can carry information. On this basis they proposed
the base-pairing solution that was rapidly verified.[38]

In short, scientists still need to attend to the connections between the
methods they employ and their implications for views of reality. Reductionism has a disquieting tendency to ignore diverse approaches to understanding human behavior. "We learn to look for underlying mechanisms—
material causes—by excluding from view the ambiguities of any larger view.
. . . Any purely genetic consideration of the human being becomes inhuman
by virtue of its narrowness."[39]

Unity and Diversity
The simple and yet complex nature of DNA inspires awe and wonder. It unites
all humankind in an intertwining web. It forms a link to all other forms of life

---

38. Gunther S. Stent, "That Was the Molecular Biology That Was," *Science* 160 (1968):
390-395.
39. Craig Holdrege, *Genetics and the Manipulation of Life,* 14, 16.

that share the same basic DNA structure. And, finally, DNA is our biological connection to our own past and to our future.

It is this vision that led Lindon Eaves to designate DNA as the central icon of biology, that "part of reality which both crystallizes reality as it is currently known and opens up new horizons for the exploration of reality."[40] Some have felt that this verges on a new idolatry, and others have been sharply critical of "DNA as a cultural icon."[41] Caution is indeed necessary, since the meaning and value of any part of creation can be distorted. Yet I must agree with Eaves that a realistic understanding and appraisal of DNA and of genetics deserves a central, but not exclusive, place in views of human nature.

It is noteworthy that genetics is involved in accounting for both the universals (that which is shared by all humans) and the particulars (the individual differences) of human behavior. Ayala's discussion of evolution stressed the universals, and I have emphasized the particulars, yet both meet in a common understanding of the transmission and expression of the genes. In another context Eaves argued that we cannot construct a theological anthropology on universals alone. [42] Here again there need be no choice between universals or particulars, since a comprehensive view of human nature requires both.

Unity and diversity also have implications for our views about the moral and spiritual life. Genes are as important for the structure and function of the brain as for the rest of the human body. Our capacities for moral and spiritual activity are genetically conditioned, but our use of them remains a matter of personal choice. We have only a limited appreciation, however, of the extent of individual diversity in these capacities.[43]

Conclusions

Genes are necessary for our human existence and for our ability to express those qualities that are thought to be important components of human nature. Genes are not sufficient, however, since interactions with environment are involved at every stage of development. Furthermore, an adequate view of human nature requires an understanding of the effects of genes at many levels, including psychological, social, and spiritual.

40. Lindon Eaves, "Spirit, Method, and Content in Science and Religion: The Theological Perspective of a Geneticist," *Zygon* 24, no. 2 (June 1989), 193.

41. Dorothy Nelkin and M. Susan Lindee, *The DNA Mystique: The Gene as a Cultural Icon* (New York: W. H. Freeman and Company, 1995).

42. Lindon Eaves, "Behavioral Genetics, or What's Missing from Theological Anthropology?" 346.

43. See Ronald Cole-Turner, *The New Genesis: Theology and the Genetic Revolution* (Louisville: Westminster/John Knox Press, 1993), 88-89.

The next decade will bring a significant expansion of genetic information, which may affect areas as diverse as self-understanding, effective modes of teaching, views of human responsibility, and theological concepts. Hence the ethical, legal, social, and theological implications of the new knowledge must be given thoughtful consideration.

Chapter Four

Brain, Mind, and Behavior

Malcolm Jeeves

THE DECADE OF THE BRAIN

Brain science in general and cognitive neuroscience in particular are prominent features of contemporary science. That is demonstrated by the number of researchers involved, the publications emerging, and the research funding allocated. The United States Congressional committee report *The Decade of the Brain*[1] noted that "scientific information on the brain is amassing at an enormous rate, and the field of computer and information sciences has reached a level of sophistication sufficient to handle neuroscience data in a manner that would be maximally useful to both researchers and clinicians dealing with brain function and dysfunction." The Senate's report succinctly captured the flavor of much contemporary brain research when it stated:

> Fundamental discoveries at the molecular and cellular levels of the organization of the brain are clarifying the role of the brain in translating neurophysiologic events into behavior, thought and emotion. . . . The study of the brain involves the multi-disciplinary efforts of scientists from such diverse areas as physiology, biochemistry, psychology, psychiatry, molecular biology, anatomy, medicine, genetics, and many others working together toward the common goal of a better understanding of the structure of the brain and how it affects our development, health and behavior. . . .

It is not only the research laboratories and scientific academies that are aware of the exciting developments in brain research. Scarcely a day passes

---

1. Joint Resolution presented in the House of Representatives in the U.S. Congress, March 8, 1989, to designate the decade beginning January 1, 1990, as the "Decade of the Brain."

without the media reporting some new discoveries that may hold out hope for the relief of suffering in conditions such as Alzheimer's disease, Parkinson's disease, and schizophrenia. Workers at the cutting edge of this research have interpreted its wider implications in differing ways. Some have suggested that the research has profound implications for the way in which we think about ourselves, about our very nature. Some see it as having profound implications for how we think about our personal freedom and responsibility. Others note that it raises questions about whether, after all, we do differ as fundamentally as past generations thought from our closest nonhuman relatives, and if so, in what ways.

This is not new. Down the millennia, our forebears have speculated about their existence. The psalmist posed the question, What then is man? Two millennia later, the poet Alexander Pope, in his famous "Essay on Man," wrote:[2]

> Know then thyself, presume not God to scan;
> the proper study of mankind is man.
> Placed on this isthmus of a middle state,
> being darkly wise and rudely great;
> with too much knowledge for the skeptic side,
> with too much weakness for the stoic's pride,
> he hangs between; in doubt to act, or rest;
> in doubt to deem himself a God, or beast;
> in doubt his mind or body to prefer. . . .
> Sole judge of Truth, in endless Error hurled:
> The glory, jest and riddle of the world!

Today, some well-known and prominent scientists believe that the advances made in our study of the brain over the past fifty years require a major rethinking of our human nature. For example, Francis Crick, Nobel laureate and joint discoverer of the structure of DNA, has written, "The idea that man has a disembodied soul is as unnecessary as the old idea that there was a Life Force. This is in head on contradiction to the religious beliefs of billions of human beings alive today. How will such a radical change be received?" Neurologist Antonio Damasio writes, "The distinction between diseases of 'brain' and 'mind' between 'neurological' problems and 'psychological' problems or 'psychiatric' ones, is an unfortunate cultural inheritance that permeates society and medicine. It reflects a basic ignorance of the relation between brain and mind."[3]

---

2. Alexander Pope, "Essay on Man," in *Poetry of the English-Speaking World,* ed. Richard Aldington (London: Heinemann, 1947), 422-424.
3. Francis H. Crick, *The Astonishing Hypothesis: The Scientific Search for a Soul* (London: Simon and Schuster, 1994).

The scientific data accumulated by researchers into brain processes, as with any other scientific data, do not come with a neat interpretative label attached. The influence of presuppositions on data interpretation is perhaps particularly acute on topics that come close to the heart of understanding our own nature. No surprise therefore that in the recent past, the marked resurgence of interest in consciousness finds equally distinguished scientists interpreting the same data in radically different ways.

In this chapter, we shall give illustrations of typical research findings, both well established as well as more recent and tentative, to indicate how and why we believe they point to the ever tightening links between brain, mind, and behavior. To write about "links" actually reflects, and to some extent conceals, our ignorance rather than resolving how best to characterize the relation between mind and brain. We believe that there is only *one set of events* but that to do justice to their complexity they must be studied and analyzed from more than one standpoint paying due attention to their mental and physical aspects.

How did we arrive at where we are today, and what can we learn from the past? How have rapid developments in three previously relatively distinct areas of science converged to produce the present situation? What implications are there in all this for some traditional Christian beliefs about human nature? For example, with the emphasis on the unity of the human person, what has become of the soul? Since it would seem that everything that happens at the level of mind is tightly coupled with what is happening in a physical system, the human brain, what about notions of human freedom and responsibility? And since many of the advances in neuropsychology come from research on nonhuman primates, what differences are there between human and non-human primates? Do animals have souls?

GAINING PERSPECTIVE

In any generation, the views of the academy filter down into the marketplace. What was happening in William Shakespeare's day well exemplifies this. Just as today we smuggle our views of the mind into our everyday expressions as when we talk about somebody being "switched on" or "switched off" (hinting at the computer analogy), or we talk about somebody being "conditioned" to do this or that (hinting at Pavlov's model of the mind), so in Shakespeare's day. No doubt aware of how for centuries the cardiovascular and encephalic views of how the soul/mind was linked to the body/brain had successively been in and out of fashion, Shakespeare, in his generation neatly sat on the fence. Thus, in *The Merchant of Venice*, Portia sings, "Tell me where is fancy bred, or in the heart or in the head." Sir John Falstaff in *Henry IV* attributes the king's apoplexy to "a kind of sleeping in the blood" and a "perturbation of the brain." And for good measure he adds in a reference to the ventricular theory when the schoolmaster Holofanes, in *Love's Labors Lost*, attributes his gift to things that are "Begot in the *ventricle* of memory, nourished in the womb of the pia mater." Thus, in the 1590s all three major views were in circulation.

Earlier Competing Views

A moment's introspection suggests that the "obvious" place to localize the mind is in the heart. Think exciting thoughts and your heart thumps in your chest. Think peaceful thoughts and your heart is quiet again. From a phenomenological point of view, one might conclude that the mind resides in the heart. Over the past 2,000 years, two views of the link between mind and body have competed and dominated thinking.

Empedocles, in the fifth century B.C.E., had no doubt that the soul (the Greek word for the mind) resided in the heart and in the blood—a theory labeled the cardiovascular theory. His views did not go unchallenged because around the same time Alcimaeon of Croton asserted that mental functions are located in the brain, a view labeled the encephalic view. Down the years, prominent figures took sides in this debate. Hippocrates around the fourth century B.C.E. held an encephalic theory, not surprisingly perhaps since one of his texts dealing extensively with epilepsy, the sacred disease, made it clear that brain and mental events were linked.

In the fourth century B.C.E., Plato and Aristotle well exemplified the continuing conflict between the two theories. Plato's views were perhaps a little ambiguous. At times he seemed to want it both ways. He located the immortal soul in the "marrow" of the head, presumably the brain, but located the passions between the neck and the midriff. Aristotle unambiguously localized the soul in the heart. At the same time, he still had a role for the brain. Being a good biologist he decided it must serve some function. Noticing that it was moist and cool to the touch he concluded that it refrigerated the blood! Aristotle's views passed on through the stoic philosophers to one of the early church fathers, Tertullian, whilst the encephalic view survived through one of Rome's outstanding physicians, Galen. He was a great anatomist and his brain dissections provided new anatomical data to support his views. Impressed with the size and location of the ventricles in the brain, he concluded that that was where the "vital spirits" or the "animal spirits" were located.

Not long after Galen died, the Germanic invasions took place in Western Europe, and as a result, for a long period it lost its knowledge of the Greek classics. By the fourth century C.E., Nemesius, bishop of Emesa in Syria, produced a new theory of the physical basis of mind. Claiming to be a follower of Galen, he took his views further, distinguishing three different mental faculties—sensation; imagination; and thought, judgment, and memory—and localizing them in the three major ventricles he observed in the brain. Interaction between the two theories, the encephalic and the cardiovascular, continued now primarily in the intellectual exchange that took place in Spain, from where the ideas of Aristotle and Galen were reintroduced into Western Europe. Thus, there were three groups of partisans forming up, holding respectively the encephalic, cardiovascular, and the ventricular theories of the mind-body link.

As recently as the late eighteenth century, the leading physicians in London seemingly saw no causal link between something wrong with the ability to speak and what was going on in the brain. Those who attended the famous English lexicographer Dr. Samuel Johnson when he suffered a stroke in 1783 (an event documented in detail in his diaries) prescribed for him the then-accepted treatment of inflicting blisters on each side of the throat up to the ear, one on the head, and one on the back together with taking regular doses of salts of hartshorn, what today we would call ammonium carbonate. Thus, they "treated" peripheral structures located in the neck and throat, believing that here was the physical basis of speech. Clearly for them, brain events and the mind events involved in speech and language were not linked. Such a view went counter to one of the prevailing views about the physical basis of mind that had competed with others for the previous 2,000 years. In the years following Dr. Samuel Johnson's experiences in 1783, views began to change rapidly. In 1825, Bouillard, a French physician, argued from his clinical observations that speech was localized in the frontal lobes of the brain. His views were supported by Gall, the distinguished anatomist and phrenologist. Shortly afterward in 1835, these views were expanded by Mark Dax, who argued that speech disorders were linked to lesions of the left hemisphere, views further reinforced in 1861, when Paul Broca reported the case of a patient who stopped speaking when pressure was applied to the anterior lobes of his brain. Thus the notion of cerebral dominance of language in the left hemisphere was enunciated.

The events described above were associated primarily with the linking of mental or cognitive processes with brain structures. In 1848, a 25-year-old foreman, Phineas Gage, working for the Rutland and Burlington Railroad Company, in New England, accidentally prematurely exploded a charge which sent a tamping iron through Gage's left cheek, piercing his skull, traversing the front of his brain and exiting at high speed through the top of his head. The detailed report of the event says that Gage was stunned! Amazingly he was still conscious and made a remarkable recovery. He became a notorious case, appearing in circuses. His employers described how, before the accident he was efficient and capable, but afterward his personality had clearly undergone a dramatic change. Not only was he feckless and irresponsible, his likes and dislikes, his aspirations, his ethics and morals, were altered. Such findings suggested that it was not just mental events that were linked to brain structures but that there may be systems in the human brain, which, if damaged, may alter the personal and social dimensions of normal life. Antonio Damasio, in his book *Descartes' Error*,[4] concluded his description of Gage's experience with the provocative question, "Is it fair to say that his soul was diminished, or that he had lost his soul?" Damasio further documented with contemporary cases the observations made on Gage, demonstrating that it was not a unique observation.[5]

The Picture Emerging
In the space of less than a hundred years the assumption that brain events and mind events were not linked changed to a recognition of the clear link between brain, language, and intellectual function generally. There were also clear hints of a link between brain and personality, including social and ethical behavior. Such moves, however, did not go unchallenged. Pierre Flourens in the early nineteenth century and a pioneer in techniques of making small lesions in the brains of animals as a way of investigating brain function, published results that were taken to imply that psychological functions are not discreetly localized in particular cerebral areas. It was a view championed a century later by Karl Lashley who put forward a theory of mass action, contending that the behavioral outcome of cortical lesions depends more on the *amount* of the brain removed than on the particular *location* of the lesion inflicted. While today, the localizationist view is dominant and well documented, it is, for our present purposes, no more than illustrative of the cumulative trend of neuropsychological research pointing to the conclusion that neural and mental processes are two aspects of one set of physical events.

During the second half of the present century, and in particular immediately after the Second World War, there was a reawakening of interest in the brain-behavior relationship. Facing the task of rehabilitating thousands of servicemen with circumscribed gunshot wounds, research began to advance rapidly. As often happens in science, the outcome was not so much the discovery of new ideas but the rediscovery of old ones. In this case, the views of some nineteenth-century neurologists, combined with the development of the new behavioral techniques of the experimental psychologists, which gave the impetus to the development of neuropsychology.

4. Antonio R. Damasio, *Descartes' Error: Emotion, Reason, and the Human Brain* (New York: Grosset/Putnam, 1994), 118.
5. Ibid.

THE CONTEMPORARY SCENE

The rapid development of cognitive neuroscience in recent years is generally attributed to the convergence of three previously relatively unrelated areas of scientific endeavor: experimental psychology, comparative neuropsychology, and brain imaging techniques. The cognitive revolution within experimental psychology freed it from earlier narrowly circumscribed behaviorist approaches to the understanding of mind and behavior. Psychologists could talk freely about mental events and not simply about stimulus-response contingencies. The development of new experimental techniques enabled cognitive psychologists to fractionate psychological processes into their component parts. Memory, for example, into long-term memory, working memory, and short-term memory.

In comparative neuropsychology, techniques found useful in studying human remembering and perceiving were adapted and applied to the study of nonhuman primates. Exciting new findings came from studies of memory and visual perception in animals. Other psychologists, following the pioneering studies of Hubel and Wiesel, used single-cell recording techniques to study perception in awake and alert monkeys. At the same time there were exciting developments in brain imaging techniques, notably nuclear magnetic resonance and most recently of all, positron emission tomography scanning techniques. These latter, combined with cerebral blood flow studies, made possible the monitoring of brain activities occurring when specified mental tasks are performed by normal people.

Localization of Cognitive Processes
One of the more consistent findings of research capitalizing on the convergence of these three approaches has been how specific mental processes or even component parts of those processes appear to be tightly linked to particular regions or systems in the brain. Within those regions, moreover, there often emerged a further specificity indicating that certain columns of cells were involved when a particular aspect of the task was being performed.

One of the best-known outcomes of neuropsychological research is from the work of Roger Sperry and his collaborators. They studied how the two hemispheres of the brain communicate and at the same time discovered more of the distinctive functions of each cerebral hemisphere. In this work, they productively and elegantly combined work in animal and human experimental neuropsychology. With Ronald Myers, Sperry studied the effects of severing the corpus callosum, the main bundle of fibers normally cross connecting the two cerebral hemispheres, in cats and monkeys. They discovered that what was taught to one hemisphere was, in such "split-brain" preparations, unavailable to the other hemisphere. Transfer between the two sides of the brain seemed to have been prevented.

Around the same time, Sperry, with neurosurgeon Joseph Bogen, studied a small group of patients in whom the same cerebral commissure had been totally severed to reduce the spread of uncontrollable epilepsy from one to the other hemisphere. Using techniques adapted from the animal studies they discovered that in these patients there seemed to be two, as Sperry put it, "centers of consciousness," so that one half of the brain was unaware of what the other one was doing. With this separation of the two hemispheres it was possible to study the specialized functions of each hemisphere with minimal interference from the other. The results are well known and confirm some of the earlier classical neurological work on hemispheric specialization described above. In right-handed people language processes are predominantly localized in the left cerebral hemisphere, and spatial visual processing is predominantly undertaken in the right hemisphere. Their studies did not end there. Language processes were fractionated down into their component parts, and it emerged that different aspects of linguistic behavior were localized in different hemispheres.

More recently, Michael Posner[6] in the United States and Christopher Frith in the United Kingdom have used MRI and PET scanning techniques to demonstrate how very specific aspects of language behavior, as well as memory, in normal people are linked to activity in circumscribed areas of the brain.

We may give one further illustration of localization of function, in this instance of face perception. The neurological literature contains occasional reports of patients who, following a stroke, suddenly lost their ability to recognize faces, including ones with which they had been familiar throughout their lives. Using CT scans it was possible to localize the damaged areas. Researchers Edmund Rolls and David Perrett, using nonhuman primates, subsequently recorded from the brains of alert monkeys performing face recognition tasks. They found that the localization already evident in human patients was even more narrowly circumscribed so that some columns of cells responded only when specific faces, familiar to the monkeys in the laboratory situation, were shown to them. Moreover, of those faces that were shown to evoke responses, only certain columns of cells responded when the faces were seen from one angle and only others when seen from another angle. In other words, increasing localization and specificity became more and more firmly established.

Our personal introspections allow us each to build up our own "folk psychology." Most of us feel that our mental life has a seamless unity to it. It

6. M. I. Posner et al., "Localisation of Cognitive Operations in the Human Brain," *Science* 240 (June 17, 1988): 1627-1631.

comes as a surprise, therefore, to discover that cognitive processes like memory may be decomposed or fractionated and that different systems go wrong when specific brain structures are damaged. For example, damage to the hippocampus or the amygdala affects what are called *declarative memories,* that is remembering names or events, whereas memories about how to do things— *procedural memories*—seem to be processed in more ancient parts of the brain.[7] There appears, therefore, to be some evidence for saying that the distinction familiar to philosophers between "knowing that" and "knowing how" may rest upon distinct neural substrates.

A further example comes from current cognitive and physiological studies of perception that suggest that the nonverbal processes involved in identifying *what* objects are, are distinct from processes involved in identifying *where* an object is in space, and both in turn are distinct from identifying the *movement* of an object.

Some of the dissociations seen by neuropsychologists further underline the tightening of the linkage between mind and brain. Some patients can write good prose but not read it,[8] some cannot identify a familiar face but can read its emotions,[9] some patients may deny seeing something but be able to discriminate it above chance level in appropriate testing, so-called blindsight.[10]

The accumulating evidence for ever-increasing localization and specificity received a timely counterbalance from work on neural networks within the brain. It emerged that psychological processes are not necessarily localized to one part of the brain but often depend upon the intact working of networks of systems of cells located in widely separated parts of the brain. In some instances psychological functions could be changed by lesions to pathways linking centers within these networks. The difference between whether functions are found to be localized versus a product of a wider network has largely to do with the *level* of definition of the function. Nevertheless, the same take-home message emerged from all of these studies, whether human or animal, namely, the remarkable localization of function in the brain and the specificity of the neural substrate underlying mental events. As each advance occurred, mind and brain were seen to be ever more tightly linked together.

7. M. Mishkin and T. Appenzeller, "The Anatomy of Memory," *Scientific American* 256, no. 6 (1987): 62-71.

8. Harold Goodglass and Edith Kaplan, *The Assessment of Aphasia and Related Disorders* (Philadelphia: Lea and Tebiger, 1972).

9. A. Damasio, "Mechanisms of Face Recognition," in *Handbook of Research on Face Processing,* ed. A. W. Young and H. D. Ellis (New York: Elsevier, 1989).

10. Lawrence Weiskrantz, *Blindsight: A Case Study and Implications* (Oxford: Oxford University Press, 1986).

Brain and Social Behavior

What is true of the high correlations between mental processes and brain processes has been paralleled by studies of the relation between social and emotional aspects of behavior and brain processes. As far back as the 1930s, clinicians had noted an apparent asymmetry in the effects of lesions either to the right or to the left cerebral hemisphere on emotional behavior. Goldstein had suggested that left hemisphere lesions produced fearfulness and depression, so-called catastrophic reactions, whereas right hemisphere lesions produce "indifference." It is now clear from more detailed and recent studies by Gainotti that a simple left/right distinction of catastrophic/indifference is too simplistic. Both the site and the size of the lesion are important in understanding the changes in emotional behavior that occur.

Another example of this brain-personality linkage that has received considerable attention is the so-called temporal lobe personality. Bear and Fedio, for example, asked patients with damage to their temporal lobes due to epilepsy to complete rating scales aimed at assessing behavioral traits such as anger, sadness, and religiosity. They reported that the epileptic patients self-reported a distinctive profile of what they called humorless sobriety, dependence, and obsessionalism; moreover, the right and left temporal lobe patients were distinguishable; the right temporal patients were described as more obsessional, the left as more concerned with "personal destiny."[11] Bear and Fedio's findings bring to mind the studies reported by Anderson in the previous chapter of a family many of whose members had shown abnormal and excessive aggression, in that instance linked to genetic factors.

The topicality of these issues is underlined by Robert Hare's suggestion that the brains of psychopaths are abnormal in that they underutilize regions that normally integrate emotion and memory with other information. Psychopaths are, he says, easily bored and crave immediate self-gratification. They are intellectually aware of society's rules but feel no guilt when they break them.[12] Joanne Intrator, a New York psychiatrist collaborating with Robert Hare, reported that normals and psychopaths differed in which areas of their brains were active when they were performing a language task earlier shown by Hare to differentiate psychopaths from normals. In normals, the ventromedial cortex and amygdala were active, in psychopaths those same parts remained inactive while processing emotion-laden words. Hare rightly cautions that further studies are required to answer definitively the question of whether psychopaths'

11. M. Bear and P. Fedio, "Quantitative Analysis of Intercital Behaviour in Temporal Lobe Epilepsy," *Archives of Neurology* 34 (1977): 454-467.
12. Robert D. Hare, *Without Conscience: The Disturbing World of the Psychopaths among Us* (Pocket Books, 1993).

brains are wired differently from those of normal people. For our present considerations these studies further illustrate, in the domain of social behavior, the tightness of the association between brain processes and behavior.

It is clear that attempts to study the relation between emotional behavior, as well as aggression, and brain processes, begins to reveal a similar picture to that which emerged from our review of cognitive processes and brain processes. The studies reviewed so far have arisen primarily from a bottom–up approach to the study of the linkages between mind and behavior on one hand and the brain on the other. That is, we have looked at what happens to mental or behavioral processes when there are identifiable changes in neural structures. A similar, although at the moment less clear-cut, picture emerges if we look at how behavior and mental life may change brain structures. Such top-down research is much harder to do (see chapter 5 by Warren Brown). Evidence in support of the influence of top-down factors comes, for example, from the discovery that the spatial position of cortical somato-sensory representations can shift significantly if motor input is manipulated.[13] Such work illustrates the potential for transfer of the biological substrate for certain cognitive functions, with shifts in both relative size and relative position. Nevertheless, the take-home message is the same, namely, the intimate link between mind, behavior, and brain.

The Relation of Human to Animal Nature

One thing that stands out very clearly from many reviews of neuroscience over the past forty years is how greatly it has depended on and benefited from experiments using animals. What is true of neuroscience in general is highlighted further in the specific domain of neuropsychological research. Here, a study of animals, not simply rats, cats, and dogs, as in other parts of neuroscience, but much more specifically of nonhuman primates, has been extremely important in increasing our understanding of human neuropsychology. In humans, for obvious ethical reasons, our understanding of the effects of changes in the structure of the brain on mental life and behavior depends on studying the consequences of brain damage, occurring through disease, accident, or at birth. While the techniques available for locating brain damage in patients have made enormous leaps and bounds in the past three decades, there remains a measure of uncertainty about the precise location and extent of any damage. That uncertainty can only be resolved if and when there is a post-mortem examination. For this reason alone, work on nonhuman pri-

13. W. M. Jenkins, M. M. Merzenich, and G. Recanzone, "Neocortical Representational Dynamics in Adult Primates: Implications for Neuropsychology," *Neuropsychologia* 28 (1990): 573-584.

mates has proved extremely valuable. With careful surgery, it is possible to produce circumscribed localized changes in the brains of nonhuman primates and
then study the differences between pre-operative and post-operative performance on a variety of experimental tasks performed by the animals. Such
studies help to reduce the uncertainties that remain if we only study people
who have been accidentally brain injured. Underlying such animal studies is
the tacit assumption that the results from them, while interesting in themselves, throw further light on the understanding of the human mind-brain
links, that is tacit assumptions about similarities between the brains of humans
and the brains of animals. This is not new in psychology. It was used by
Köhler, by Skinner, and by Pavlov, to name but three well-known researchers.
Such research raises two distinguishable issues relevant to our present discussions. The first is the way in which the results from animal neuropsychological research further strengthen the grounds for seeing mental processes as
embodied in localized structures, or localized or distributed systems or subsystems in the brain. The second indicates how research in nonhuman primate
neuropsychology, while adding further support to the tightness of the men-
tal-neural linkages, may be interpreted as a further warning against reifying
"soulishness" and then making it something that humans have and nonhuman
primates do not.

George Ettlinger argued that "The majority of neuropsychologists would
agree that within the primates, brain size (relative to body weight) increased
suddenly with the emergence of modern man; that a large mass of brain tissue endowed man with a step wise superior intelligence; and that language
followed from man's superior intelligence." He continued, "In humans language has more than a communicative role—it also organizes the representation of information within one individual's mind. It is yet to be shown that
language competent apes can solve any of the kind of cognitive problems
more proficiently than can non-trained apes. By contrast, aphasic patients can
be shown to be impaired on a variety of cognitive tasks." [14] Richard
Passingham also raised the question "What is the distinctiveness of the brain
in humans?" [15] He suggested there are three different ways we can consider
this: first, in terms of size; second, in terms of relative proportions assigned to
particular functions in the brain; and third, whether there are specialized areas
in human brains not found in other brains. As for size, certain facts become
obvious. Elephants and whales have much bigger brains than we have. So
sheer size does not provide very good grounds from which to argue the

14. G. Ettlinger, "Humans, Apes and Monkeys: The Changing Neuropsychological
Viewpoint," *Neuropsychologia* 22, no. 8 (1984): 685-696.
15. R. Passingham, *The Human Primate* (Oxford: Oxford University Press, 1982).

uniqueness of *Homo sapiens*. Considering the primates, Passingham plots brain weight against body weight and comes up with a regression line for the non-human primates. Against this line, the human brain is 3.1 times as big as we might expect for a nonhuman primate of the identical weight. On the basis of this, one may therefore say that we are indeed special creatures. The human brain is unique in terms of overall size in relation to body weight. If size alone is important, there are grounds for asserting difference. But there are other ways of thinking about a typical primate brain. You could ask, "Is there any-thing special about the *proportions* of the brain assigned to different functions, such as areas that receive sensory information or control motor output? Regarded in this way, is there anything special about our brains as compared to the typical primate brain?" Passingham concludes that the human brain seems to fit very nicely the typical primate brain, but he says that such dif-ferences as there are, are predictable—that is, predictable from the model of a typical primate brain—but because they are predictable it does not say they are unimportant. The question then becomes, is our brain just an expanded brain of another primate, such as the chimpanzee? Is there something distinct about the human brain, and if so, what is it? Passingham notes that there are two specializations that are often said to be unique to the human brain: cere-bral asymmetries and the existence of speech areas in the neocortex. Two areas of the brain, the cerebellum and the neocortex, are largely responsible for associating information that comes from other parts of the brain as a system. These areas in the human brain are roughly three times the size they should be for a typical primate of our size. On these grounds, Passingham concludes that the gap between human and chimpanzee is probably much greater than we had earlier supposed. Thus, specialization does provide some clue to a dif-ference between humans and animals. Passingham points out that the account he gives lacks mystery. It attributes peculiarly human forms of mental life to relatively simple changes in the human brain. Finally, he says that it is, with-out doubt, language that has led to the transformation of society. Rules can be issued by means of it, strategies can be discussed, roles can be laid down, and traditions can be passed on.

Clearly, for Passingham, the crucial difference is language. And he is not sim-ply talking about communication. Right across the animal phyla, animals com-municate subtly and elegantly with one another. For Passingham, it is that aspect of language that enables us to handle not just symbols—chimps and apes can do that—but to represent words to ourselves, to manipulate internal sym-bols. It is this aspect of symbolic behavior, conferred by language, that he believes is the crucial difference between humankind and nonhuman pri-mates, and in this regard, he reaches a conclusion very similar to that of

Ettlinger mentioned earlier. The wisdom of the conclusions drawn both by Passingham and Ettlinger is underlined by the more recent results of studies on animals, designed to investigate the hypothesis that one aspect of language, auditory temporal processing, regarded as a precursor to speech processing, may be in evidence in species other than humans. Some researchers have identified left hemisphere specialization for the discrimination of species-typical calls in monkeys and mice, results that have been interpreted as evidence of left hemisphere specialization for communicative information processing. Other researchers, however, have called this interpretation into question, pointing out that monkeys exhibit left hemisphere specialization for performing complex auditory discriminations of stimuli that have no communicative relevance. It seems clear that left hemisphere specialization for auditory temporal processing is present in species other than humans, and that it is this mechanism that is critical to the discrimination of both coo-calls in monkeys and ultrasonic noise bursts in mice. Such results do not deny the points made by Passingham and Ettlinger about the aspect of symbolic behavior conferred by language as being crucial to the differences we now observe between humankind and nonhuman primates. It may well be with increased complexity of the neural networks in humans, that there has been a "phase change" that makes possible this property of symbolic behavior.

The logic of the argument about what similarities and differences imply needs watching carefully here, however. It has often been pointed out that a weak mixture of gas and air may contain the same kinds of molecules and lie on the same continuum as a richer mixture that burns, but that does nothing to prove that some kind of flame must be possible in the weaker mixture. Below a certain minimum concentration in the mixture it is simply not flammable. By the same token, the fact that the human brain organized in a specific way can embody conscious mental and spiritual life does nothing to prove that similar mental and spiritual capacities must be present in the brains of animals.

In thinking about how the human brain as a system may change with increasing complexity and differ from the nonhuman primate brain we may wonder whether there is an analogy here with the change in our understanding of superconductivity. Polkinghorne has pointed out that "after more than fifty years of theoretical effort, an understanding of current flow in metals was found which subsumed ordinary conduction and superconductivity into a single theory. The different behaviors correspond to different regimes, characterized by different organizations of the states of motion of the electron in the metal. One regime changes into another by a phase change (as the physicists call it) at the critical temperature."[16] Complete continuity of biological devel-

16. John C. Polkinghorne, *One World* (London: SPCK, 1986), 75.

opment, phylogenetically and ontogenetically, does not rule out the possibility of a radical change in cognitive/spiritual capacities at some point along a process of continuity at the physical level. No amount of evidence for continuity can deny a distinction between the two ends simply because thus far we have failed to identify a decisive moment when such a phase change occurs. We ask, therefore, could it be that the same material "stuff"—brains of animals as well as humans—due to changes in structural complexity, at some point undergo something analogous to a "phase change" so that new properties of mind, consciousness, and a capacity for spiritual awareness emerge in humans? Patient hard work by dedicated psychologists and neuroscientists may yet give us fresh insights into how, indeed, "we are marvelously and wonderfully made" in this regard. There will always be a delicate balance to be maintained. Pascal, we believe, had it right when he wrote, "It is dangerous to show man too clearly how much he resembles the beast, without at the same time showing him his greatness. It is also dangerous to allow him too clear a vision of his greatness without his baseness. It is even more dangerous to leave him in ignorance of both." [17]

THE TIGHTENING OF THE BRAIN-MIND-BEHAVIOR LINKS: WHAT DOES IT ALL IMPLY?

Dualism versus Materialism

We have given a few illustrative examples of how research points to the ever-tightening link between mind, behavior, and brain. Like any other research data, they do not arrive with a label attached telling us what they all mean. Not surprisingly some of the leading researchers when asking themselves what it may all imply for wider questions about human nature offer radically differing interpretations. The published views of Nobel laureates with an interest in neuroscience well illustrate these differences. Francis Crick, a reductionist materialist, had no doubts that "You are *nothing but* a pack of neurones" and that "you are . . . *no more than* the behavior of a vast assembly of nerve cells and their associated molecules." Of consciousness, he concluded that "to repeat: consciousness depends crucially on thalamic connections with the cortex. It exists only if certain cortical areas have reverberatory circuits (involving cortical layers 4 and 6) that projects strongly enough to produce significant reverberations." Having put forward his tentative theory, like any good scientist, he was immediately self-critical, commenting "While writing it down, my mind was constantly assailed by reservations and qualifications. If anyone else produced it, I would unhesitatingly condemn it as a house of cards. Touch it, and it collapses. This," he says,

17. Pascal, *Pensées* (1659), fragment 347.

"is because it has been carpentered together, with not enough crucial experimental evidence to support its various parts. Its only virtue is that it may prod scientists and philosophers to think about these problems in neural terms, and so accelerate the experimental attack on consciousness." [18]

By contrast, Sir John Eccles, from his earliest writings to his most recent publications, has advocated a strong dualist view. On the specific question of consciousness he writes, "It is dependent on the existence of a sufficient number of such critically poised neurons, and, consequently, only in such conditions are willing and perceiving possible. However, it is not necessary for the whole cortex to be in this special dynamic state." And, he continues, "On the basis of this concept (of activity of the cortex) we can face up anew to the extraordinary problems inherent in a *strong dualism. Interaction of brain and conscious mind*, brain receiving from conscious mind in a willed action and in turn transmitting to mind in conscious experiences." But, he continues, "Let us be quite clear that for each of us the primary reality is our consciousness—everything else is derivative and has a second order reality. We have tremendous intellectual tasks in our efforts to understand baffling problems that lie right at the center of our being. . . ." [19]

Roger Sperry, like Crick and Eccles, a Nobel laureate in Medicine and Physiology, but having worked more closely with problems at the coal face in understanding brain and mind, adopted a view diametrically opposed to that of Francis Crick's "nothing buttery," and was unwilling to accept the form of dualism advocated by Eccles. Sperry held a nonreductive physicalist view. Writing of consciousness he says "Consciousness is conceived to be a dynamic emergent property of brain activity, neither identical with nor reducible to, the neural events of which it is mainly composed," and "Consciousness exerts potent causal effects on the interplay of cerebral operations," and "In the position of top command at the highest levels in the hierarchy of brain organization, the subjective properties were seen to exert control over the biophysical and chemical activities at subordinate levels." His view is clearly a top-down view where mental events, as in the case of Eccles, are given ontological priority, but he wishes to avoid any suggestion of dualism of substance. Sperry's view is well captured in his words, "We do not look for conscious awareness in the nerve cells of the brain, nor in the molecules or the atoms in brain processing." Like many other neuroscientists, he believes that there has been "a move away from the mechanistic, deterministic and reductionist doctrines of the pre-1965 science to the more humanistic interpretations of the 1970's."

18. See Crick, *The Astonishing Hypothesis*.
19. J. C. Eccles, ed., *Brain and Conscious Experience* (Berlin: Springer-Verlag, 1966), 312, 327.

Sperry's own form of interaction is not without its problems. He has no doubt, however, that "the new model adds downward to traditional upward micro-determinism and is claimed to give science a conceptual foundation that is more adequate, valid and comprehensive." [20]

A formulation of the nonreductive physicalist view that we believe does justice to the evidence currently available would regard mental activity and correlated brain activity as inner and outer aspects of one complex set of events which together constitute conscious human agency.[21] The two stories that may be written about such a complex set of events, the mental story and the brain story, were argued by the late Donald MacKay to demonstrate logical complementarity. The irreducible duality of human nature is on this view seen as duality of aspects rather than duality of substance. Thus, the tightening of the link between mind and brain does not in any way minimize the importance of the mind or of mental activity in general. It does not mean that the mind is a mere epiphenomenon of the physical activity of the brain. We may think of the way the mind "determines" brain activity as analogous to the relation between the software and the hardware of our computers. In this sense in complementary fashion mental activity and behavior depend on the physically determinant operations of the brain, itself a physicochemical system. When that system goes wrong or is disordered, there are changes in its capabilities for running the system that we describe as the mind or as mental activity. And, likewise, if the mind or the mental activity results in behavior of particular kinds, this in turn may result in temporary or chronic changes in the physicochemical makeup and activity of the brain, its physical substrate. Thus, this ever-tightening link does not minimize the importance of the mind or the brain in this unitary complex system.

According to this view, we regard mental activity as *embodied in* brain activity rather than as being *identical with* brain activity. To go beyond that and to adopt what is sometimes called the materialist view is to confuse categories that belong to different logical levels. There is nothing within brain science or psychology that offers any justification for asserting that a materialist view is more compatible with the evidence than the view outlined above.

One cannot overemphasize the dangers of sliding into a form of thinking about human beings that relegates the conscious cognitive agent to second place. To go down that road is to adopt the reductionist gospel. All our knowledge of brains and minds and computers comes only through our experience and activity as conscious agents. It is only in and through that experience that

20. C. Trevarthen, ed., *Essays in Honor of Roger W. Sperry* (Cambridge: Cambridge University Press, 1990), 382-385.
21. See Murphy, chapter 6 this volume.

we gain scientific or any other kind of knowledge and that means that the conscious agent has what philosophers call ontological priority. Donald MacKay put it well when he wrote, "Nothing could be more fraudulent than the pretence that science requires or justifies a materialist ontology in which ultimate reality goes to what can be weighed and measured, and human consciousness is reduced to a mere epiphenomenon."[22]

Jean Delacour in 1995 noted an emerging consensus among scholars that rejects dualism as well as what he calls "eliminative monism." He writes, "The sterility of dualism has been stressed repeatedly and it is now a classical introduction to a text on consciousness with Descartes playing the role of a straw man. The insufficiency of eliminative monism is obvious, since it can be easily masked by scientific arguments; moreover, this philosophical position fits well with reductionism, which until recently was dominant in neurosciences. "However," he goes on, "consciousness as a fact of experience withstands any form of reductionism."[23]

Are There Challenges to Traditional Christian Beliefs?

Was Francis Crick right in asserting that most religious people assume that there are two separate things, the body and the soul? Was he right to assert that "there is broad agreement (in religions) on at least one point. People have souls in the literal and not merely the metaphorical sense"? The answer to these questions is probably yes and no. Crick was probably right to assume that a knee-jerk reaction to the question, what about the soul? is to assume that it is some separate thing that dwells within the body, and the answer is no if we are to take seriously what biblical scholars have been saying for at least a hundred years.[24] Are there any special issues at stake here for the Christian believer? Are there any claims from within neuropsychological research or any implications to be taken from it that challenge traditionally held Christian beliefs? We believe not.

Despite Crick's attempt to set up a conflict between what he takes as the religious view of human nature, that is belief in a "hypothetical immortal soul," in a "literal and not merely metaphorical sense," we believe there is no necessary conflict between the biblical pictures of human nature[25] and the emerging pictures from scientific research. Both point to one set of events that

22. Donald M. MacKay, *The Open Mind and Other Essays: A Scientist in God's World* (Leicester: Inter-Varsity, 1991).

23. J. Delacour, "The Biology and Neuropsychology of Consciousness," *Neuropsychologia* 33, no. 9 (1995): 1061-1192.

24. For detail, see Green, chapter 7, this volume.

25. Ibid.

require analysis from two (at least) distinct perspectives in order to begin to do justice to what we know.

Biblical scholars[26] emphasize that a dominant view found in Scripture is of the *unity* of the human person. She is a unified being who manifests several different aspects of her nature as she lives and acts in this world. At the same time we are encouraged to recognize the many-sidedness of our mysterious nature. It seems that we must hold in delicate balance three aspects of our nature that are highlighted by Old and New Testament writers alike: our physical make-up; our capacity for mental life; and our capacity for making moral decisions, including an appreciation for the importance of a spiritual dimension to life. Working harmoniously together, these are involved in maintaining a right relationship with God and our fellows.

A key aspect of the human person is what may be loosely defined as the spiritual aspect. This very important and intangible quality gives a person her special significance. It seems that if you can say something about this aspect of a person, you reveal something of what she is really like; you say what it is that inspires her for her daily living. Know what people set their hearts on and you know a great deal about their essential character, their spiritual dimension. So, for example, in Proverbs 20:27 we read, "The human spirit is the lamp of the LORD, searching every innermost part."

Commenting on past debates about the spiritual aspect of a person in the Christian tradition, the authors of *What Then Is Man?* wrote helpfully, "The word spirit is used over and over in the sense of what might be termed the operational content and direction of man's thoughts, words and actions. Spirit, then, is a fruit, an outcome of the individual's life and experience." They went on, "If spirit is regarded as a functional outcome rather than a separate structural entity, the difficult and troublesome trichotomy theory becomes entirely unnecessary." [27] In similar vein, Dallas Willard has written,

> Spirituality in human beings is not an extra or "superior" mode of existence. It's not a hidden stream of separate reality, a separate life running parallel to our bodily existence. It does not consist in special "inward" acts, even though it has an inner aspect. It is, rather, a relationship of our embodied selves to God that has a natural and irrepressible effect of making us alive to the kingdom of God—here and now in the material world.[28]

The rich fabric of the varied pictures of humankind given to us in Scripture[29] brings to mind the similarly rich complexity of the pictures of human nature

26. Ibid.
27. *What Then Is Man?* (St. Louis: Concordia Publishing House, 1958), 319.
28. Dallas Willard, *The Spirit of the Disciplines* (San Francisco: Harper and Row, 1988), 31.
29. See Green, chapter 7, this volume.

given to us through the scientific enterprise today. Both emphasize the complexity of human nature, the need to understand and study it from several aspects or perspectives, and the need to recognize that essentially human nature is a unity. A unity now in this present life, and by the grace of God, a unity in the life to come. Thus, our spiritual existence is not immune from neurological change. Indeed, the effects of brain damage on personality are, at times, extremely subtle, so that sometimes the essential spirit of the person is remarkably preserved despite massive deterioration of function. The story is very complex.

Neuroscience and the Spiritual Dimension

In the light of the emerging consensus among neuroscientists that the human person is most properly regarded as essentially a psychobiological unity, it follows that the brain, mind, and spirit are not to be regarded as separate entities, but rather as different aspects of our identity. Does it make any sense therefore to suggest that our spirit, independent of our mind and brain, has a state of well-being of its own? Is the spiritual dimension of our existence immune to the changes and chances of this fleeting world? There are several lines of inquiry that help us to answer these questions.

Today we are much more aware than in the past of the sufferings experienced by those with conditions like Alzheimer's disease. Like the rest of the body, the brain is affected by the passing of the years. We all experience the occasional lapse of memory, but for some, that turns into something much worse—senile dementia. Dementia is a consequence of a variety of different diseases of which Alzheimer's is by far the most common. Intensive research has established that many of the symptoms of Alzheimer's dementia are caused by damage to the nerve cells in the brain, some of which can be visualized using modern scanning techniques. Changes in brain structure have predictable psychological consequences. As the disease progresses three distinguishable stages are evident. First is forgetfulness, second comes confusion, and finally dementia. In the final stage, psychotic-like delusions and hallucinations occur. The suffering patient may then manifest not only psychological consequences but also dramatic changes in spiritual awareness. Subjective appreciation of their relationship with God may be severely compromised. Detailed studies of devout Christians in the terminal stages of Alzheimer's show that they are frequently deeply troubled about their relationship with God. They feel personally responsible for falling away from their close walk of discipleship, they may violate the commands of their nurses, and they may describe bizarre sexual disturbances. They may believe that they have committed sins that have provoked God's wrath. In due course, they lose all interest in their daily devotions and prayer. They are, as the psalmist has portrayed, often cry-ing out from the depths of chaos. With the neural changes of which we have considerable knowledge, there are psychological consequences, which in turn affect spiritual awareness.

Some forms of epilepsy, or what the Greeks called "the sacred disease," provide examples of how brain processes may be linked to religiosity. There was a long history of the association of religious hallucinations with epilepsy. Often those suffering from the disease showed an intense religiosity. The mood of exultation at times associated with the onset of an epileptic seizure may simulate the expression of religious sentiment. More recent study indicates that although hyperreligiosity and temporal lobe epilepsy may co-occur in some individuals, there does not appear to be a direct causal relationship between repeated seizure discharge in the temporal lobes and hyperreligiosity. This remains the case despite some speculations (e.g., Persinger[30]) that normal religious people, that is the seizure-free population, may report mystical or paranormal experiences because they are suffering what he calls microseizures in the brain. Studies carried out by Persinger to investigate this are seriously flawed methodologically and will need repeating more carefully.

Religious experience associated with brain seizure (or drugs), although undeniably a contributor to the conversions of some individuals, has a number of weaknesses as a general neuropsychological model of religious conversion. Certainly the accounts of mystical/religious experiences in the clinical epilepsy literature are not characteristic of *typical* Christian or other forms of religious conversion. From a theological point of view, nothing is established by demonstrating that a particular conversion has been related to abnormal brain activity; the epistemological problem of the *truth* of the content of the experience is not solved. In the case of St. Paul, if the Damascus road experience happened to involve a seizure, it would have little relevance to the theological question of the truth of what he subsequently preached, taught, and wrote.

The Mind / Brain Link, Determinism, and Free Will

The accumulating evidence for the ever-tightening link between mind and brain has led some Christian psychologists to re-examine with a fresh urgency

30. A. Persinger, "Religious and Mystical Experiences as Artifacts of Temporal Lobe Function: A General Hypothesis," *Perceptual and Motor Skills* 557 (1983): 1225-1262; A. Persinger, "People Who Report Religious Experiences May Also Display Enhanced Temporal Lobe Signs," *Perceptual and Motor Skills* 58 (1984): 163-197; A. Persinger, "Propensity to Report Paranormal Experiences Is Correlated with Temporal Lobe Signs," *Perceptual and Motor Skills* 59 (1984): 583-586; A. Persinger, "Striking EEG Profiles from Single Episodes of Glossalalia and Transcendental Meditation," *Perceptual and Motor Skills* 58 (1984): 127-133.

the question of the determinism of human behavior and of whether we enjoy any real freedom of choice. The general flavor of the debate is well illustrated by some of the views currently held by leading thinkers in the field. While sharing many basic Christian beliefs their solutions to the problem differ. Some take the view that freedom and determinism are concepts belonging to different language systems. Others point out that while determinism is a useful postulate *within* science, that does not mean that it is a universal rule.

Some, such as John Eccles, have seen a possible solution to the problem by appealing to the Heisenberg principle of indeterminacy in physics. On his view, some form of mind-brain liaison occurs in the cerebral cortex, and it is here that the will can influence neural activity without violating physical laws, because the energy involved in such influence is within the limits of the Heisenberg uncertainty principle. Eccles argues that mind, being a nonphysical factor, either may influence individual quantum events, these effects then being amplified throughout the cortex, or, more probably, there could be a coordinated shifting of probabilities in many such events simultaneously. There are, however, problems with this view. The indeterminacy allowed by the Heisenberg principle becomes more and more negligible the bigger the object we are studying. For the studying of electrons, it is far from negligible, but by the time we get to the size of the neuron, which is a million million times heavier than the electron, it is already becoming negligible. Furthermore, the brain, as far as we can tell at the moment, seems to be organized on a teamwork basis, so that one brain cell's behaving unpredictably would make no significant difference to the overall function of the brain. Finally, the random fluctuations in the brain, attributable to Heisenberg's principle, are very small compared with other fluctuations known to us, such as those due to thermodynamic changes, random fluctuations in the blood supply, and so on. Such unpredictable disturbances could, in fact, as easily be used to excuse from responsibility as to credit with responsibility for choices made.

John Polkinghorne refers to the "perpetual puzzle of the connection of mind and brain." It is easy, he says, if you are a thoroughgoing reductionist to answer the puzzle that is posed: mind is the epiphenomenon of brain, a mere symptom of its physical activity. But, he points out, the reductionist program in the end subverts itself. It destroys rationality and replaces thought with electrochemical neural events. Such events cannot confront one another in rational discourse; they are neither right nor wrong, but just happen. On this view, he says, the world of rational thought dissolves into the absurd chatter of firing synapses, and that cannot be right; none of us believes it to be so.[31]

---

31. See Polkinghorne, *One World*.

Others have seen chaos theory, regarded as nothing less than the third great revolution in the physical sciences, as a clue to the problems posed by mind related to the physical substrate of the brain. On this view, the simplest systems now seem to create extraordinarily difficult problems when it comes to predictability. They suggest that only a new kind of science could begin to cross the great gulf between knowledge of what one thing does, whether it be one water molecule or one neuron of the brain, and what billions of them will do. A *Scientific American* article in 1986 concluded that "Chaos provides a mechanism that allows free will within a world governed by deterministic laws." [32]

While these several attempts to solve the free-will problem scientifically are not at all promising, this does not mean we should deny human freedom. There is nothing remotely scientific in ignoring or minimizing the importance of our primary experience that we make choices all the time. To try and pretend, on any ideological reductionist grounds, that the common human experience of freedom to choose is an illusion is blatantly unscientific special pleading. It amounts to sweeping universally shared and agreed empirical data under the carpet.

Philosophers will hasten to point out that discussions of determinism and freedom of choice have a long history. What is new is how the accumulating evidence, examples of which we gave earlier, seems to pose the old questions with a fresh urgency. Some writers have distinguished between the liberty of spontaneity and the liberty of indifference. To understand the difference between the two, consider a situation where a person is faced with a choice of selecting porridge or stewed fruit for breakfast. She chooses porridge. Now if we were able to set up the exact same circumstances in force at the moment when the choice was made, and that would include a specification of the state of the whole universe including the person's brain, then so it is said, two possibilities exist:

1. The liberty of spontaneity, according to which the person would always choose porridge, since choosing porridge is what the person wanted to do.
2. The liberty of indifference, according to which the person would have the ability to take either porridge or stewed fruit.

The liberty of spontaneity is often referred to as a compatiblist view of freedom. This is because it is compatible with determinism. The liberty of indifference is referred to as a libertarian view of freedom.

32. J. P. Cruchfield et al., "Chaos," *Scientific American* 225 (1986): 38–49.

Many authors believe that freedom of indifference may give us too great an independence in that it produces an independence from our own selves; we are not the source but only the scene of the choice.[33]

Donald MacKay took a different view and gave the whole debate on free will a new twist by defining freedom in a new way, consistent with the other definition of liberty, liberty of spontaneity. To make his argument, MacKay assumed what he called a worst case scenario. He wrote, "We are going to set ourselves the toughest case; we are going to be asking what if—and it is a *strong* if—the whole of this system (i.e., the neurobiological substrate of cognitive activity) as summarized here were a determinate system in the physical sense? That is to say, if every physical event had its adequate determinacy, in other and earlier physical events, would it follow that we have no choice, everything is inevitable, and we couldn't have done otherwise?" MacKay has no desire to appeal to unpredictability to retain the kind of freedom that he believes we require. Thus, no doubt with Eccles's view in mind, he comments, "In so far as quantum events disrupted the normal cause and effect relationship between the physical correlates of my rational deliberation, such events might be held to diminish rather than enhance my responsibility for the outcome." [34]

In presenting his views, Donald MacKay asks us to imagine the following scenario. We consider a person (call him *A*), whose behavior we are studying and whose next choice we seek to predict. We can think of a superscientist who is able to look into *A*'s brain to see its complete state and on the basis of this, so it is claimed, the scientist would be able to predict the future brain state of *A*. But, asks MacKay, would *A* himself be correct to believe the prediction being made by the superscientist if it were offered to him? His answer is no. MacKay argues that if the superscientist's predictions were presented to *A*, then it would in fact alter *A*'s brain state, and so the prediction would immediately be invalidated. Since, therefore, by definition no change can take place in what *A* believes without a correlated change in his brain state, it follows that no completely detailed specification of the present or immediately future state of his brain would be equally correct whether or not *A* believed it. If it were correct before *A* believed it, then it must be incorrect in some detail after *A* comes to believe it.

MacKay envisages the further situation that supposes that our superscientist could, in fact, formulate a new prediction that would take into account the

33. J. Dole et al., "Contemporary Perspectives in Chance, Providence and Free Will: A Critique of Some Modern Authors," *Science and Christian Belief* 7 (1995): 117-139.
34. For example, Donald M. MacKay, *Behind the Eye* (Oxford: Blackwell, 1991), 193.

effect of offering it to *A* and would only be correct if *A* believed it. The question, then, is, would such a prediction command *A*'s unconditional assent? MacKay answers no. *A* would obviously be entitled to believe it. However, *A* would be equally entitled to disbelieve it, as a prediction is true if and only if *A* believes it. Putting this in a more formal way, we can say there does not exist a complete description of *A*'s future, which would have an unconditional claim to *A*'s assent in the sense that *A* would be correct to believe and mistaken to disbelieve it, if only *A* knew it. MacKay argues that in this sense *A*'s future is logically indeterminate and that from *A*'s point of view the future is open and up to *A* to determine. For MacKay this is the essence of freedom, as he asserts that it is not brains but persons who choose. It is at the level of our conscious experience that there is indeterminacy, irrespective of any indeterminacy at the level of the brain. MacKay remained uneasy with other definitions of freedom that do not explicitly distinguish between these two levels and he suggested that it is a mistake to try to secure our freedom by trying to exploit physically indeterminate processes in the brain, along the lines of Eccles's arguments. On balance, MacKay's approach seems to be the most promising in the literature published so far.[35]

CONCLUSIONS

Human curiosity about the mind, how it is related to the body, and more specifically to the brain, has left a rich legacy of possible models from Plato and Aristotle, through Galen and Nemesius, to Descartes. Most, but not all, have leaned towards some form of dualism. In the past 200 years, the accumulated scientific evidence has pointed steadily, and in the last 40 years at an ever-accelerating pace, toward recognizing the intimate link between mind and brain. As research proceeds simultaneously at several different levels from the molecular to the cognitive, the pictures of the mind/brain relations become very complex. The basic fact remains, however, that when something happens in the mind, something also happens in the brain and vice-versa. The cognitive happenings may not always be conscious, but may nonetheless be detectable using some of the subtle scientific techniques available today to brain scientists.

To be sure, changes occur in our brain which take place through no choice of our own. One example of this, which receives a lot of publicity today, is Alzheimer's disease. At the same time, we recognize increasingly that our self-motivated thoughts and actions affect the workings of the neural substrate (for example, alcoholism and other forms of drug abuse). The cumulative effect of

35. See also Murphy, chapter 6, this volume.

such increasing self-knowledge should enable us to become more responsible for our actions while becoming more compassionate and attentive to the plight of those who, through no fault of their own, suffer from diseases of the mind.

Our consciousness of the presence and power of God, often labeled spiritual awareness, is not immune to changes in our brains. This comes as no surprise to those who pay attention to the biblical pictures underlying our psychobiological unity.[36] That does not mean that our spiritual experience is nothing but the outcome in changes in our neural substrate. The true value of any beliefs that we may espouse, whatever the state of our biological substrate, must be judged, not from our understanding of the likely mediating neural processes, but by examining in each case the relevant evidence.

In attempting to take a balanced view of developments in neuroscience, we find the reductionist trap always set before us. Personal presuppositions enter readily into wider interpretations of what all the new data in neuroscience mean for our understanding of persons. Some continue to espouse a dualist view, some an identity hypothesis, others a psychophysiological parallelism. Our view is that the evidence is best understood in terms of a nonreductive physicalist view of the mind–body relationship. On this view, the irreducible duality of human nature is seen as duality of aspects rather than as duality of substance.

36. See Green, chapter 7, this volume.

Chapter Five

Cognitive Contributions to Soul

Warren S. Brown

THE CONCEPT OF SOUL

How did humans become souls? If, as the scientific record tells us, God's work in the creation of human persons was progressive, what was the nature of the step from intelligent ape to human person? How could biological and cultural development (described in a previous chapter by Ayala) result in a race of souls? If there is a direct link between neurological processes and psychological events, as described by Jeeves, how does a neurocognitive system have a soul in the sense often presumed by Jewish and Christian theology?

A frequent and historically dominant answer within Christian tradition has been that humans are endowed by a special act of creation with a separate entity which is the soul; that the soul has separate existence and perhaps even a separate realm of awareness and agency. This is the dualist position. One of the attractive aspects of this point of view is that one does not have to attempt to understand rationally or scientifically what exactly a soul might be like or how it operates because the soul is of an entirely different nature and existence than the physical or psychological world. We presume that we have one, with our understanding of the soul's nature dependent on our theological preferences. Physical or psychological realities are not presumed to be relevant to our understanding of the soul, nor are they thought to affect the soul's status or well-being.

The chapters of this book argue for a second possibility, that the soul of humans is a physiologically embodied property of human nature and thus not an entity with distinctive existence, awareness, and agency. This nondualist position (which Murphy in a following chapter describes as nonreductive physicalism) has its own explanatory problem: If we are physically embodied, we must ask ourselves how the properties attributed to soul arise out of a neurocognitive system? How is soul embodied and what are some of its underlying properties?

It is not the purpose of this chapter to construct a systematic theology of an embodied soul. However, I would suggest the usefulness of differentiating two functions of the soul concept. The first meaning of the soul concept is to designate a realm of presumably unique human capacity and experience (which might include concepts such as consciousness of self, personal agency and responsibility, ability to give and receive love, communication with God, the experience of transcendence, etc.). It is this concept of soul that this chapter addresses. The second function of the soul concept is to designate that part of the self that continues beyond death. Here I agree with Donald MacKay in suggesting that our eternal existence would not be the continuation of some aspect of our current embodiment but would be a new creation, outside of the time and space we currently occupy. Thus, the nature of our eternal existence would be up to God to determine within this new creation and not dependent on a currently existing separate nonphysical essence that survives death. MacKay writes:

> If the concept of creation is to be thought of by any analogy with creation as we ourselves understand it—as, for example, the creation of a space-time in a novel—then a new creation is not just the running on and on of events later in the original novel: it is a different novel. A new creation is a space-time in its own right. Even a human author can both meaningfully and authoritatively say that the new novel has some of the same characters in it as the old. The identity of the individuals in the new novel is for the novelist to determine. So if there is any analogy at all with the concept of a new creation by our divine Creator, what is set before us is the possibility that in a new creation the Author brings into being, precisely and identically, some of those whom He came to know in and through His participation in the old creation.[1]

This chapter attempts to describe the cognitive capacities that might contribute to the soulfulness of human experience. In so doing, I will attempt to move the realm of our portraits of human nature from the evolutionary,[2] the genetic,[3] and the neurocognitive,[4] closer to what we might call the "soulish" as described by Jewish and Christian Scripture.

1. Donald M. MacKay, *Behind the Eye* (Oxford: Basil Blackwell, 1991), 260.
2. See Ayala, chapter 2, this volume.
3. See V. E. Anderson, chapter 3, this volume.
4. See Jeeves, chapter 4, this volume.

Despite the physicalist accounting we are attempting in this volume, it is difficult to avoid use of the word "soul" in this discussion as well. The word designates something within us that is at once both deep and transcendent. While arguing for a more embodied understanding of this aspect of our experience, the experience itself cannot be denied. Thus, "soul" (or at times "soulful" or "soulish") is used herein to designate not an essence apart from the physical self, but the net sum of those encounters in which embodied humans relate to and commune with God (who is spirit) or with one another in a manner that reaches deeply into the essence of our creaturely, historical, and communal selves.

HUMAN COGNITION, PERSONAL RELATEDNESS, AND AN EMERGENT SOUL

Humans have a substantial advantage over the most intelligent of primates in the power, scope, and complexity of mental processing. As Ayala pointed out in a previous chapter, the increasing cognitive capacities of humans allowed for a process of cultural development, including language, art, technology, and culture. An even more important consequence of the significantly increased mental powers of humans is expanded horizons of personal relatedness. Based on the assumption of an embodied soul and the *nonreductive physicalism* that we are exploring in this book,[5] I will argue that soul as a dimension of human experience arises out of *personal relatedness,* and that personal relatedness is an emergent property of human cognition.[6]

As we attempt to bring together the dimensions of human persons traditionally termed body, mind, and soul into a singularity, we must be concerned about preserving in our picture the critical properties and attributes of human nature and potentials for human experience that have been described in Scripture and traditionally assigned to the soul. These include, for example, some measure of free will, sin and the experience of guilt, acceptance of redemption, the experience of grace, righteousness and ethical behavior, worship and an inner "life in the spirit," the experience and expression of love, participation in community, ability to understand the nature of God's revelation, and participation in the work of God's kingdom. To be theologically adequate, a cognitive (physicalist) portrait of human persons must allow for such soulish capacities and experiences as those that are assumed or described in Scripture.

There is, however, a fundamental core capacity running through this list of human soulful experiences and attributes. A critical feature of the biblical por-

---

5. See Murphy, chapters 1 and 6, this volume.
6. "Cognition" herein is meant to include emotions and affects as they interact with other aspects of mental processes. See the section following on Human Emotions as Complex Codes.

trait of human nature is the potential for *personal relatedness.* The Bible presumes a unique depth and scope of human relatedness that is not presumed for the rest of the animal kingdom. The term "personal" is meant to capture this uniqueness (in quality or quantity). "Relatedness" is meant to encompass three important dimensions: (1) *subjective* processes of self-relatedness and self-representation; (2) *inter-individual* relatedness; and (3) *relatedness to God.*

If soul, mind, and body are one indivisible essence, then "soul" becomes a semantically designated portion of the soul-mind-body whole. The portion of this whole which is most directly related to our soulful potentialities and experiences are those capacities that allow for the depth, scope, and richness of human interpersonal relationships. Thus, in this view, it is experiences of relatedness to others, to the self, and most particularly to God that endow a person with the attributes that have been attached to the concept of "soul." Experiences of personal relatedness, in their deepest and richest, create in us that which is semantically designated as "soul."

The capacity for personal relatedness can in turn be seen as an *emergent property* of certain critical cognitive abilities.[7] An emergent property is a unique mode of functioning that becomes possible on the basis of both a significant increase in the capacity of some number of lower-level abilities and the interaction among these capacities. Emergenesis of this sort is consistent with the idea of a "phase change" in the operation of a system when a certain level of complexity has been reached, as mentioned by Jeeves in the preceding chapter. Emergent properties are *non-reducible* in two senses: (1) Whereas the emergent property is dependent on the lower-level abilities (i.e., cannot exist in the absence of these lower abilities), the emergent property *cannot be understood by close scrutiny of the lower abilities,* nor can the behavior in the realm of the emergent property be totally accounted for using the descriptive concepts of the lower-level phenomena. (2) Functioning of the neurocognitive system at the level of the emergent property has a *downward causative influence* on the ongoing and future activity of the lower-level processes (i.e., top-down causation). The activity of the whole system, created by the interactive play of the lower-level processing modules, exerts a unique level of control and influence on the entire system. Mental processes that operate at the level of the cognitive, psychological, and psychosocial determine the course of the neurophysiological systems that instantiate them.[8]

---

7. A treatment of the concept of emergence within the literature on philosophy of mind can be found in A. Beckermann, H. Flohr, and J. Kim, eds., *Emergence or Reduction? Prospects for Nonreductive Physicalism* (New York: Walter DeGruyter, 1992).

8. This higher level "determination" does not imply nonbiological interference in the ongoing neurobiological processes of the brain. Rather, these processes are shaped and

To make explicit the perspective of this chapter, I suggest that the soulful aspects of human experience are engendered by the experiences of *personal relatedness*. This relatedness is, in turn, an emergent property of certain critical *human cognitive capacities*. Just as the properties of soul presumed by Jewish and Christian Scripture emerge from personal relatedness, so also personal relatedness emerges from the operation of the incredibly enhanced mental powers of humans. In the plan and design of God, the richness and depth of human interpersonal relatedness was made possible by an evolutionary explosion of our mental capacities.[9] Nevertheless, personal relatedness and the soulful capacities of humans are not the same as these cognitive systems or reducible to nothing but cognition. Rather, the human experiences of soul are conditioned by but cannot be reduced to the underlying mental processes from which they emerge.

CRITICAL COGNITIVE CAPACITIES FOR PERSONAL RELATEDNESS

Nearly every fundamental human mental ability or function exists in some form or to some degree in nonhuman species. However, the remarkable expansion of certain areas of the brain endowed humans with notably enhanced mental powers that have far-reaching implications for the scope and quality of relatedness. Among the capacities that are significantly superior to those of our closest nonhuman fellows and that are critical for personal relatedness are the following:

1. *language:* the capacity to communicate a potentially infinite number of propositions; to relate regarding complex, abstract ideas, as well as about the past and the future
2. *a theory of mind:* an ability to consider the most likely thoughts and feelings of another person
3. *episodic memory:* a conscious historical memory of events, persons, times, and places (i.e., more than memory for actions and their consequences)
4. *conscious top-down agency:* conscious mental control of behavior; the ability to modulate ongoing behavior in relationship to the conscious process of decisionmaking
5. *future orientation:* ability to run mental scenarios of the future implications of behaviors and events

influenced by the pattern of activity in the totality of information being processed in the interactive network of brain processing modules.
9. See Ayala, chapter 2; and Jeeves, chapter 4, this volume.

    6. *emotional modulation* by complex social and contextual cognition that serves to guide ongoing behavior and decisionmaking

Several important points must be made regarding this list of human capacities important for personal relatedness and soul. First, it is meant to be suggestive rather than either exhaustive or theoretically systematic. Second, it is not presumed that lower primates do not possess some measure of any or all of these capacities. This point will be clear from the comparative analyses of these human capacities that follow. Finally, these capacities are neither unitary nor independent of one another. For example, episodic memory interacts with language in that memory is enhanced by capacities for verbal labeling of events. Similarly, affective responsiveness does not contribute uniquely to personal relatedness other than via its interaction with other human higher cognitive information processing.

Language

Perhaps the greatest chasm between the mental life of the most intelligent non-human primates and that of human beings lies in the use of language in communication and mental representation. However, the apparent size of the chasm has been moderately reduced by the extensive work done over the last 20 years in attempting to teach great apes a language system. The research on ape language has revealed much not previously known about the capacity of apes to communicate using an abstract system of symbols or gestures (including the ability of some to understand human speech). Nevertheless, the linguistic performance of apes is limited and dependent on the availability of the support of a human linguistic community.

    The natural signaling systems that apes use in the wild have been found to be semantically *closed,* that is, "there is a finite—and actually a rather small—number of basic [signal] types." [10] These basic types relate primarily to emotional states of the signaler. Such complexity as exists in primate natural signaling systems can be shown to result not from a large number of semantic and syntactic items, but from gradations and modulations of a small number of basic signals types. However, there are significant limits to this form of signal complexity. "The effectiveness of signals in mediating social action is limited to the degree that different signals are confusable, and confusability is heightened when the signals continuously intergrade and blend with each other." [11] These

10. Jarvis Bastian, "Primate Signaling Systems and Human Language," in *Primate Behavior: Field Studies in Monkeys and Apes,* ed. Irven DeVore (New York: Holt, Rinehart and Winston, 1965), 588.
11. Ibid., 589.

continuous intergradations of basic signals (not unlike prosody in human language) can subserve no more than a closed and limited natural communication system. Thus, the ape in the wild cannot be considered to have developed language.

Explicit attempts to teach expanded, abstract communication systems to apes have met with some success.[12] Most of these experiments have involved trying to teach chimpanzees to communicate with a human using abstract symbols or tokens, or using the gestures of American Sign Language. However, conclusions about the exact linguistic nature of what apes have learned in these attempts at explicit teaching has been controversial. Apes clearly have an intent to communicate using the abstract system, a multiword vocabulary (i.e., can learn different semantic referents to different lexical items), and an ability to use multi-word expressions (two to at most six words) in which the combinations appear to make sense.[13] However, it remains uncertain whether apes taught in this manner use these abstract communication systems in a manner that indicates possession of a structured, rule-governed grammar. In this sense many linguists would argue that these apes have been taught a somewhat more sophisticated signaling system, but not a language.[14]

For example, in a paper that is now nearly 20 years old, Terrace analyzed 19,000 multi-sign utterances of the explicitly linguistically trained chimpanzee Nim Chimpsky and found no evidence of *grammatical constructions,* that is, constraints of word order, use of grammatical words (articles, prepositions, connectives), phrase nesting, or words inflected for tense or number. What is more, there were relatively few instances in which Nim used language to express what had not been previously said by his teachers, that is, there did not appear to be critical levels of *creativity* in his linguistic competence.[15] Thus, the majority of the expressions of explicitly linguistically trained chimps do not show the rule-governed manipulation of a basic set of lexical items in such a way as to create an unlimited number of novel expressions, as is characteristic of language even in young children. In contrast, human language is marked by *regularity* (a grammar) and *creativity* (creation of a potentially infinite variety of novel sentences), as well as by a unique form of *semanticity* (assignment of meaning) within the lexicon. Very young children (three years old) have a much more sophisticated expres-

12. Richard Byrne, *The Thinking Ape: Evolutionary Origins of Intelligence* (Oxford: Oxford University Press, 1995).

13. Ibid.

14. Steven Pinker, *The Language Instinct* (New York: William Morrow and Company, 1994), chapter 11.

15. Herbert Terrace, Laura Petito, Richard Saunders, and Tom Bever, "Can an Ape Create a Sentence?" *Science* 206 (1979): 892-902.

sive grammar and much greater linguistic creativity than that of the best examples of language performance in the explicitly trained primates.

While Terrace's analysis may somewhat underestimate the potential language competence of apes, his report nevertheless suggests the domain of limitations in the linguistic abilities of apes explicitly trained as adolescents or adults. However, recent reports suggest that significantly higher levels of ability are attained by raising chimps in a language-rich environment. Sue Savage-Rumbaugh and Roger Levin describe the remarkable language capacity of the bonobo (or pygmy chimpanzee) Kanzi, who as an infant was a passive participant in unsuccessful attempts to teach language to his mother. When finally allowed to express himself via the language system that was being taught to his mother, Kanzi seemed to know spontaneously how to communicate via the symbols, and to have developed an unusual (for a chimpanzee) general language processing capacity. Most remarkable was Kanzi's grasp of spoken English. Kanzi was eventually capable of understanding a wide variety of spoken sentence types (13 in all), including sentences with embedded phrases. Kanzi responded correctly on 74 percent of 660 novel sentences, showing "sensitivity to word order as well as to the semantic and syntactic cues that signaled when to ignore word order and when to attend to it."[16] This capacity was comparable to that of a two-and-one-half-year-old human.

Based on the earlier work with explicitly trained older apes, Bickerton classifies the language competence of apes as *protolanguage,* similar to the linguistic competence of a human two-year-old child, or the language behavior of a severely environmentally deprived older child, or the "pidgin" of a second language user in the very early stages of learning.[17] However, impressed by the remarkable capacities of Kanzi, Duane Rumbaugh suggests that "apes have vaulted the language barrier."[18] Nevertheless, neither real language or protolanguage emerge spontaneously in apes, but is dependent for its development on the support of a human linguistic community. Apes in the wild develop no more than a contextually and emotionally modulated set of vocal signals. Adolescent or adult apes specifically trained by human researchers can learn to use symbols or gestures to communicate with humans in a manner with some linguistic properties. Chimpanzees raised in an environment with extensive exposure to human language develop a capacity to understand language that

16. Sue Savage-Rumbaugh and Roger Levin, *Kanzi: The Ape at the Brink of the Human Mind* (New York: John Wiley and Sons, 1994).
17. Derek Bickerton, *Language and Species* (Chicago: University of Chicago Press, 1990), chapter 5.
18. Duane Rumbaugh, "Primate Language and Cognition: Common Ground," *Social Research* 62 (1995): 711-730.

is not measurably different than a normal two-year-old human, although language expression is more limited. In all cases, it is the presence or absence of a rich human language environment that allows for the emergence of proto-human, or childlike, language in apes.

Beyond the various linguistic competencies and limitations of apes, the lexicon of the human may be unique in another important sense. According to Jarvis Bastian, the early vocabulary and phonetics of children are most likely learned by repetition, conditioning, and/or direct visual-auditory experience, not unlike the context in which apes learn vocabulary. However, once a certain level of grammatical competence has been reached such as to enable generation of new formations and transformations, "further enlargement of the learner's vocabulary may be achieved through definitional procedures, through learning the relations the new lexical items have to others in the practices of the linguistic community, and not through the direct conditioning required for the first items."[19] This means that interactions with the linguistic community suffice to enhance vocabulary, with little or no need for direct sensory appreciation of the referent of the new word. "Many human concepts of the greatest social significance . . . may pass through their entire histories almost exclusively within the linguistic matrices in which they were constructed, with only the most fragile, indirect, and shifting connections to extralinguistic conditions." Bastian cites as examples of such concepts: "$\sqrt{1}$," "gene locus," and "holy ghost."[20] It is this second-order vocabulary learning process that allows humans access to the knowledge, ideas, and experiences of others distant in time and space. There are no experiential limits to the acquisition of new semantic/lexical items. This process in language is not unlike what Ayala described as "cultural evolution," where a critical level of cognitive ability resulted in a process of cultural and linguistic development which is not itself biological.

The unique power of human language makes possible important dimensions of personal relatedness that could not exist independent of language. Among the capacities critical to the quality of personal relatedness are the ability to:

1. transmit a complex idea, proposition, or image from the mind of one individual to the mind of another
2. represent and communicate the conscious and affective state of one's own mind, or describe the state of the mind of another person

19. Bastian, "Primate Signaling Systems," 588, 601.
20. Ibid., 602-603.

3. represent in conversation complex aspects of interpersonal relations, that is, interpersonal relationships become self-referential and self-modifying through language

4. represent details of the past and thus create a shared memory

5. describe to another individual aspects of a future the two are likely to share

6. preserve in written language the thoughts and experiences of an individual for the benefit of those distant in time or space

While neither personal relatedness nor our soulful experiences can be reduced to nothing more than the operation of linguistic processes within the human cognitive system, such attributes of human relations as the above list are clearly rooted in our linguistic capacities. Thus, possession of a significantly enhanced language capacity endows humans with dimensions of relatedness not within the realm of possibility for nonhuman primates. This is not to imply that primates, or other animals, are not relational in important ways. Certainly Savage-Rumbaugh and Levin describe a strong sense of relatedness between themselves as experimenters and Kanzi. [21] However, with the limited language capacity of chimps comes limitations in the depth and richness of human-primate relatedness.

Theory of Mind
As important as language is to the emergence of personal relatedness, there are other cognitive abilities that are significantly enhanced in humans and must be considered. Among the important additional contributors to relatedness are *metacognitive skills,* particularly the possession of a reasonably valid theory of mind. Metacognition is "thinking about thinking"—the awareness of the workings of one's own mind. "Theory of mind" is the ability accurately to attribute mental states to other people, as in "I think she thinks" or "I think she thinks that he thinks."

The sense of "self" can be understood as an aspect of a metacognitive theory of mind. To be able to think about one's own thinking, deciding, and doing is to have a mental representation of the self as a center of conscious agency. Thus, in the sense that personal relatedness is meant to extend to our relatedness to ourselves, metacognitive ability and a theory of mind are clearly necessary.

Neuroscientist Donald MacKay described in his 1986 Gifford Lectures the aspects of information flow and mental representation that must be present when two conscious agents (i.e., persons) are in dialogue (relatedness).

21. Savage-Rumbaugh and Levin, *Kanzi.*

According to MacKay, each person in the dialogue must gain from the communication a mental representation of the mind of the other individual. Dialogue involves a reciprocal situation where *B* must keep in mind a little map of *A*'s mind; and *A*'s mental map must include a little map of *B*. "This of course results in a feedback loop, a closed loop, a re-entrant situation . . . ," which constitutes dialogue.[22] Along the lines of MacKay's analysis, I have already suggested above that *A* and *B* each must have a mental representation of her or his own self (a sense of "self"). In addition, within the processes of dialogue each would have some understanding of the other's representation of them (e.g., *A*'s understanding of *B*'s understanding of *A*), as well as the other's self-representation (e.g., *A*'s understanding of *B*'s understanding of *B*). Thus, MacKay's analysis makes clear the importance of a theory of mind to personal relatedness.[23] To have an adequate representation of the state of one's own mind and the mind of the other is a necessary condition for (as well as a result of) interpersonal dialogue.

There has been considerable research on the development of metacognition in children. The basic attributes of a theory of mind appear to develop in children between three and nine years of age, with increasing expertise accumulating during adolescence.[24] At the age of three, children are beginning to manifest a rudimentary theory of mind. This includes an understanding of what distinguishes people and animals; what distinguishes animate and inanimate; and the idea that people's thoughts and feeling may differ in relating to the same circumstance. A first-order theory of mind ("I think she thinks. . . .") begins to appear by around four years of age. The concept of false belief (that I or someone else could believe something that is untrue) develops by about age five. Second-order theory of mind ("I think she thinks he thinks. . . .") appears somewhat later. However, the exact ages of the development in children of these various aspects of a theory of mind is not yet entirely agreed upon.

Whatever the precise timing of development of the various subskills of a theory of mind, it is nevertheless clear that these skills develop over a time domain at least as long, if not longer, than that of the development of the basic skills of language. These progressively acquired metacognitive skills allow the child to understand increasingly more of the subtle nuances of social interactions and to extend the depth and scope of their personal relatedness.

The relevance of a theory of mind to personal relatedness is clearly illustrated in the experiences of the high functioning autistic individual. Autism

22. MacKay, *Behind the Eye,* 149.
23. W. S. Brown, "MacKay's View of Conscious Agents in Dialogue: Speculations on the Embodiment of Soul," *Journal of Philosophy and Psychology* 4 (1997): 497–505.
24. J. H. Flavell, F. L. Green, and E. R. Flavell, "Young Children's Knowledge about Thinking," *Monographs of the Society for Research in Child Development* 60 (1996).

in an individual with normal measured IQ is often referred to as Asperger's Syndrome.[25] This syndrome manifests itself by the following characteristics:

1. a severe impairment in reciprocal social interactions, including lack of normal desire for age-peer company and lack of appreciation of social cues
2. a failure to grasp much in the way of nonverbal interpersonal communication
3. speech and language problems, including delayed language development, a somewhat formal, pedantic, and flat mode of expression, and a mild comprehension impairment involving concrete misinterpretations
4. an all-absorbing, circumscribed interest that is adhered to in a repetitive way (often producing circumscribed areas of unusual ability) and that tends to rely on powers of rote memory rather than an understanding of underlying meaning
5. a stereotyped way of imposing routines on all or most all aspects of life

Individuals with Asperger's Syndrome have been thought to have an underlying deficit in the metacognitive skill of a theory of mind.[26] Baron-Cohen, for example, found that no autistic under the age of 11 years showed signs of a theory of mind.[27] Many of the symptoms of Asperger's Syndrome that involve interpersonal interactions can be understood as a deficit in understanding the cognitive processes and mental life of other individuals, and a consequent failure of normal relatedness and empathy. In fact, some researchers believe that the entire syndrome of autism can be attributed to a disability in the area of metarepresentational skills.

Oliver Sacks makes it clear that Asperger's Syndrome is relevant to a discussion of the cognitive contributions to soul. Sacks writes, "Autism as a subject touches on the deepest questions of ontology, for it involves a radical deviation in the development of the brain and mind."[28] Particularly telling is Sack's account of Temple Grandin, a very high-functioning autistic who is a profes-

25. Lorna Wing, "The Continuum of Autistic Characteristics," in *Diagnosis and Assessment in Autism*, ed. E. Schopler and G. B. Mesivob (New York: Plenum, 1988), 91-111. See also Sally Ozonoff, Sally J. Robers, and Bruce F. Pennington, "Asperger's Syndrome: Evidence of an Empirical Distinction from High-Functioning Autism," *Journal of Child Psychology and Psychiatry* 32 (1991): 1107-1122.
26. Dermont M. Bowler, "'Theory of Mind' in Asperger's Syndrome," *Journal of Child Psychology and Psychiatry* 33 (1992): 877-893.
27. S. Baron-Cohen, "The Autistic Child's Theory of Mind: A Case of Specific Developmental Delay," *Journal of Child Psychology and Psychiatry* 30 (1989): 285-297.
28. Oliver Sacks, *An Anthropologist on Mars* (New York: Vintage Books, 1995), 247.

sor of agriculture at a large university. The title of Sacks' book, *An Anthropologist on Mars,* is taken from a statement made by Temple in a conversation with Sacks regarding her understanding of myths and dramas:

> She was bewildered, she said, by Romeo and Juliet ("I never knew what they were up to"), and with Hamlet she got lost with the back-and-forth of the play. Though she ascribed these problems to "sequencing difficulties," they seemed to arise from her failure to empathize with the characters, to follow the intricate play of motive and intention. She said that she could understand "simple, strong, universal" emotions but was stumped by more complex emotions and the games people play. "Much of the time," she said, "I feel like an anthropologist on Mars."[29]

Asperger's individuals thus have severe difficulty in understanding human interpersonal relationships. While use of their rational powers may compensate to a degree, their intuitive understanding of the complexity and subtlety of personal relations and the subjective experiences of others (i.e., a theory of mind) is severely deficient. Sacks further describes Temple's difficulties in the area of personal relatedness:

> One cannot say that she is devoid of feeling or has a fundamental lack of sympathy. On the contrary, her sense of animals' moods and feeling is so strong that these almost take possession of her, overwhelm her at times. She feels she can have sympathy for what is physical or physiological—for an animal's pain or terror—but lacks empathy for people's states of mind and perspectives. When she was younger, she was hardly able to interpret even the simplest expressions of emotion; she learned to "decode" them later, without necessarily feeling them.[30]

This difficulty in understanding social cues makes Temple ingenuous and gullible with an "innocence and guilelessness arising not from moral virtue but from failure to understand dissembling and pretense. . . ."[31] Sacks quotes Temple as saying, "I had to learn to be suspicious, I had to learn it cognitively. I could put two and two together, but I couldn't see the jealous look on his face."[32] Of the emotional life of the Asperger's patient, Sacks suggests that "it is not affect in general that is faulty but affect in relation to complex human experiences, social ones predominantly, but perhaps allied ones—aesthetic, poetic symbolic, etc."[33] Thus, Temple, as with most high-functioning autistics, has

29. Ibid., 259.
30. Ibid., 269.
31. Ibid., 260
32. Ibid., 260.
33. Ibid., 288.

few friends. One autistic individual has been described as unable to compre-
hend the idea of a friend. While Temple has excellent comprehension of technical writing, she has difficulty understanding allusion, metaphor, presupposition, and irony. She does not respond deeply to music.

Theory of mind has been studied in nonhuman primates. According to
Byrne, the critical diagnostic criteria for knowing that an animal possesses a
theory of mind is that it treats other individuals as if they have mental states.
There is some evidence accumulating suggesting that the behavior of some primates satisfies this diagnostic criterion. Apes have been shown to understand
the visual perspective of another, to have an understanding of what other individuals know or do not know, and to understand intentions versus accidents
in the behavior of others. Both in laboratory situations and in the wild, apes
seem to use intentional tactics of deception based on an understanding of the
perspective of another individual, as well as intentional teaching based on an
understanding of the lack of knowledge of another younger animal. Such
behaviors are seen in the great apes, but not in lesser primates. Byrne writes,
"It seems that great apes, but not other animals, are able to carry out their social
manipulations aided by a real appreciation of what other animals can know or
be led to think."[34] Forms of social manipulation based on an understanding of
the knowledge, intentions, and social relationships of other individuals (i.e.,
forms of a theory of mind) has been termed by Byrne and Whiten
"Machiavellian intelligence."[35] Interestingly, Byrne found that the frequency
of tactical deception among different species of primates correlated very
strongly with the size of the neocortex relative to the size of the rest of the
brain, a scale of brain size on which humans far exceed chimpanzees or other
great apes.

Thus, as with language, a form of theory of mind appears to be present in
the great apes (but not lesser monkeys). While research is still ongoing, there
nevertheless appears to be a large gap between the ape form of theory of mind
and that possessed by humans. Perhaps apes have a proto-theory of mind, similar in kind to that of the human but of lesser power and complexity, akin to
the metacognition of a young child. In light of the consequences of a failure
of a metacognitive theory of mind seen in a highly intelligent Asperger's patient
such as Temple Grandin, the critical contribution of a theory of mind to personal relatedness is clear (*res ipsa loquitur*).

34. Byrne, *The Thinking Age,* 134.
35. Richard Byrne and A. Whiten, *Machiavellian Intelligence: Social Expertise and the
Evolution of Intellect in Monkeys, Apes and Humans* (Oxford: Clarendon Press, 1988).

Episodic Memory

Memory is not a unitary function of the mind or brain, but encompasses several sub-processes. For example, there is a clear distinction between procedural and declarative memory; the former being memory for bodily skills and cognitive operations (i.e., how to do things), and the latter being memory for facts and information.[36] Declarative memory is experienced consciously, whereas procedural memory is by-and-large unconscious. Our conscious, declarative memory is further divided by Endel Tulving into semantic and episodic memory.[37] Semantic memory is memory of general information—our knowledge of the world. All the things we have learned to be true and can think consciously about, but which are not tied to any specific past life event, make up the totality of our semantic memory. Episodic memory, however, is our recall of the events of our past that are marked in our recollection by specifics of time and place. "Episodic memory stores the cumulated events of one's life, an individual's autobiography."[38] In describing the nature of episodic memory, Tulving states that "For a rememberer to remember something means that he or she is autonoetically aware of a past happening in which he or she has participated."[39]

The line between semantic and episodic memory appears to be permeable. For example, many of the new things we learn are remembered over short periods of time within the context of a memory for when and where we encountered the information. "I remember that so-and-so told me this last week over lunch." However, over time the same information, having been encountered in several other situations or brought to mind in multiple new contexts, may begin to lose its temporal markers within our memories. We now know that such-and-such is true, but we no longer remember how or when we came to know it to be true. Information that was previously episodic within our memory has lost its episodic markers and merged into our general semantic knowledge. Memory for one aspect of an episode, the context within which information was learned, has been differently affected by the passage of time from the content of the information itself, suggesting at least a functional episodic-semantic difference.

However, not all memories lose their temporal markers. Much that we can recall continues to be attached to memories of important specific life events. These memories form our autobiographical knowledge, providing us with a

36. Larry R. Squire, *Memory and Brain* (New York: Oxford University Press, 1987).
37. Endel Tulving, *Elements of Episodic Memory* (Oxford: Clarendon Press, 1983).
38. Squire, *Memory and Brain,* 169.
39. E. Tulving, "What Is Episodic Memory?" *Current Directions in Psychological Science* 2 (1993): 67-70.

sense of continuous historical personal identity, including a record of important events in our interpersonal and community relationships.[40] The previous section described the role of a theory of mind in the formation of a sense of "self." A personal narrative memory is another important contributor to the experience of being a unique center of conscious agency and to the potential for relatedness to one's self. Personal relatedness is a phenomenon that depends on both the nature of the events and experiences of our relations at the particular moment, and our sense of a continuity of relatedness based in our memory of those instances of our personal history that involved the same individuals.

Episodic memory appears to develop during early childhood, being not fully developed until after the third year of life.[41] That other forms of memory are fully functional prior to this is attested to by the vast amount of procedural and semantic learning that takes place during these early childhood years. The term "infantile amnesia" refers to our inability to remember events (episodes) from our very early childhood, although we are typically able to remember significant events from later childhood. Infantile amnesia is due to the fact that episodic memory is not yet well developed, thus specific life events cannot be recalled.[42]

Although it is difficult to imagine life without autobiographical memory, there are cases in the neuropsychological literature that suggest the consequences of a deficient episodic memory. The classic case of anterograde amnesia (loss of the ability to form new episodic memories) is H.M.[43] Due to bilateral damage to important structures of the limbic system of the brain, H.M. lost the ability to form a new conscious, declarative memory. If you met H.M. and carried on a short conversation with him, then walked out of the room for a few minutes, then returned again, H.M. would express no knowledge of the previous meeting. Any new information that passes out of his immediate memory (also called "short-term" or "working" memory) is lost forever to

40. The long-term accuracy of human episodic memory is controversial. See E. F. Loftus, "Psychologists in the Eyewitness World," *American Psychologist* 48 (1993): 550–580.

41. P. A. Ornstein, B. N. Gordon, and L. E. Baker-Ward, "Children's Memory for Salient Events: Implications for Testimony," in *Development of Long Term Retention,* ed. M. L. Howe, C. J. Brainerd, and V. F Reyna (New York: Springer Verlag, 1992), 135–158.

42. J. Perner and T. Ruffman, "Episodic Memory and Autonoetic Consciousness: Developmental Evidence and a Theory of Childhood Amnesia," *Journal of Experimental Child Psychology* 59 (1995): 516–548.

43. B. Milner, S. Corkin, and H. L. Teuber, "Further Analysis of the Hippocampal Amnesic Syndrome: 14-year Follow up Study of H. M," *Neuropsychologia* 6 (1968): 215–234.

conscious recall. Thus, H.M. is trapped within a narrow window of the memories of immediately preceding events, a window no wider than the amount of information he can keep consciously in mind at one time. Episodic and semantic memories formed prior to the onset of H.M.'s brain pathology are well remembered, but all events occurring during the intervening years continue to be permanently lost.

A somewhat similar story can be told of patient N.A. who received an accidental injury to a brain structure slightly different in location but within the same system as case H.M. Like H.M., N.A. appears normal on first encounter. Yet his memory difficulties are considerable. Although he continues to score in the superior range on tests of general intelligence, he does very poorly on tests of memory. "His memory impairment is best understood as a difficulty in retaining the events of each passing hour and day. . . . He loses track of his possessions, forgets what he has done, and forgets whom he has visited."[44]

The consequences of such memory impairment to interpersonal relationships is well described by Squire with regard to N.A. "He has no close friends. His socializing is limited by his difficulty in keeping a topic of conversation in mind and in carrying over the substance of social contacts from one occasion to another. . . . He says that watching television is difficult, because he forgets the story content during commercial breaks."[45] In an expression that reflects the pathos of a person without memory of a recent past, Milner quotes H.M. as saying, "Every day is alone in itself, whatever enjoyment I've had, and whatever sorrow I've had. . . . Right now, I'm wondering. Have I done or said anything amiss? You see, at this moment everything looks clear to me, but what happened just before? That's what worries me. It's like waking from a dream; I just don't remember."[46] Thus, it can be seen in these two tragic cases that personal relatedness is deeply affected by an inability to access consciously memories of our not-too-distant past.

Episodic memory is another cognitive domain in which it would appear that humans have considerably more capacity than nonhuman primates. Although it is obviously impossible to know directly the mental experience of an ape, conscious semantic memories clearly seem to be present. These semantic memories are not (or seldom) "declared" through language, but they can be fairly strongly inferred from behavior. However, the nature or existence of an episodic, autobiographical memory in apes is uncertain. For example, chimps are very good at remembering where they saw a trainer hide a desirable stash

44. Squire, *Memory and Brain,* 178.
45. Ibid., 178.
46. B. Milner, "Memory and the Temporal Regions of the Brain," in *Biology of Memory,* ed. K. H. Pribram and D. E. Broadbent (New York: Academic Press, 1970), 37.

of food and can return without error to the spot after many hours or days. However, whether the memory is of the nature of "I-remember-the-trainer-hiding-food-there-yesterday" or "I-know-food-is-hidden-there" is not yet known. There are a few anecdotal reports of expressions of an episodic memory in the more language competent chimpanzees. Nevertheless, the existence or capacity of an episodic memory in subhuman primates has not been established.

However, two points suggest that human episodic memory is apt to be of greater scope and complexity than that which might exist in the nonhuman. First is the capacity of human language to preserve historical detail, providing an incredible economy for memory. To be able not only to preserve an experience as a specific, historical sensory memory, but to add to it a memory of verbally encoded labels (such as "on my wedding day" or "at my twenty-first birthday party," or "my first day on the job") adds important dimensions of temporal coding to memory storage. Language can form temporally coded linkages in the network of semantically remembered information that would endow the human with a richer autobiographical memory.

Second, certain aspects of autobiographical memory may be more developed in humans due to the remarkably expanded size and complexity of frontal lobes in humans relative even to the highest nonhuman primates. Frontal lobes are important for what Joaquin Fuster has referred to as the "temporal organization of behavior." [47] Behaviors that are complex and require sequences of purposive behavior extending over long periods of time rely on frontal lobe function. We shall return shortly to the issue of the prospective nature of these purposive behaviors, but for the moment we must focus on the retrospective nature of this frontal lobe function. Based in part on the remarkable development of frontal neocortex, humans have the capacity to remember the previous steps in, and current status of, very complex plans that have extended over considerable periods of time, that is, we have episodic memories for the events that constitute progress thus far in carrying forward a complex plan.

In summary, a personal, autobiographical memory forms the basis of a continuous personal identity and adds a critical retrospective dimension to interpersonal relatedness. Whether or not a historical, episodic memory provides a qualitatively or quantitatively unique aspect of human nature, it serves an important core of the cognitive abilities necessary for the personal relatedness we have been discussing.

---

47. Joaquin M. Fuster, *The Prefrontal Cortex: Anatomy Physiology, and Neuropsychology of the Frontal Lobe* (New York: Raven Press, 1980).

Conscious Top-Down Agency and Future Orientation

The capacity for conscious top-down agency and the ability to represent in mind long-term future possibilities are interrelated and, thus, can be described together. *Top-down agency* refers to the ability to modulate behavior in relationship to conscious thought and intention. That is, the phenomena at the top of the hierarchy of cognitive activity that we experience as conscious thought are not epiphenomenal mirages passively formed by the workings of a physically determined neural system, but are efficacious in creating top-to-bottom influences such that neurally embodied conscious intentions can modulate the very neural processes on which they are dependent. A *future orientation* is meant to denote the ability to run a conscious mental simulation or scenario of future possibilities for the actions of oneself and others, and to evaluate these scenarios in such a way as to regulate behavior and make decisions now with regard to desirable future events. The goals and priorities that determine current behavior are set with regard to a long-term perspective, rather than being predominantly a response to the current perceptual field. Thus, the behavioral output of a conscious agent is determined not only by the immediate stimulus environment but also by an evaluation of the contingencies represented in images and ideas of potential future states, events, and actions.

The cognitive revolution of the last half century has reestablished within the realm of scientific study the idea of conscious mental states and subjective phenomena. The primary influence in this revolution has been an information processing model of cognition in which various processing modules can be identified that intervene between the stimulus world and the pattern of behavioral responses. Important in the cognitive revolution has been the concept of top-down influences. The concept has been worked out most clearly in the realm of perception, where it has been recognized that that perception of sensory information is influenced both by the nature of the stimulus itself (bottom-up) and the expectancy set up in the mind of the individual regarding the stimulus (top-down).[48] Extrapolated from top-down phenomena in perception has been the concept that higher-level conscious processes of attention, expectancy, intention, and planning (manifestations of the highest levels of integrative brain processing) are influential in the future operations of lower-level neurocognitive systems and modules.

Baddeley proposes that the recall and manipulation of information from memory within consciousness (which he calls "working memory") necessitates a central executive processor. The central executive selects information for attention, determines strategies for mental or behavioral problem solving, plans

48. For example, see Margaret M. Matlin, *Cognition,* 3d ed. (Fort Worth: Harcourt Brace Publishers, 1994), 29, 37–40.

and controls behavior, and attempts to gather any information necessary from inner (memory) or outer (perceptual) sources. In that Baddeley's "central executive" works within the context of conscious working memory to plan and order behavior, it fulfills the necessary criteria for conscious agency.[49]

The concept of efficacious top-down conscious agency has been represented by Donald MacKay as a "supervisory system" within his information-flow analysis of brain-mind events. This system is responsible for goal setting and switching, assessing the current state of affairs with reference to these goals and priorities, and updating the conditional readiness for responding. The self-supervisory system is the process whereby the system "undertakes the task of setting its own goals and goal priorities. . . . In this *supervisory activity* . . . we have an information flow structure with some of the necessary features to serve as a direct correlate of our conscious experience. The most characteristic aspect of being conscious is that we both evaluate the ongoing state of affairs, and determine or revise at will our goal priorities and criteria for evaluation."[50] It is the work of such a system that is consciously experienced as decision and volition. Thus, MacKay rejects both the notion that consciousness is epiphenomenal, and the concept that consciousness in some way interferes with brain processes. Rather, he suggests that the two phenomena are interdependent. "Yet I would insist," says MacKay, "on the *determinative efficacy* of our thinking, valuing, choosing, and so forth."[51]

There is reasonable evidence to suggest that at least the great apes have conscious agency. This is best seen in behaviors that indicate that they understand that other individuals are intentional agents with knowledge and desires different than their own. Laboratory studies of chimpanzees have shown that they understand others as causal agents, can assume the cooperative role of another individual in a task, understand the difference between accidents and intentions, and have a sense of self that allows them to respond appropriately to their own mirror image. Thus, conscious agency is an important but not a unique part of a portrait of human cognition. However, as Byrne points out, the evidence of such capacities in the great apes is somewhat patchy and suggestive of considerably less sophisticated abilities than that seen in humans:

> Although all great apes make and use a range of tools in captivity, and appear to understand the cause-and-effect logic of their use, only chimpanzees regularly make tools for several purposes in the wild. Only gorillas have so far been shown to use complex, hierarchical task organization in their normal environment. Certainly, most great apes can understand their reflection in a

49. Alan D. Baddeley, *Working Memory* (Oxford: Oxford University Press, 1986).
50. MacKay, *Behind the Eye*, 142, 53.
51. Ibid., 63.

mirror, but they do not use the image to adorn themselves for the benefit of others. Great apes can impersonate actions, but this has only been shown clearly in home-reared individuals, not in the wild. Occasionally great apes show pretense, but this is also largely in home-reared animals, and pretense anyway has an uncertain relationship to belief attribution. Experiments with single chimpanzees have suggested empathy with others' problems, and comprehension of accident versus design. Only twice has intentional teaching of infants been recorded convincingly in chimpanzees, never in other apes. All species of great ape sometimes show that they can attribute deceptive intentions to others, to judge from observational data. A few intriguing chimpanzee behaviors imply anticipatory planning for the future. This imperfect set of evidence has taken a lot of getting, partly because the diagnostic signs are intrinsically hard to observe, partly perhaps because most observers aren't looking for them.[52]

The behaviors cited above suggest a measure of conscious agency on the part of the great apes. These same behaviors also suggest that they have a modicum of future orientation represented in an ability to run mental scenarios:

They (like humans) are able to mentally simulate actions. To the extent that great apes can select or make tools appropriate for the job, in advance of feedback from the task itself, or structure skilled behavior without trial-and-error learning, they are simulating physical action. To the extent that they intentionally deceive and teach, and solve the various artificial tests of intentional understanding, great apes are simulating social action. What the data show, therefore, is that in a limited way *great apes can think.*[53]

What is ultimately the meaning of the qualifier "in a limited way" to Byrne's statement that "great apes can think" is a matter of continuing research. However, there are aspects of human future orientation and mental simulation that are at least quantitatively (if not qualitatively) unique and are critical attributes of human cognition. The accounts of the most sophisticated behavior of apes that suggest conscious agency and a future orientation also suggest a limitation in the temporal extent of planning. Whereas apes can plan behavior extending over the course of hours, maybe days, humans project and plan over periods of weeks, months, and years. Humans can mentally imagine potential scenarios and set relevant current goals and agendas with reference to goals even decades in the future. As an example, humans are uniquely aware of their own mortality, that is, we can elicit mental scenarios regarding the long-term consequences and meaning of our own death and regulate our current be-

52. Byrne, *The Thinking Age,* 158.
53. Ibid., 150.

havior accordingly. Herbert Benson has suggested that "the price we pay . . . for (our) intelligence, for (our) referential ability, is the knowledge of our mortality. We are arguably the only species . . . that know we are going to die."[54] Certainly the angst related to our knowledge of the physical mortality of ourselves and our friends and family is a critical contribution to the experience of soul.

The ability to regulate one's behavior effectively with reference to conscious intentions is of obvious importance to personal relatedness. Altruism, for example, is best understood in this context. A very involved and, in my opinion, tortuous literature exists on what is termed the "genetics of altruism."[55] The attempt in this literature is to understand how humans could have been endowed with the capacity for altruism by genetic selection, as if altruism were the direct manifestation of some complex of genetic determinants. It is more reasonable and intuitively satisfactory (and, I think, scientifically parsimonious) to consider altruism to be a property emerging out of the cognitive capacities of conscious agency and a future orientation. For example, we are able to give a highly valued possession, like a check for $1,000, to a friend in need with no hope or expectation of being repaid only because we are able to simulate mentally our friend's future with and without the help and our own future without the money but with a certain sense of satisfaction. Within the context of such a simulated future, we are able to intentionally plan and regulate our behavior to write the check, send the money, and so forth. The genetic process has endowed humans with levels of cognitive capacity that allow for personal relatedness with a long-term perspective that can be used to mediate altruism. This point is consistent with Ayala's argument in a previous chapter for a distinction between biological-genetic evolution and cultural evolution. Other critical attributes of personal relatedness, such as commitment, loyalty, trust, and promise making and keeping, can similarly be understood as aspects of human relatedness made possible by the capacities for a long-term perspective and an efficacious conscious agency, both of which have emerged from expanded neurocognitive abilities.

Human Emotions as Complex Codes
Any discussion of human personal relatedness that does not consider emotions is obviously incomplete. We judge the qualities of our interpersonal (and

54. Herbert Benson, personal communication in comments given to the authors of this volume, 1996.
55. Arguments along this line can be found in E. O. Wilson, *Sociobiology: The New Synthesis* (Cambridge, Mass.: Harvard University Press, 1975). Also see R. Dawkins, *The Selfish Gene* (Oxford: Oxford University Press, 1989).

intrapersonal) relatedness almost exclusively by what we sense in our affections and emotions. Toward others we "feel" love, friendship, a spirit of cooperativeness, like and dislike, hatred, disgust, sympathy, and care. Toward ourselves we might "feel" joy, bliss, contentment, fear, anxiety, and depression.

Damasio, in his book *Descartes' Error*, has made a compelling case for the rationality, intelligence, and tacit knowledge posited in our emotional reactions.[56] For example, the prospective mental scenarios mentioned above are evaluated primarily on the emotional reactions created in us when we imagine the potential events. The images or ideas that constitute thinking about a future possibility elicit evaluative emotional responses. Normally, we decide to do one thing versus another dependent more on these emotional reactions than on any conscious verbal, rational analyses we might produce. What is more, these emotionally guided decisions are generally socially correct, that is, they encompass whatever social wisdom we have learned. Our emotional reactions inform us (many times unconsciously) of things we know but may not be able to formulate in rational discourse or conscious mental images. Our tacit knowledge is communicated to awareness via our emotional responses.

The consequences of a deficit in the elicitation of such visceral, emotional reactions to our thoughts and plans is illustrated by individuals with damage to the prefrontal area of the cerebral cortex. The most widely known example of such prefrontal lobe damage is the nineteenth-century case of Phineas Gage.[57] Gage's frontal lobe injury occurred in an accidental dynamite explosion when a tamping iron was blown through the frontal portion of his skull. As a result of his brain damage, Gage became irresponsible, unreliable, and puerile, loosing much of the constraints on behavior that were learned from years of life experience. Whereas Gage's intelligence itself did not seem to change, the considerable wisdom he had possessed as a manager of workers and responsible member of a community and family were lost. Important qualities of Gage's personal relatedness were lost or altered.

More revealing to our discussion of the role of evaluative emotional reactions is the case of Elliot described by Antonio Damasio as a modern Phineas Gage. Elliot had a frontal lobe meningioma that was surgically removed but left him with a damaged prefrontal cortex. After the surgery and recovery, Elliot still presented as an intelligent, engaging, and sophisticated person, retaining his premorbid superior level of testable intelligence. What is more, Elliot's performance on laboratory tests of social judgment was impeccable. "Elliot had a normal ability to generate response options to social situations and to consider

56. Antonio R. Damasio, *Descartes' Error: Emotion, Reason, and the Human Brain* (New York: G. P. Putman's Sons, 1994).
57. Previously described by Jeeves, chapter 4.

spontaneously the consequences of particular response options. He also had a capacity to conceptualize means to achieve social objectives, to predict the likely outcome of social situations, and to perform moral reasoning at an advanced developmental level."[58] However, Elliot's ability to function in real life situations, to make wise and responsible decisions with respect to everyday alternatives, was seriously defective. He could no longer effectively manage his time, either becoming easily distracted from completing important tasks or developing a perseverative concern for unimportant detail. He made extremely poor financial decisions, even in the face of clear and explicit advice to the contrary. He was not able to maintain a marriage relationship. He had been a successful businessman, a reliable manager of his time and resources, and a responsive husband, but after the damage to his prefrontal cortex he eventually lost his job, all his money, his family and friends.

According to Damasio, the critical feature of Elliot's behavioral and social deficits was the decoupling of the process of thinking through options (running mental scenarios) and the elicitation of anticipatory evaluative emotional responses. In a gambling game set up in the laboratory, Elliot would persist in making unwise decisions with respect to the very obvious reward contingencies of the game. Whereas normal individuals would soon learn to respond on the basis of the game's reward contingencies, Elliot never seemed to respond in a way that suggested he had learned the contingencies. Most interestingly, psychophysiological recordings revealed that normal individuals would develop anticipatory negative autonomic responses as they considered and, in the early stages of the game, executed wrong decisions. However, Elliot's autonomic system never responded negatively to what should have become predictably inappropriate plays in the gambling game. As the game progressed, Elliot never developed the ability to make the correct (most rewarding) decisions because his system could not generate anticipatory emotional responses to alternatives being considered that would serve as pre-response warning signals.

Damasio theorizes that individuals like Elliot and Phineas Gage have lost the coupling between high-level, rational thought processes and evaluative emotional responses ("somatic markers" in Damasio's terminology). Somatic markers provide experience-based feedback in relationship to the ongoing processes of thought. With respect to our cognitive portrait of human nature, Damasio clearly describes the dire consequences of the operation of the higher cognitive process of the human mind in the absence of a dynamic interaction with our limbic, emotional brain systems. In conversation Elliot seemed rational, but his rational evaluations had no impact on his bodily emotional reactions.

---

58. Damasio, *Descartes' Error,* 48.

Consequently, when life forced him to make choices, he would choose to act in ways that seemed obviously irrational. The power of language, an understanding of the minds of others, a rich episodic memory, the ability to formulate scenarios of alternative potential future events and situations, and the ability consciously to choose one's actions on the basis of these complex and sophisticated mental processes—all lose relevance to real-world decisionmaking when cut off from learned emotional reactions.

There is no reason to believe on the basis of either neuroanatomy or cognitive psychology that the "somatic marker" system is itself substantially different in humans from that of other primates (or most other mammals). Thus, what is unique about human mental systems is the power of the cognitive processes that interact with the emotional evaluative system. It is most likely the complexity and sophistication of the information that is evaluated, rather than the affective response system itself, that characterizes human mentation. What is clear from cases like Elliot and Gage is that these relatively unique higher cognitive systems are without particular value in the exigencies of daily life if they are not modulated and informed by feedback from emotional systems. Disengagement of cognition from emotional modulation has dire consequences for the quality of personal relatedness.

A Critical Caveat: Human Soul and Reduced Cognitive Capacity

This chapter has attempted to describe human soul in terms of the cognitive capacities that allow for personal relatedness, asserting in the process that the experience of "soul" emerges from relationship. It should not be construed, however, that the implications of this argument diminish the worth of humans with less-than-normal cognitive abilities. I do not mean in this description of cognitive contributions to soul to imply, for example, that prior to the development of language or a theory of mind or other critical cognitive skills a child is in some way a "lesser soul." Although such a conclusion might seem to follow from the arguments above, other perspectives need to be considered.

I distinguished earlier between two theological uses of the concept of soul, one as that substantial entity that survives death, and the other as a designator of our deepest experiences of personal relatedness. The theological status of a human person with respect to eternal life need not be dependent on a preexisting nonphysical soul, but on God's re-creation in another space and time; whereas soul-as-experience is embodied, emerging out of personal relatedness. In the case of both of these concepts of soul, the worth and status of each person would be up to God to determine. God may deal with individuals outside of this creation as he wishes. God may also relate to whom he chooses within his current creation, allowing for one form of relatedness that is not dependent on human capacity. The scriptural narrative suggests that it is God's will to relate to all humankind. Thus, our theological status now or eternally would not rely either on the existence of a separate nonphysical entity or on our human cognitive capacities to reciprocate personal relatedness.

In addition, it is critical to keep in mind that personal relatedness involves being related *to* by other persons, as well as being a person who is capable of initiating and sustaining personal relatedness. Certainly an infant is related *to* personally by its parents (and from the perspective of Christian theology is related to by God) prior to the development of the capacities critical for relatedness. Thus, even in the context of human experience, soul can be considered a state that is initially endowed by the process of being related *to*. However, the personal qualities of relationships deepen as the human individual develops in cognitive and social understandings. Nearly all parents feel deeply related to their infant children, but few parents would want to return to the level of relatedness experienced when the child was an infant after the child was, for example, eight years of age. Indeed, to be forced by neurological or psychiatric disorder to return to (or not to be able to progress beyond) this level of interrelationship is rightly viewed by the family and the community as a significant tragedy. However, the persistent relationship of the family and community to an individual, even within the context of a severe cognitive disability, continues to endow the individual with significant experiences of personal relatedness and soul.

What then is to be said of the souls of the individual with Asperger's syndrome, or of the lesser functioning autistic, or the severe amnesiacs such as H.M. and N.A., or the individual without sufficient evaluative emotional reactions to be socially responsible? To the degree that the attribute of soul is endowed by our Creator's choice to relate to them, soul is undiminished in essence. However, certain qualities or experiences of "soulishness" as they emerge from interhuman personal relatedness must be considered to be diminished in some degree by the cognitive disability. Yet, even a severe autistic, while incapable of appreciating the subtleties and complexities of human relationships, still responds in clear, albeit unusual, ways to human relationships. While the surrounding human community may need to expend greater effort and devise new strategies of relationship with the autistic, some degree of relationship is nonetheless possible.

Finally, comment must be made with respect to a competence versus performance difference in the relatedness of the normal adult human. It is obvious that within the cognitively competent community, not everyone develops, or allows themselves to express, the capacity for personal relatedness to the same degree. I am not speaking here of the person whose relationships are negative, distressing, or troubled, rather of the one who, for reasons of inadequate personality or character development, or impoverished social environment, participates minimally in human community. The thesis of this chapter has been that the experience of soul emerges from interpersonal relatedness. When such relatedness is diminished not by limitations in cognitive competence, but by a psychological makeup or a social history that does not lead to relatedness, experiences of soul can shrivel. In fact, individuals with diminished cognitive capacity (e.g., Down's syndrome) who are provided with and participate in a rich social environment may well have richer and deeper experiences of personal relatedness than some others with normal capacity who for reasons of psychological inadequacy have an impoverished realm of relatedness.

Thus, as Post develops more completely in a following chapter, the responsibility of the human community to the cognitively (or psychologically) deficient is not diminished, in the sense that these individuals can be seen and treated as lesser souls. To the contrary, the human community assumes a greater responsibility to extend personal relatedness to such individuals. It is a matter of the quality of their embodied experience of soul whether or not those with normal human capacities are responsive to those with a lesser capacity to reciprocate. "From everyone to whom much has been given, much will be required; and from the one to whom much has been entrusted, even more will be demanded" (Luke 12:48b).

CONCLUSION

This chapter has proposed one possible answer to the question, "How can a neurobiological organism be thought to have a soul if we are to adopt the position of nonreductive physicalism?" Working backward from biblical descriptions, I suggested that the concept of soul is fundamentally meant to point to the capacity for, and experience of, deep and rich forms of personal relatedness. I have further suggested that personal relatedness is an emergent property of the enhanced and interactive functioning of a number of fundamental cognitive abilities. These capacities would include (but are likely not limited to) language, a theory of mind, episodic memory, conscious top-down agency, a future orientation, and subtle emotional modulation by complex cognition. Each of these capacities is present to some degree in lower animals, substantially enhanced in humans, and plays a critical role in the richness of personal relatedness. Finally, I argued that a physicalist understanding of soul need not reduce the dignity of persons with diminished cognitive ability since (1) those with normal capacity have the potential (and the moral obligation) to relate to those with lesser capacity; and (2) it is ultimately God's sovereign choice to be in relationship with us, and not our ability to reciprocate, that bestows ultimate value and worth. While cognition contributes to soul, it is in the final analysis, God's act of relating that engenders soul in each human being.

Chapter Six

Nonreductive Physicalism: Philosophical Issues

Nancey Murphy

ISSUES FOR REFLECTION

Chapter 1 of this volume listed two competitors for a nonreductive physical-ist account of the person: dualism (of one sort or another) and reductive (or eliminative) materialism. Chapters 2 through 5 each in its own way provided reasons for choosing physicalism over dualism but also argued against the reductionist conclusions that are often drawn from those same scientific devel-opments. In the process, a number of issues have arisen that may profit from further philosophical reflection. I shall address three:

First, all of the authors have claimed that "higher" human characteristics such as morality, rationality, and the ability to enter into personal relationships cannot be reduced to evolutionary advantage, or genetic endowment, or neurobiology. In contrast, as Warren Brown says, these features are *emergent properties*. The first task of this chapter will be to examine more closely what is meant by *reduction* of higher-level properties to lower and explain why reductionist accounts fail (in some cases). A closely related issue is free will. Elving Anderson has already noted that recognition of genetic factors in human behavior does *not* entail genetic determinism; Malcolm Jeeves has made some useful distinctions regarding the nature of free will. I hope to contribute to these analyses.

Second, Jeeves has pointed out, rightly, that no amount of evidence from the neurosciences can ever *prove* dualism to be false or physicalism true. It is note-worthy that three Nobel laureates look at the evidence and each draws a dif-ferent conclusion: John Eccles maintains a dualist account, Francis Crick argues for a reductive materialist account, and Roger Sperry advances a nonreductive physicalist account. In the next section of this chapter I shall attend to the *epistemological* status of nonreductive physicalism, and argue that recent scientific advances do indeed provide scientific evidence for this position.

Third, I noted in chapter 1 that the focus in philosophy shifted in the modern period from the soul to the mind. Cognitive and neural sciences have followed suit in seeking to understand the *mental* processes once attributed to the soul. In medieval theology and still in many Christian circles the soul is understood, in addition, to be the locus of the person's ability to be in relationship with God. Warren Brown has made a significant contribution to the question of how, in terms of cognitive science, we are to understand our ability to relate to God. I hope to extend his account by examining in some detail various forms of *religious experience* and showing in each case that we need not postulate anything beyond the neural equipment involved in ordinary experience in order to account for our ability to be in conscious relationship with God.

PHYSICALISM AND REDUCTIONISM

Hierarchies

Westerners seem always to have attempted to understand the world in terms of hierarchies. For the ancient Greeks, reality was thought of as a hierarchy of *beings.*[1] A "generic" Greek view would go something like this:

divinities (including heavenly bodies)

humans

animals

plants

inanimate objects

During the modern period (beginning around 1600) a different hierarchical understanding has gradually supplanted the Greek. This is not a hierarchy of beings, but a hierarchy of *complex systems.* This hierarchy can be represented by a correlative hierarchy of the sciences that study reality in its varying levels of organization:

biology

chemistry

physics

1. See Arthur O. Lovejoy, *The Great Chain of Being* (Cambridge, Mass.: Harvard University Press, 1936).

Here physics is at the bottom because it studies the most basic constituents of reality; chemistry studies these "atoms" as they relate in complex structures (molecules)[2]; biology studies a number of levels of structure, from the biochemical through the levels of organelles, cells, tissues, organs, organisms, to colonies of organisms in their environments.

A contentious issue throughout the modern period has been whether psychology and the social sciences could be added in turn to this natural-science hierarchy—psychology being the study of the *behavior* of whole organisms, the social sciences being the study of human behavior in groups.

Another contentious issue has been reductionism. Here we need to distinguish among various sorts of reductionist theses:[3] *Methodological reductionism* is a research strategy of analyzing the thing to be studied into its parts. *Causal reductionism* is the view that the behavior of the parts of a system (ultimately, the parts studied by subatomic physics) is determinative of the behavior of all higher-level entities. Thus, this is the thesis that all causation in the hierarchy is "bottom-up." If this thesis is true, it would follow that the laws pertaining to higher sciences in the hierarchy should be reducible to the laws of physics.

Another sort of reductionism is the claim that higher-level entities are "nothing but the sum of their parts." However, this thesis is ambiguous; we need names here for two distinct positions. One is the view that as one goes up the hierarchy of levels, no new kinds of metaphysical "ingredients" need to be added to produce higher-level entities from lower. No "vital force" or "entelechy" must be added to get living beings from nonliving materials; no immaterial mind or soul is needed to get consciousness; no *Zeitgeist* is needed to form individuals into a society. Let us use the term *ontological reductionism* for this position. There is a stronger claim than the previous one that also sees the higher-level entities as nothing but the sum of their parts, but with the addition that only the entities at the lowest level are *really* real; higher-level entities—molecules, cells, organisms—are only composites of atoms. This thesis we here designate as *reductive materialism*. It is important to stress that it is possible to hold ontological reductionism without subscribing to this thesis. Thus, one might want to say that higher-level entities, such as human beings, are real—

---

2. Of course this is an oversimplification: physics itself is now many-layered, and atoms as understood by chemists are no longer "atoms" in the philosophical sense of being the most basic constituents of matter.

3. Cf. Ayala's "Introduction" in *Studies in the Philosophy of Biology: Reductionism and Related Problems*, ed. F. J. Ayala and T. Dobzhansky (Berkeley and Los Angeles: University of California Press, 1974); Ian Barbour, *Religion in an Age of Science: The Gifford Lectures*, vol. 1 (San Francisco: Harper and Row, 1990), 165-168; and Arthur Peacocke, *God and the New Biology* (London: J. M. Dent and Sons, 1986), chapters 1 and 2.

as real as the entities that compose them—and at the same time reject all sorts of vitalism and dualism.

A variety of philosophers, biologists, and others have taken care to distinguish these latter two theses. For example, "organicists" in biology rejected both vitalism and reductive materialism. The American philosopher Roy Wood Sellars developed a view of the entire hierarchy of the sciences that he called, variously, "emergent realism," "emergent naturalism," and "evolutionary naturalism." Sellars argued that organizations and wholes are genuinely significant; they are not mere aggregates of elementary particles. Reductive materialism, he believed, overemphasizes the "stuff" in contrast to the organization. The levels Sellars countenanced were the inorganic, the organic, the mental or conscious, the social, the ethical, and the religious or spiritual.[4]

So Sellars, and a number of contemporary thinkers as well,[5] accept ontological reductionism but vehemently reject reductive materialism. In addition, they say that while methodological reductionism has been a crucially important strategy in all the sciences, it is a limited strategy and needs to be balanced by studies of how entities at one level relate to higher levels—for example, organisms to their environments. They reject causal reductionism—one has to take account of causal influences of the whole on the part, as well as of the part on the whole. This is referred to as "downward causation,"[6] "top-down causation," or "whole-part causation."[7]

Let us use the term "nonreductive physicalism" to refer to this constellation of positions: the acceptance of ontological reductionism, but the rejection of causal reductionism and reductive materialism. Applied to the specific area of studies of consciousness, it denies the existence of a nonmaterial entity, the

4. *The Philosophy of Physical Realism* (New York: Russell and Russell, 1966), first published in 1932; and *idem, Principles of Emergent Realism: The Philosophical Essays of Roy Wood Sellars,* ed. W. Preston Warren (St. Louis, Mo.: Warren H. Green, Inc., 1970).

5. See Ian G. Barbour, *Issues in Science and Religion* (Engelwood Cliffs, N.J.: Prentice Hall, 1966); *idem, Religion in an Age of Science;* and Arthur Peacocke, *Creation and the World of Science* (Oxford: Clarendon Press, 1979); *idem, Theology for a Scientific Age: Being and Becoming—Natural, Divine, and Human,* 2d enlarged ed. (Minneapolis, Minn.: Fortress Press, 1993).

6. Donald Campbell " 'Downward Causation' in Hierarchically Organized Systems," in *Studies in the Philosophy of Biology,* ed. Ayala and Dobzhansky, 179-186.

7. See Arthur Peacocke, *Theology for a Scientific Age;* and *idem,* "God's Interaction with the World: The Implications of Deterministic 'Chaos' and of Interconnected and Interdependent Complexity," in *Chaos and Complexity: Scientific Perspectives on Divine Action,* ed. Robert J. Russell, Nancey Murphy, and Arthur R. Peacocke (Vatican City State and Berkeley, Calif.: Vatican Observatory and Center for Theology and the Natural Sciences, 1995), 263-288.

mind (or soul) but does not deny the existence of consciousness (a position in philosophy of mind called eliminative materialism) or the significance of conscious states or other ment*al* (note the adjectival form) phenomena. In brief, this is the view that the human nervous system, operating in concert with the rest of the body in its environment, is the seat of consciousness (and also of human spiritual or religious capacities). Consciousness and religious awareness are emergent properties and they have top-down causal influence on the body. This is the view advocated here. As mentioned above, there are a number of philosophical issues that need investigation in order to show that this position is coherent and intelligible. That is, can one consistently say that the neural system performs all of the functions once assigned to mind (and soul), and that this entails no significant loss to our understanding of human life? I believe that this general issue is best considered under the heading of causal reductionism: is it possible to accept ontological reductionism without causal reductionism? I begin with this issue.

Defeating Causal Reductionism
The central question to be addressed here is, how can a physicalist account of the person *fail* to be reductive? The question of *causal* reduction seems to be the one that matters for retaining our traditional conceptions of personhood. There are several related issues. First, if mental events can be reduced to brain events, and the brain events are governed by the laws of neurology (and ultimately by the laws of physics), then in what sense can we say that humans have free will? Are not their intendings and willings simply a product of blind physical forces, and thus are not their willed actions merely the product of blind forces?

Second, if mental events are simply the product of neurological causes, then what sense can we make of *reasons?* That is, we give reasons for judgments in all areas of our intellectual lives—moral, aesthetic, scientific, mathematical. It seems utter nonsense to say that these judgments are merely the result of the "blind forces of nature."

If free will is an illusion and the highest of human intellectual and cultural achievements can (*per impossible*) be counted as the mere outworking of the laws of physics, this is utterly devastating to our ordinary understanding of ourselves, and of course to theological accounts, as well, which depend not only on a concept of responsibility before God, but also on the justification (not merely the causation) of our theories about God and God's will. So, how to avoid this unacceptable outcome of a physicalist account of the mental realm?[8]

---

8. Recall that a dualist account does not escape similar problems. Here the problem is also causal: how can a nonmaterial mind have any causal impact on the brain? See chapter 1, sections 7–9.

Supervenience. I claim that it is only with the assistance of recent conceptual developments that physicalist accounts of the mental can avoid causal reductionism. We saw in chapter 1 that there have been a variety of strategies proposed for understanding the relation of mental events to brain events, and all run into difficulties: for dualists there is the problem of psychophysical interaction; for identity theorists there is the problem that mental events become the result of neurological causes rather than conscious reasons.

To see where the problem lies, let us begin with the vague thesis that every mental event (state, property) is *related to* some brain event. Add to this the assumption of causal connections among the neurological events, and we inevitably get a picture like the following, where M_1 through M_3 represent a temporal series of mental events, and the arrows represent causal connections among the brain events:

$$
\begin{array}{ccccc}
M_1 & & M_2 & & M_3 \ldots \\
| & & | & & | \\
B_1 & \rightarrow & B_2 & \rightarrow & B_3 \ldots
\end{array}
$$

Until recently only two relations were conceivable between mental events and brain events: identity and causation.[9] So we can make the picture more specific in one of two ways (arrows represent causal relations, || represents an identity relation):

$$
\begin{array}{ccccc}
M_1 & & M_2 & & M_3 \ldots \\
\uparrow & & \uparrow & & \uparrow \\
B_1 & \rightarrow & B_2 & \rightarrow & B_3 \ldots
\end{array}
$$

or:

$$
\begin{array}{ccccc}
M_1 & & M_2 & & M_3 \ldots \\
|| & & || & & || \\
B_1 & \rightarrow & B_2 & \rightarrow & B_3 \ldots
\end{array}
$$

In either case, if we assume causal connections at the physical level, causal reductionism seems inevitable. The mental events appear as mere epiphenomena.

In order to explain how reductionism can be avoided it is advantageous to consider the relation between consciousness and the neural system as but one instance of hierarchical ordering of complex systems because we can see analogies and borrow concepts from less problematic levels. Recall that Sellars included both the conscious and the ethical as levels in the hierarchy of complex systems. In 1952, R.M. Hare introduced the term "supervenience" as a

9. Mere correlation is also a possibility, but this runs into all the problems of dualism.

technical term to relate evaluative judgments (including ethical judgments) to descriptive judgments. Hare says:

> First, let us take that characteristic of "good" which has been called its supervenience. Suppose that we say, "St. Francis was a good man." It is logically impossible to say this and to maintain at the same time that there might have been another man *placed exactly in the same circumstances* as St. Francis, and who behaved in exactly the same way, but who differed from St. Francis in this respect only, that he was not a good man.[10]

So the higher-level property or description "good" *supervenes* on a collection of descriptions of Francis's character traits and actions. Or, to say the same thing, these character traits and actions constitute Francis's goodness.

In 1970 Donald Davidson introduced the concept of supervenience to describe the relation between mental and physical characteristics. Davidson describes the relation as follows:

> Mental characteristics are in some sense dependent, or supervenient, on physical characteristics. Such supervenience might be taken to mean that there cannot be two events alike in all physical respects but differing in some mental respect, or that an object cannot alter in some mental respect without altering in some physical respect. Dependence or supervenience of this kind does not entail reducibility through law or definition. . . .[11]

The concept of supervenience is now widely used in philosophy of mind,[12] but there is as yet no agreement on its proper definition. Terrence E. Horgan writes:

> The concept of supervenience, as a relation between properties, is essentially this: Properties of type A are supervenient on properties of type B if and only if two objects cannot differ with respect to their A-properties without also differing with respect to their B-properties. Properties that allegedly are supervenient on others are often called consequential properties, especially in ethics; the idea is that if something instantiates a moral property, then it

10. From *The Language of Morals* (1952); quoted by Terence E. Horgan in "Supervenience," in *The Cambridge Dictionary of Philosophy*, ed. Robert Audi (Cambridge: Cambridge University Press, 1995), 778-779. My italics.
11. *Essays on Actions and Events* (Oxford: Clarendon Press, 1980), 214. Reprinted from *Experience and Theory*, ed. Lawrence Foster and J. W. Swanson (Boston: University of Massachusetts Press and Duckworth, 1970).
12. See, for instance, Jaegwon Kim, *Supervenience and Mind: Selected Philosophical Essays* (Cambridge: Cambridge University Press, 1993); John Heil, *The Nature of True Minds* (Cambridge: Cambridge University Press, 1992); and David J. Chalmers, *The Conscious Mind: In Search of a Fundamental Theory* (New York: Oxford University Press, 1996).

does so *in virtue of,* i.e., as a (non–causal) *consequence of,* instantiating some lower-level property on which the moral property supervenes.[13]

Notice that there are two distinguishable notions of supervenience in this passage. In the first sentence (substituting 'S' for 'A' for clarity, so that S-properties are *supervenient* and B-properties are subvenient or *base* properties):

1. Properties of type S are supervenient on properties of type B if and only if two objects cannot differ with respect to their S-properties without also differing with respect to their B-properties.

But from the last sentence we can construct the following definition:

2. Properties of type S are supervenient on properties of type B if and only if something instantiates S-properties in virtue of (as a noncausal consequence of) its instantiating some B-properties.

These two possible definitions are not equivalent; *1* does not entail *2*. The reason can be seen in Hare's original use of the term. Francis's character traits and actions (B-properties) only constitute him (or someone like him) a good person (an S-property) *under certain circumstances.* That is, it is conceivable that identical behavior in different circumstances would *not* constitute goodness. For example, we would evaluate Francis's life much differently if he had been married and the father of children.[14]

The difference between these two accounts of supervenience is absolutely crucial. If mental properties or events are supervenient in the first sense, this ensures the reducibility of the mental to the physical and raises all the problems mentioned above. If mental events or properties are supervenient only in the second sense, then, I claim, reduction is not a necessary consequence. Thus, I offer the following definitions (which I take to be equivalent):

3. Property S is supervenient on property B if and only if something instantiates S in virtue of (as a non–causal consequence of) its instantiating B under circumstance *c*.

13. Horgan, "Supervenience," in *The Cambridge Dictionary of Philosophy,* 778-779.
14. A qualification needs to be added here. Someone who wanted to argue for the reducibility of supervenient properties in all cases would point out that anyone whose life was like Francis's in *all* (nonmoral) respects, including his relations to everyone else and everything else in the universe would necessarily have the same moral properties. That is, even if moral properties do not supervene "locally" (in the first, stronger sense), it must be the case that moral properties supervene "globally" on nonmoral properties. We cannot imagine a possible world like this one in all nonmoral respects but differing only in moral respects. I believe that this claim about global supervenience is true but uninteresting for the issues at hand.

4. Property S is supervenient on property B if and only if something's being B constitutes its being S under circumstance c.

An important feature of the supervenience relation, which has long been recognized, is that supervenient properties are often *multiply realizable*. This is a term from computer science—different configurations of hardware (vacuum tubes versus circuits) can realize, constitute, the same machine considered at the functional level. So if S supervenes on B (given circumstance c), then something's being B entails its being S, but its being S does not entail its being B. For example, goodness is multiply realizable; there are many life patterns different from Francis's that also constitute one a good person. Thus, from the statement "R. M. Hare was a good man" we cannot infer that he lived as St. Francis did. This is one respect in which supervenience relations fail to be identity relations ($S \leftrightarrow B$) since it is not the case that S entails B ($S \rightarrow B$). (Here arrows represent entailment rather than causation.)

My definition of supervenience recognizes another way in which supervenience relations fall short of identity. The fact that S supervenes on B does not mean that B entails S ($B \rightarrow S$) because of the dependence upon circumstances. Under c_1, $B \rightarrow S$, but under c_2 it may be the case that B → not -S. For example, under the circumstance of having a family to support, giving away all one's money may not constitute a good act.

For the purposes of getting clear about the use of these terms, we need a very simple example, one not complicated by the added perplexities associated with either the mind-brain issue or moral issues. Suppose that I have a light in my window and that I have arranged with a friend to use it as a signal to let her know if I am at home or not: on means yes; off means no. I flip the switch; one state of affairs ensues, with two levels of description.

> *supervenient:* the message is "I'm home"
> *subvenient:* the light is on.

It is important to emphasize that there is one state of affairs, two descriptions. Turning the light on *constitutes* my sending the "at home" message under the circumstances of our having made the appropriate prior arrangement.

The "at home" message is multiply realizable. We could have agreed instead that I'd leave the light off if I were home, or we could have agreed to use some other device altogether, such as leaving the window shade up or down.

We need a term to call our attention to an opposite sort of failure of the two descriptions to be identical. Not only is it the case that a *variety* of subvenient states can *realize* the *same* supervenient state (light on, shade up), but also, *again depending on circumstances,* the same subvenient state can *constitute* a variety of supervenient states. Suppose, for example, that we have agreed that the light's being on means I'm home only on Mondays, but on any other day the light's being on means I'm out. So depending on the circumstances of the day of the week, the same subvenient state constitutes either one message or the other. I suppose we could refer to this as "multiple constitutability."

It is this latter feature of the supervenience relation that I mean to highlight by emphasizing the role of *circumstances.* The variability in circumstances and their role in such cases is what makes for the difference between a supervenience relation and ordinary identity relations, and thus explains why some supervenient descriptions are not reducible to the lower level. This is the aspect that Horgan's first definition in the quotation above leaves out of account.

Let us now summarize the factors that distinguish between cases where reduction is and is not possible. The issues that matter are the following: (1) whether there are multiple circumstances such that B constitutes S in circumstance c but it is not the case that B constitutes S in circumstance c'; and if so (2) whether or not c, c' etc. are describable at the subvenient level; (3) whether S is multiply realizable; and if so (4) whether there is a finite disjunctive set of realizands.

Reduction will be possible in the limiting case where B constitutes S under all circumstances and S is not multiply realizable.[15] Reduction will not be possible when:

1. there are multiple circumstances that make a difference to the supervenience relation and these circumstances cannot be defined in terms of the subvenient level; or
2. when S is multiply realizable and there is no finite disjunctive set of realizands.

The example above wherein the light's being on has opposite meanings on Monday and Tuesday is an example of the first type of nonreducibility: days of the week cannot be defined the language of electrical phenomena.

For an example of the second type of nonreducibility we cannot use agreed signals because this will necessarily be a finite list. Instead consider the variety of natural signs or evidence of someone's being home: lights on, television on, car in the garage, etc. Here there is no finite list of states of affairs that consti-

15. For a justification of these claims, see Nancey Murphy, "Supervenience and the Nonreducibility of Ethics to Biology," in *Molecular and Evolutionary Biology: Scientific Perspectives on Divine Action,* ed. Robert J. Russell, William R. Stoeger, and Francisco J. Ayala (Vatican City State and Berkeley, Calif.: Vatican Observatory and Center for Theology and the Natural Sciences, forthcoming).

tute the supervenient state "evidence of someone's being home"; thus, there can be no laws relating the two levels.

I emphasize that my conclusions here depend on using my more complex definition of supervenience, which gives due attention to circumstances. One might wonder why the disagreement over the definition of supervenience. (John R. Searle, in fact, claims that in philosophy of mind the supervenience relation is a *causal* relation and sharply distinguishes its use there from previous use in moral philosophy.)[16] It is important to recognize that many of the theorists working in this area are in favor of reductionism. Thus, the matter cannot be left to mere stipulation; we have to pursue the more difficult task of judging which definition better fits the facts: mine, in which circumstances at a higher level of description need to be taken into account, or the more common definition in which they do not.

Many cases will fit the simpler definition of supervenience. However, there will also be a number of cases (perhaps most) where only the more complex definition does justice to the phenomena. A clear case where non-neural *circumstances* are widely recognized to make a difference is the role of *mental set* in perception. Two subjects induced to hold different expectations will often have different perceptual experiences resulting from the same physical stimulus. Mental set is a variable easily describable at the mental level, but in most cases (all cases?) will not be definable in terms of a finite set of neural realizands. For example, consider a well-known experiment in which subjects receive a small electrical shock on the back. Depending on their mental set, they will experience the sensation either as a burn or as ice. So at the subvenient level there is a series of physical events including the application of the shock, the transmission of a nerve impulse to the brain, and the set of brain events that realize the sensation of either heat or cold. The mental set will, of course, be realized neurologically, but it is multiply realizable: it could be the realization of a variety of perceptions of the environment (ice-cube tray on the counter, burn ointment), or the result of statements by the experimenters, or any one of an unbounded set of other devices resulting in what we can only meaningfully describe at the mental level as the *expectation* of heat or of cold.

Another example: children asked to estimate the size of disks will generally estimate coins to be larger than other disks of the same size. The concept of economic value simply does not translate to the neurological level of discourse.

This last example is important. If we take the hierarchy of levels to include the moral and the social (with its political, economic, legal dimensions) we can see that we will have here a vast array of concepts that most philosophers would agree are not logically reducible to neurological variables. So these

16. *The Rediscovery of Mind* (Cambridge, Mass.: MIT Press, 1992), 124-126.

higher levels of reality are not in danger of causal reduction to the biological level. This, I claim, is exactly what is needed to protect traditional views of the meaningfulness of human intellectual endeavors. In Warren Brown's terms, there are *emergent levels* as we go from the neurological to the cognitive, to the interpersonal, to the political, economic, and legal, to the moral, and finally to the spiritual. While all human behavior supervenes on the biological (genetic and neurological), little of it is reducible to biology.

Free Will

It would be foolhardy to attempt to solve the problem of free will in one short section of one chapter. However, the reflections in the previous subsection are certainly relevant to this issue. Clearly, if I have succeeded in defeating causal reductionism with regard to the mental and the neurobiological, this opens the door to treatments of human freedom that do not depend on denying either physicalism or the law-governed character of neurobiological processes. That is, one of our strongest reasons for denying free will in the modern period has been the supposition that causal determinism applies to the human body.[17] Rebut this supposition and the burden of proof shifts to those who would deny the freedom that seems an obvious fact of human experience.

As Malcolm Jeeves has pointed out,[18] discussions of free will often distinguish between compatibilist and incompatibilist accounts. An incompatibilist view maintains that free will is incompatible with a determinist view of the natural world. A compatibilist view, in contrast, maintains that human freedom means being able to act as one chooses. It is irrelevant whether one's choices themselves can be shown to be a product of prior causes of certain sorts. The important issue, it seems, is whether our choices are determined by the kinds of factors that we believe to be operative, or whether we are self-deceived. For example, is one's choice motivated by the reasons one gives, consistent with one's values, a true reflection of one's character; or is it instead, unbeknown to the actor, a product of genetic predisposition, unconscious drives, or social manipulation?

The argument of the previous subsection is relevant here. In addition to the above list of suspicions, the physicalist has to answer the question whether what appear to us to be reasoned choices are not actually the products of the laws of physics (with the laws of neurophysiology being but special cases). It was the intent of the previous argument to show that we can sometimes (and

17. This supposition has also been a powerful motivator for dualist accounts of the person; the body may be caught up in the laws of Newtonian mechanics, but the mind is free.

18. See chapter 4.

I would actually want to make the stronger claim—*usually*) only make causal sense of a series of human actions by attending to the mental-level description, which includes reasons, judgments, and so on. Yet this is *compatible* with causal determinism at the neurobiological level.

Now, it is one thing to rebut determinist arguments; it is another to give a positive account of how free will is embodied in neurological functioning. My guess is that such an account will come from appreciating the multiple interacting layers of information processing in the brain.

EMPIRICAL SUPPORT FOR NONREDUCTIVE PHYSICALISM

It has long been recognized that substance dualism cannot be *disproved* by empirical evidence. For example, no matter how much evidence accumulates suggesting that the brain performs mental operations (in John Searle's pithy phrase: "Scoop out the brain and the darned thing doesn't work."), it is still possible to claim that there is a substantial mind and that its operations are neatly *correlated* with brain events; as Jeeves has pointed out, Sir John Eccles, one of the most noted of neuroscientists, holds exactly this view. It follows, then, that no amount of evidence from neuroscience can *prove* a physicalist view of the mental. This may seem a vexing state of affairs to philosophers who expect conclusive arguments, but most scientists are well aware that adequate evidence can be provided for a thesis without it ever amounting to proof.

I suggest, then, that we look at the epistemological status of nonreductive physicalism, not as a philosophical thesis, but as a scientific theory. Philosopher of science Imre Lakatos has provided the most illuminating account to date of the structure of science.[19] Reacting to Thomas Kuhn's rather ambiguous account of the history of science as a series of *paradigms*,[20] Lakatos described it instead as a series of competing *research programs*. A research program is a vast network of theories, logically related to one another and supported by a variety of data. What unifies this network of theory and data is the "hard core," a thesis, often of a metaphysical nature, about the character of the part or aspect of reality under investigation. A clear example of the role of metaphysics can be seen in the development of early modern physics, where atomism, one of the competing views of matter in ancient Greek *philosophy*, became the core of a very successful *scientific*

19. See "Falsification and the Methodology of Scientific Research Programmes," in *The Methodology of Scientific Research Programmes: Philosophical Papers, Volume 1*, ed. John Worrall and Gregory Currie (Cambridge: Cambridge University Press, 1978), 8–101.
20. Thomas Kuhn, *The Structure of Scientific Revolutions*, 2d ed. (Chicago: University of Chicago Press, 1970).

research program. So I propose that we think of the metaphysical thesis of nonreductive physicalism as the hard core of a scientific research program.

A scientific research program also has a "positive heuristic"; that is, a formal or tacit plan for development of the program that specifies the work to be done—the domain of phenomena that need to be explained using the basic concepts and principles of the program. The positive heuristic in this case will be the plan to explain physicalistically all of the operations once attributed to the mind or soul. Insofar as researchers (in neurophysiology and anatomy, neuropsychology, psychiatry, cognitive science, and other related fields) make progress in explaining "mental" phenomena, the program as a whole is making empirical progress and its core thesis is thereby corroborated.

As can be seen from the previous chapters, great advances have been made in recent years in giving neurobiological accounts of these faculties. I find brain localization studies to be some of the most impressive pieces of evidence for the physicalist program. Besides simply locating and modeling mental processes as previously understood, these studies sometimes *improve* our understanding of the mental processes themselves. For example, Antonio Damasio's account of patients with localized brain lesions causing a combination of anhedonia and deficits in everyday decisionmaking shows that contrary to what has often been supposed, the emotions contribute positively to practical reasoning.[21]

One area of brain research to which I shall attend in some detail is moral reasoning. I select this example because it is often considered one of the highest of human faculties. If progress can be made in explaining it neurobiologically (but without reducing it to mere biology) this will be a dramatic instance of empirical confirmation for nonreductive physicalism.

Here I follow Paul Churchland's work. Churchland and others are engaged in an attempt to supplant an earlier approach to computer modeling of neural processes.[22] The earlier approach was algorithmic; that is, it attempted to model mental processes by writing rules to govern a linear sequence of transformations. This is the way most computers are programmed, but all computer users suspect it is not the way human thinking works—computers are much better at some things than we (computation), but maddeningly worse at others (recognizing the same intention in the command "\n\ch6" as in "\n\ch-6").

---

21. Antonio R. Damasio, *Descartes' Error: Emotion, Reason, and the Human Brain* (New York: G. P. Putnam's Sons, 1994).
22. See Paul M. Churchland, *The Engine of Reason, the Seat of the Soul: A Philosophical Journey into the Brain* (Cambridge, Mass.: MIT Press, 1995); and also Gerald M. Edelman, *Bright Air, Brilliant Fire: On the Matter of the Mind* (New York: HarperCollins, 1992).

An alternative model employs the notion of *prototypes* created by trial and error. For example, a computer can learn to distinguish an underwater mine from a rock if appropriate data are fed to it, the computer repeatedly "guesses," and is informed after each trial whether its guess was correct. The hypothesis is that human brains work the same way. One of Churchland's examples is learning to recognize the taste of a peach. We have four different types of taste receptors (sour, bitter, sweet, salty). On a four-dimensional graph we could represent a region within the space of all possible taste combinations that contains the exact combination of flavors of a number of peaches. The theory is that through repeated trials one develops a tendency to respond when a combination of signals from the tongue fall into that region. A strong "peach" signal will then be sent if the combination falls in the center of that region; weaker signals will be sent when combinations fall closer to the periphery.[23]

Now, what is the relevance of all of this to ethics? Churchland argues that much of moral or ethical learning is the development and refinement of *prototypes;* it is a process of learning how to recognize and categorize a variety of social situations and to respond to them appropriately. For example, it involves learning to distinguish lying from kidding and "white lies." Churchland writes: "The intellectual tradition of Western moral philosophy has focused on *rules,* on specific laws or principles. These are supposed to govern one's behavior, to the extent that one's behavior is moral at all."[24] However, human capacities for moral reasoning out-pace philosophers' ability to identify the rules it follows, just as children's ability to speak grammatically precedes any knowledge of the rules of grammar.

> It may be the case that a normal human's capacity for moral perception, cognition, deliberation, and action has rather less to do with rules, whether internal or external, than is commonly supposed. What is the alternative to a rule-based account of our moral capacity? The alternative is a hierarchy of learned prototypes, for both moral perception and moral behavior, prototypes embodied in the well-tuned configuration of a neural network's synaptic weights.[25]

It is interesting to note that (quite independently of Churchland's work) many moral philosophers and theologians have made a significant turn away from rule-based analyses and toward approaches to morality that focus on

---

23. Churchland, *The Engine of Reason,* 21–24.
24. Ibid., 144.
25. Ibid.

virtues (prototypically good human qualities), recognizable only in narrative contexts. The topic of moral *description* has become central as well.[26]

So what does this mean for the topic at hand? One particular subsidiary research strategy within the broad research program of physicalism provides a competing account of the nature of moral reasoning (prototypes rather than rules). This thesis, if true, would explain in biological terms not only what is happening neurophysiologically when one engages in moral reasoning, but also why the predominant rule-based strategy in modern Western ethics has turned out to be inadequate. It explains neurobiologically why an approach to moral analysis and moral education based on narrative accounts of virtuous lives should be more effective than its competitor.

So far, I have not said anything about a nonreductive physicalist program that distinguishes it from a reductive materialist program. I shall not pursue that general question here, but it is clear that an important issue arises from Churchland's work. Is it adequate to say that moral reasoning is *nothing but* developing moral prototypes, and (as Churchland seems to assume) that moral motivation is *nothing but* the recognition that one gets along better in the social world by complying with moral expectations? Churchland writes: "From this perspective, the traditional question posed by the moral skeptic, namely, 'Why should I be moral?', looks peculiar and uncomprehending. As well ask, 'Why should I acquire the skills of swimming?' when one is a fish."[27]

Owen Flanagan argues, rightly, that to reduce ethics to a combination of moral perception and prudence omits the crucial *normative* aspect of ethics. It disallows the question, *should* it be the case that this society is such that one gets along better in it by conforming to prototype *x*?[28] I would argue that the reduction of the moral "ought" to a social-prudential "ought," or to biology, or to both is to fail to understand the meaning of the moral "ought." It is a species of the incoherence into which reductive materialist accounts of the

---

26. In philosophical ethics, Alasdair MacIntyre has done more than anyone else to encourage this shift; see *After Virtue* (Notre Dame, Ind.: University of Notre Dame Press, 1981; 1984). In theological ethics, Stanley Hauerwas has been most influential; Hauerwas has a series of books, beginning with one aptly titled *Vision and Virtue: Essays in Christian Ethical Reflection* (Notre Dame, Ind.: Fides Publishers, 1974). See also James Wm. McClendon Jr., *Ethics: Systematic Theology, Volume 1* (Nashville, Tenn.: Abingdon Press, 1986), for a "three stranded" analysis of Christian morality, which could nicely be interpreted as an account of three supervenient levels of moral reflection: the bodily, the social, and the level pertaining to the community's ongoing relation with God.
27. Churchland, *The Engine of Reason,* 150.
28. Owen Flanagan, *Self Expressions: Mind, Morals, and the Meaning of Life* (New York: Oxford University Press, 1996), chapter 8.

person regularly fall, and against which I have attempted to guard in the previous section.[29]

So I conclude that if we take nonreductive physicalism to be not merely a
philosophical thesis, but also the hard core of a scientific research program,
there is ample scientific evidence for it. It can be shown to be consistent with
our everyday concepts of the significance of the mental, but also confirmed
by a burgeoning body of research showing that mental capabilities are realized neurobiologically. I have also hinted, in my critique of Churchland's
view of ethics, that a *nonreductive* program would be more coherent and adequate to experience than a reductive materialist program. However, I cannot
argue that here.

A NONREDUCTIVE-PHYSICALIST ACCOUNT
OF RELIGIOUS EXPERIENCE

Many concerns of a theological nature that arise from the replacement of dualist accounts of the person by a nonreductive-physicalist account will be
addressed in the following chapters. My goal here is to address but one issue.
Some earlier conceptions of the soul in the Christian tradition saw it as the
means of contact with God. So the question arises how we are to explain
divine-human interaction using the resources of this new account of the person.

Religious Experience
Philosopher of religion Carolyn Franks Davis has provided a useful list of
kinds of religious experiences: interpretive experiences, quasi-sensory experiences, revelatory experiences, regenerative experiences, numinous experiences,
and mystical experiences. I argue that these experiences *supervene* on combinations of ordinary experiences. That is, there is no special faculty needed in
order to experience religious realities. What makes the experience religious is
a meaningful combination of ordinary experiences, under *circumstances* that
make it apparent that God is involved in the event in a special way. My case is
easiest to make for Franks Davis's first category. She writes:

29. I argue that the reduction of ethics to something else (pleasure calculus, reason-
ableness, prudence, and now biology, whether neurobiology or genetics) is a confusion,
but an understandable confusion in our secular society. Ethics is intrinsically dependent
on a higher (theological) level of analysis. See Nancey Murphy, "Supervenience and the
Nonreducibility of Ethics to Biology," in *Anglo-American Postmodernity: Philosophical
Perspectives on Science, Religion, and Ethics* (Boulder, Colo.: Westview Press, 1997), chapter 10; and Murphy and George F. R. Ellis, *On the Moral Nature of the Universe: Theology,
Cosmology, and Ethics* (Minneapolis, Minn.: Fortress Press, 1996), chapters 6 and 8.

Sometimes a subject sees an experience as religious not because of any unusual features of the experience itself, but because it is viewed in the light of a prior religious interpretive framework. Common examples of such experiences are seeing a misfortune as the result of sins . . . , going through an illness with joy because it is a chance to "participate in Christ's suffering," experiencing love for all things of this world because of the belief that they are permeated by the divine, seeing an event as "God's will," and taking an event to be the answer to a prayer.[30]

Here it is clear that no special faculty is needed to account for the religious experience. For instance, in Franks Davis's example, the "misfortune" is experienced in the same way as any other event in human life. The higher-level description of "punishment from God" is seen as appropriate because of the circumstances: the prior sin, the belief that God chastises. Her second example is more interesting and more complex. Again, there is a lower-level description of an event, experienced in the ordinary way: "the person is ill." The sufferer's Christian worldview, however, allows for higher-level description: participating in Christ's suffering. In addition, this higher-level perception is causally efficacious at the psychological level; in a top-down manner it affects the mood of the subject, producing joy, where depression would otherwise be more likely. A more striking top-down effect is the enhancement of immune function that is a likely outcome of the elevated mood.

Franks Davis's second category is quasi-sensory experiences: "Religious experiences in which the primary element is a physical sensation or whose alleged percept is of a type normally apprehended by one of the five sense modalities are 'quasi-sensory' experiences. These include visions and dreams, voices and other sounds, smells, tastes, the feeling of being touched, heat, pain, and the sensation of rising up (levitation)."[31]

The most common instances of this type discussed in the literature are visions. There are two ways to understand such experiences: (1) spiritual beings are really present in some way, and they are visible to the eye; or (2) the experience is akin to a hallucination, but may be a genuine religious experience in that the vision was *caused* by God for some special purpose, or at least the person derives some religious value from it. The second account seems to this author the more plausible. Here again no special faculty is required to understand it as a genuine religious phenomenon—presumably the same or similar neural capacities are involved as in hallucinating or dreaming.

30. Carolyn Franks Davis, *The Evidential Force of Religious Experience* (Oxford: Clarendon Press, 1989), 33.
31. Ibid., 35-36.

This type of religious experience raises the issue of divine action. That is, the description of, say, "a vision of Christ" *justifiably* supervenes on the description "experience of a man in white" under the circumstance of the experience truly having been caused by Christ as opposed to, say, the mere wishing of the recipient or the effect of drugs. More on divine action below.

Franks Davis's third category is revelatory experiences:

> Religious experiences of this category comprise what their subjects may call sudden convictions, inspiration, revelation, enlightenment, "the mystical vision," and flashes of insight. They may seem to descend upon the subject out of the blue, unaccompanied by any other feature which would make the experience religious, in which case it is their religious content which makes them "religious experiences;" or, more frequently, they are the "revelatory" element in a more complex religious experience, very often a mystical experience. These experiences have distinctive features: (i) they are usually sudden and of short duration, though the after-effects may last a lifetime (especially in the case of conversion experiences); (ii) the alleged new knowledge seems to the subject to have been acquired immediately rather than through reasoning or sense perception; (iii) the alleged new knowledge usually seems to the subject to have been "poured into" or "showered upon" him (metaphors abound) by an external agency; (iv) the "revelations" carry with them utter conviction, somehow even more than that which attaches to sense perception; and (v) the insights gained are often claimed to be impossible to put into words.[32]

With the possible exception of "the mystical vision," these are clearly experiences that depend on the same neural functions as ordinary experiences. I want to emphasize the role of narrative context in justifying the description of these experiences in religious terms. Their happening "out of the blue" is often counted as a sign of divine action in the Christian tradition. For example, Ignatius of Loyola describes *consolation,* an experience confirmatory of God's action in a person's life as an

> interior movement in the soul . . . through which the soul comes to be inflamed with love of its Creator and Lord; and when it can in consequence love no created thing on the face of the earth in itself, but in the Creator of them all.
>
> Likewise, when it sheds tears that move to love of its Lord, whether out of sorrow for one's sins, or for the Passion of Christ our Lord, or because of other things directly connected with His service and praise.

32. Ibid., 39–40.

Finally, I call consolation every increase of hope, faith and charity, and all interior joy which calls and attracts to heavenly things and to the salvation of one's soul, quieting it and giving it peace in its Creator and Lord.[33]

Ignatius emphasized that consolation could be distinguished from more ordinary experiences partly by the fact that one had not done anything to induce it. This provides some grounds for believing it to have been effected by God. The long-lasting positive effects in the recipient's life that Franks Davis mentions add powerful confirmation to the judgment that these experiences are indeed revelations *from God*. In short, the church has developed *criteria* for discerning whether an experience is merely a human phenomenon or a true experience *of* or *from* God, and this discernment relies heavily on the narrative context of the event.[34]

Franks Davis writes that regenerative experiences are the most frequent type of religious experience among ordinary people. These are experiences that tend to renew the subject's faith and improve his or her spiritual, moral, physical, or psychological well-being. Again, the circumstances are the key: "This category includes a wide range of experiences: experiences of new hope, strength, comfort, peace, security, and joy, seen as 'religious' because they are obtained during religious activity such as prayer...."[35]

Numinous experience has been defined by Rudolf Otto as a combination of awe, dread, or terror with a sense of attraction or fascination.[36] Here we have, again, ordinary human experiences, although in an unusual combination.

There is much disagreement about the nature of mystical experience. Franks Davis describes it as having the following features: "(i) the sense of having apprehended ultimate reality; (ii) the sense of freedom from the limitations of time, space, and the individual ego; (iii) a sense of 'oneness': and (iv) bliss or serenity."[37] I shall not attempt an adequate account of these experiences, but will only point out that qualitatively similar experiences have been reported by people taking psychoactive drugs. What then distinguishes the true mystical (i.e., religious) experience from one phenomenally very similar is, as Franks Davis says: "mystical experiences are usually ... the pinnacle of the spiritual

---

33. Ignatius Loyola, *The Spiritual Exercises: A Literal Translation and a Contemporary Reading,* ed. and trans. David L. Fleming (St. Louis: Institute of Jesuit Sources, 1978), 206.

34. For an account of discernment practices, see Nancey Murphy, *Theology in the Age of Scientific Reasoning* (Ithaca, N.Y.: Cornell University Press, 1990), chapter 5.

35. Franks Davis, *Evidential Force,* 44–45.

36. Rudolf Otto, *The Idea of the Holy,* trans. J. W. Harvey (London: Oxford University Press, 1936).

37. Franks Davis, *Evidential Force,* 54.

journey."[38] Thus, it is the setting of the experience in the (often lifelong) quest of the recipient that distinguishes it as a religious experience.

In conclusion, then, I want to suggest that religious experiences do not depend on any special faculties over and above humans' ordinary emotional and cognitive faculties.[39] Their religiousness consists in (sometimes) their special content, but, more importantly, in their circumstances—circumstances that justify their being interpreted as acts of or encounters with the divine. In brief, religious experience supervenes on cognitive and/or affective experience in the context of an encounter with God.

Now, in the above account I have been assuming a view of divine action such that God is not only the creator and sustainer of the universe, but also an agent in a special way in particular events. This is a common view of divine action in conservative Christian circles, but many liberal theologians would reject or seriously qualify the account of special divine acts. For instance, Maurice Wiles restricts God's action to enacting the whole of history. Revelation is not the result of special action on God's part, but is to be explained in terms of special sensitivity of some people to God's general action.[40] The reason for such accounts of divine action is largely that more robust accounts of special divine actions (whether this be of miracles or merely of special providence) have been made problematic by modern science. The same problems arise in attempting to account for the action of a nonmaterial God as in attempting to explain how a nonmaterial mind could have a causal effect on the body.

The nonreductive physicalist account of religious experience is valuable in that it allows believers to accept and make use of research on the biological, psychological, and social realization of religious experience. However, without an account of divine action, religious experience will be reducible to these lower levels in the hierarchy. The nonreductive physicalist account of nature needs to be completed by a theological account in which descriptions of divine action supervene on descriptions of natural and historical events, but without being reducible to them. We need to conceive of the hierarchy of the

38. Ibid., 55.
39. And perhaps in conjunction with a physiological component. "For example, a 'meditative' religious experience could include a cognitive/mental component, a behavioral component, and a physiological component (or components) all of which could be potentially identified, none of which is uniquely religious but in their clustering become a religious experience" (Dan Blazer, personal correspondence, August 28, 1996).
40. Maurice Wiles, "Religious Authority and Divine Action," in *God's Activity in the World: The Contemporary Problem,* ed. Owen C. Thomas (Chico, Calif.: Scholars Press, 1983), 181-194.

sciences as incomplete without theology, and especially to maintain the nonreducibility of theology to other disciplines.[41]

Recognizing the role of Newtonian science in creating problems for an account of divine action, a number of theologians and scientists have called for reconsideration of the problem in light of more recent scientific developments.[42]

CONCLUSION

Nonreductive physicalism is an important new concept in the philosophical world. While dualism has gradually come to appear untenable in philosophical circles, most philosophers of mind have sought alternatives with a reductive intent. Recent developments in neurobiology and psychology have given aid and comfort to the reductionists. However, radical reductionism (reductive or eliminative materialism) is utterly unacceptable to the Christian. Thus, much needs to be done by scholars in a variety of fields to clarify nonreductive physicalism and to relate it to science, to discussions in fields such as ethics, and finally to relate it to the Christian tradition.

I have attempted to make a few steps in this direction, arguing for the coherence of a view that is ontologically reductionist but not causally reductionist, and claiming that this avoids unacceptable consequences such as the denial of human freedom and the meaninglessness of the entire intellectual order. I have also provided a suggestion for how to view the epistemological relations between nonreductive physicalism and the accumulating scientific evidence. Finally, I have suggested a nonreductive physicalist account of religious experience.

41. When lecturing on the topic of this chapter I have often been surprised to find that some of the audience take the denial of the existence of a substantial soul to imply the denial of the existence of God. This is, emphatically, not my position. Christians need two basic metaphysical categories: God and creation. The claim that God's creation is purely physical does not entail that there is no (nonphysical) creator.

42. See Peacocke, *Theology for a Scientific Age;* Robert J. Russell, Nancey Murphy, and C. J. Isham, eds., *Quantum Cosmology and the Laws of Nature: Scientific Perspectives on Divine Action* (Vatican City State and Berkeley: Vatican Observatory and Center for Theology and the Natural Sciences, 1993); Robert J. Russell, Nancey Murphy, and Arthur Peacocke, eds., *Chaos and Complexity: Scientific Perspectives on Divine Action* (Vatican City State and Berkeley: Vatican Observatory and Center for Theology and the Natural Sciences, 1995); and Russell et al., eds., *Molecular and Evolutionary Biology: Scientific Perspectives on Divine Action*.

Chapter Seven

"Bodies—That Is, Human Lives": A Re-Examination of Human Nature in the Bible

Joel B. Green

BIBLICAL CONCERNS

Recent fervor among persons representing the sciences, philosophy, and other disciplines regarding the nature of the human person has begun to generate at least two related outcomes. The first, and most obvious, is growing support for a monist, or physicalist, account of the human being. Second, though perhaps less celebrated, is a pointed affirmation of the essentially social character of the human person, who is qualitatively distinguished from other creatures by the capacity for personal relatedness and ethical comportment. The fundamental question facing us in this chapter is, how might reflections of this sort be correlated with biblical concerns regarding the nature of the human person? For Christians, what might Scripture add to this discussion?

In fact, questions concerning the nature of the human person are not simply a product of the history of philosophical reflection or a focus of contemporary scientific study. For Christians, "portraits of human nature" are also deeply rooted in the biblical traditions of the people of God. Even if speculative attention to these issues is lacking in the Christian Scriptures, biblical writers nevertheless worked with an assumed depiction(s) of the human person—sometimes in order to counter competing portraits.

A Preliminary Example
A preliminary example, found in the Bible's last book, Revelation, will help to focus our concerns. Writing in Revelation 18, John divulges the contents of

the Rome-bound seafaring cargo in order to portray the center of the Roman Empire as a mistress-harlot who maintains a luxurious lifestyle at the expense of her lovers, the conquered peoples of the Roman empire. He thus exposes a network of economic interests—including kings, merchants, and mariners, who have most to gain from Roman economic dominance, as well as common subjects, exploited but bedazzled by Roman opulence and propaganda. According to the New Revised Standard Version (NRSV), this cargo record consists of "gold, silver, jewels and pearls, fine linen, purple, silk and scarlet, all kinds of scented wood, all articles of ivory, all articles of costly wood, bronze, iron, and marble, cinnamon, spice, incense, myrrh, frankincense, wine, olive oil, choice flour and wheat, cattle and sheep, horses and chariots, slaves—and human lives" (18:12-13). What interests us about this inventory are the occupants of its climactic finale. Where the NRSV reads "slaves—and human lives," the Greek text may be translated more literally "bodies—even the souls of humans" or "bodies—that is, human lives" *(stomaton kai psychas anthropon).* Strictly speaking, the NRSV is not inaccurate in its translation, as *somata* could denote "slaves,"[1] but it masks the reductionism inherent in such usage and overlooks John's criticism of this debasement of human beings. Even slaves are more than their physicality; they are human beings wrongly catalogued by their materiality, like so many carcasses, alongside cattle and sheep.

That is, we find in this one textual exemplar evidence (1) for the presence of body-soul dualism in the Greco-Roman world,[2] and (2) of the distortion that might emanate from duality. In fact, where some form of body-soul dualism was accepted in the Greco-Roman world, the soul was typically accorded privilege and the body denigrated. Also well represented among our contemporaries, belief in a body-soul dualism is similarly implicated in its own travesties—for example, with reference to the biomedical paradigm that prevails in Western medicine, with its primary focus on the body of the patient as the

---

1. William F. Arndt and F. Wilbur Gingrich, *A Greek-English Lexicon of the New Testament and Other Early Christian Literature,* 2d ed., rev. F. Wilbur Gingrich and Frederick W. Danker (Chicago: University of Chicago Press, 1958), 799. John has thus linked an ordinary term for "slaves" with language borrowed from Ezek. 27:13.

2. It might be argued that the denigration of human beings assumed by Rev. 18:12-13 is equally consistent with the philosophical position of reductive physicalism (see Murphy, chapter 1). As we will indicate, however, this position seems to occupy no place within the presupposition pool of Greco-Roman antiquity. On the other hand, an important aspect of the ideology of slavery in the Hellenistic and Roman periods was the argument from "nature"—namely, though slaves might possess the physical qualifications of a free person, they lacked "the soul's beauty" (cf. Yvon Thébert, "The Slave," in *The Romans,* ed. Andrea Giardina [Chicago: University of Chicago Press, 1993]), 138-174).

source of sickness, its locus of attention at or beneath the skin, and its concomitant indifference to the mind and to human life in its social embeddedness;[3] or with reference in many Christian circles to evangelism as "winning souls," without regard to the promise and embodiment of peace and justice.[4] Finally, (3) this text evidences the capacity of at least one early Christian prophet to give written expression to what for many in the Greco-Roman world would have been a common view, body-soul duality, while at the same time criticizing that view of human nature for its denigration of the body—indeed, of human life.

The Problem

This brief example from the Book of Revelation helps to surface the issues with which this chapter is concerned. Popular Christianity has tended to assume anthropological duality,[5] and some streams of biblical scholarship have contended for it, usually by insisting that the New Testament materials are dualistic in their understanding of the human person.[6] With reference to this one text, however, we see immediately that duality cannot simply be taken for granted. Given the state of the current discussion,[7] we need to ask with refer-

---

3. See Robert A. Hahn, *Sickness and Health: An Anthropological Perspective* (New Haven, Conn.: Yale University Press, 1995), 28.

4. *Contra* biblical visions for the church's mission, on which cf. William A. Dyrness, *Let the Earth Rejoice! A Biblical Theology of Holistic Mission* (Westchester, Ill.: Crossways, 1983); Joel B. Green, "Proclaiming Repentance and Forgiveness of Sins to All Nations: A Biblical Perspective on the Church's Mission," in *The World Is My Parish: The Mission of the Church in Methodist Perspective,* ed. Alan G. Padgett, Studies in the History of Missions 10 (Lewiston, N.Y.: Edwin Mellen, 1992), 13-43.

5. This view is propagated by the enormously influential Chinese Christian writer of the last half of the twentieth century, Watchman Nee; see especially his *The Spiritual Man,* 3 vols. (New York: Christian Fellowship, 1968).

6. This is especially true of evangelical scholarship—cf., e.g., Robert H. Gundry, *Soma in Biblical Theology with Emphasis on Pauline Anthropology,* Society of New Testament Studies Monograph Series 29 (Cambridge: Cambridge University Press, 1976); John W. Cooper, *Body, Soul, and Life Everlasting: Biblical Anthropology and the Monism-Dualism Debate* (Grand Rapids: Wm. B. Eerdmans, 1989). J. Knox Chamblin, "Psychology," in *Dictionary of Paul and His Letters,* ed. Gerald F. Hawthorne, Ralph P. Martin, and Daniel G. Reid (Downers Grove, Ill.: InterVarsity, 1993), 765-775 [esp. 766-768], writes from this perspective as well, though he notes that most contemporary scholars argue for some form of monism in Pauline thought.

7. Cf. Rudolf Bultmann, *Theology of the New Testament,* 2 vols. (New York: Charles Scribner's Sons, 1951/55) 1:192-203; Cooper, *Body, Soul, and Life Everlasting;* Gundry, *Soma;* Robert Jewett, *Paul's Anthropological Terms: A Study of Their Use in Conflict Settings,* Arbeiten zur Geschichte des antiken Judentums und das Urchristentums 10 (Leiden: E. J. Brill, 1971); Peter Müller, *Der Soma-Begriff bei Paulus: Studien zum paulinischen*

ence to the biblical writings, Are soul and body indivisible (even if conceptually and/or rhetorically distinguishable) or divisible (even if functionally or ideally inseparable)? As we will see, however, by attending to the biblical witness with questions of this sort, additional questions regarding the nature of the human person, arising from the texts themselves, will be invited.

Interestingly, the findings of colleagues in evolutionary biology, genetics, and cognitive psychology, for example, already portend our discussion of biblical concerns with human identity that move beyond body-soul issues. By speaking of a "capacity for ethics,"[8] "moral accountability,"[9] or "personal relatedness,"[10] these colleagues come close to what we will see is a fundamental concern, witnessed throughout the biblical canon, with the embodiment of humanity in relationship to all creation, the full integration of the human being within the human family and, indeed, within the whole cosmos.

In the same way that the body-soul dualism of Greco-Roman antiquity has its counterpart in contemporary life in the West, so do these concerns with human relatedness have immediate relevance. The contemporary context for our examination is set not only by popular conceptualizations of human beings as bipartite (body and soul) or even tripartite (body, soul, and spirit), but also by either principled or functional affirmations of what Robert Bellah and his research team refer to as "ontological individualism": a pattern of dispositions and practices that defines life's ultimate goals in terms of personal choice, freedom in terms of being left alone by others to believe and act as one wishes, and justice as a matter of equal opportunity for individuals to pursue happiness as each person has defined it for her- or himself.[11] As our examination will indicate, this prevalent view of the human person runs counter to the understanding of humanity assumed and fostered within Scripture.

The Approach

Our discussion of Revelation 18 also brings to center stage the critical question of method. Since biblical teaching on the nature of the human person is at best indirect, how might we best have access to it? Previous study has often

---

Menschenbild und seine Bedeutung für unsere Zeit (Stuttgart: Urachhaus, 1988); John A. T. Robinson, *The Body: A Study in Pauline Theology,* 2d ed., Studies in Biblical Theology (London: SCM, 1977); N. T. Wright, *Christian Origins and the Question of God,* vol. 1: *The New Testament and the People of God* (Minneapolis: Fortress, 1992), 252-256.

8. See Ayala, chapter 2, this volume.

9. See E. Anderson, chapter 3, this volume.

10. See Brown, chapter 5, this volume.

11. Robert N. Bellah, Richard Madsen, William M. Sullivan, Ann Swidler, and Steve M. Tipton, *Habits of the Heart: Individualism and Commitment in American Life* (Berkeley: University of California Press, 1985).

taken a "word study approach," either examining in succession those texts wherein previously identified vocabulary—typically, "body," "soul," or "spirit" —is found, or studying the origins of these terms and using their respective etymologies to help discern their usage in biblical texts. According to this approach, once the word "body" is seen to have a particular meaning, for example, that meaning becomes a presupposition applied to its usage in those texts where it appears. Such an approach is severely limited as a linguistic option, however, since (1) conceptualizations of human nature are not necessarily tied to particular vocabulary, (2) the biblical writers did not develop a highly specialized, or denotative, vocabulary for describing human existence, and (3) the crucial question is not, what does this word mean? but, how would this word be understood given the literary co-text[12] and sociolinguistic context within which it has been communicated?[13]

An alternative approach has been to focus primarily on the question, what happens when we die? That is, eschatology has determined semantics and anthropology. This is particularly the case among those who have correlated Christian dogmas like "general resurrection" or "eternal life" with the need for a personal "essence" that outlives the decaying corpse. This approach is problematic on three grounds. First, anxiety regarding "what happens when we die" was not rampant in Greco-Roman antiquity, and viewpoints ranged from skepticism or agnosticism about any form of afterlife to suggestions of continuing embodied existence, to a belief in the soul's immortality;[14] and, second, within contemporary Judaism one finds a diversity of expectations about what might follow death.[15] Third, evidence of this nature is necessarily analogical and speculative, since discussion of the afterlife in our texts is carried on by

12. "Co-text" refers to the string of linguistic data within which a text is set, the relationship of, say, a sentence to a paragraph, and a paragraph to the larger work.
13. See Eve E. Sweetser, *From Etymology to Pragmatics: Metaphorical and Cultural Aspects of Semantic Structure,* Cambridge Studies in Linguistics 54 (Cambridge: Cambridge University Press, 1990); Max Turner, "Modern Linguistics and the New Testament," in *Hearing the New Testament: Strategies for Interpretation,* ed. Joel B. Green (Grand Rapids: Wm. B. Eerdmans; Carlisle: Paternoster, 1995), 146-174. That is, such studies often assume what they go on to argue.
14. See Ramsey MacMullen, *Paganism in the Roman Empire* (New Haven, Conn.: Yale University Press, 1981), 53-57; Dale B. Martin, *The Corinthian Body* (New Haven, Conn.: Yale University Press, 1995), 108-117.
15. Some Jewish texts speak of the immortality of the soul, for example; others fail to speak of any afterlife or reject outright such an existence, while still others anticipate some form of resurrection; cf. George W. E. Nickelsburg Jr., *Resurrection, Immortality, and Eternal Life in Intertestamental Judaism,* Harvard Theological Studies 26 (Cambridge, Mass.: Harvard University Press, 1972); E. P. Sanders, *Judaism: Practices and Beliefs (63 B.C.E.— 66 C.E.)* (London: SCM; Philadelphia: Trinity Press International, 1992), 298-303.

those who have no firsthand knowledge on which to draw. Hence, for our purposes in this chapter it is better to ask, given the biblical evidence regarding the nature of the human person on this side of the eschaton, what can we say about human nature on the other? than to ask, given our theories about eschatology, what must we say about the nature of the human person in the present?

Although other modes of investigation may find their champions,[16] our discussion of Revelation suggests an alternative approach. If biblical writers never explicitly take up the problem of the construction of the human person as a topic, but nevertheless work with an assumed portrait(s) of the human person, then our attention is fixed on how biblical authors articulate with and/or over against the norms available to them and shared by their audiences.[17] Since all language is culturally embedded,[18] since literary texts like those found in Scripture are themselves cultural products,[19] it behooves us to grapple with how those texts have both absorbed and censured their social values and contexts—that is, with how their perspectives on the human person might have corroborated or challenged commonly held presumptions. Because there is general agreement that, in the Hebrew Bible, human beings are depicted as body and soul—that is, humans do not possess a body and soul, but are human only as body and soul—the problem of articulation, acute in the New Testament, is less pressing with reference to the Old Testament. Hence, the particular focus of our investigation will be on how New Testament writers critically engaged the range of options available to them regarding the characterization and portrayal of human beings.

In what follows, then, our agenda is twofold. First, we need to explore the conceptual background available to writers and readers/listeners of the New Testament period. This includes accounting for the view(s) of the human person in the Old Testament, both because of its (potential) influence on New Testament writers and because, as the Bible's First Testament, it provides rele-

16. See, for example, the importance in early dogmatic anthropology of attempts to determine the origin of the soul, discussed in H. Wheeler Robinson, *The Christian Doctrine of Man*, 3d ed. (Edinburgh: T. & T. Clark, 1926), 161-163.

17. This approach is adapted from Robert Wuthnow, *Communities of Discourse: Ideology and Social Structure in the Reformation, the Enlightenment, and European Socialism* (Cambridge, Mass.: Harvard University Press, 1989).

18. Cf. Michael Stubbs, *Discourse Analysis: The Sociolinguistic Analysis of Natural Language* (Chicago: University of Chicago Press, 1983), 8; G. Gillian Brown and George Yule, *Discourse Analysis,* Cambridge Textbooks in Linguistics (Cambridge: Cambridge University Press, 1982), 27-31.

19. Cf. Stephen Greenblatt, "Culture," in *Critical Terms for Literary Study*, ed. Frank Lentricchia and Thomas McLaughlin (Chicago: University of Chicago Press, 1990), 225-232, at 227.

vant testimony for our construction of biblical portraits of human nature. We must also account for Hellenistic views of the human person, especially as these would have been mediated to New Testament writers by Hellenistic Jews of the Second Temple Period. Second, we will examine relevant texts from two New Testament writers, Luke and Paul, in order to inquire into pertinent features of their understandings of human nature.[20] This will lead us to a series of important, programmatic observations about how Scripture contributes to our understanding of human nature.

THE HUMAN PERSON AND THE
SCRIPTURES OF ISRAEL

The imago dei

From a biblical point of view, the most succinct way of underscoring the uniqueness of humanity within the cosmos is the affirmation of the nature of human beings in Genesis 1:26-27:

> Then God said, "Let us make humanity in our image, after our likeness. Let them have dominion over the fish of the sea, over the birds of the air, over the cattle, over the whole earth, and over every creeping thing that creeps upon the earth." So God created humanity in his own image, in the image of God he created them; male and female he created them. And God blessed them, and said to them, "Be fruitful and multiply, and fill the earth and subdue it. Have dominion over the fish of the sea, the birds of the air, and over every living thing that moves upon the earth" (my translation).

Of all the creatures mentioned in this story, only humanity is created after God's own likeness, in God's own image *(imago dei)*. Only to humanity does God speak directly. Humanity alone receives from God this divine vocation.

In this case, however, succinctness cannot be equated with clarity, and the *imago dei* tradition has been the focus of diverse interpretations among Jews and Christians—ranging from some physical characteristic of humans (such as standing upright) to a way of knowing (especially the human capacity to know God), and so on.[21] Taken within its immediate narrative co-text in Genesis 1, "the image of God" in which humanity is made transparently relates to the

---

20. Study of New Testament anthropology often takes as its focus "human nature" vis-à-vis "the human condition"—the implication of sin, the possibility of reconciliation, and the like (e.g., Udo Schnelle, *The Human Condition: Anthropology in the Teachings of Jesus, Paul, and John,* trans. O. C. Dean Jr. [Minneapolis: Fortress, 1996]). This is not our preoccupation here.

21. See the helpful survey in Claus Westermann, *Genesis 1-11: A Commentary* (Minneapolis: Augsburg, 1984), 147-158.

exercise of dominion over the earth on God's behalf. But this observation only begs the question, for we must then ascertain what it means to exercise dominion in this way—that is, in a way that reflects God's own style of interaction with his creatures. What is more, this way of putting the issue does not grapple with the profound word spoken over humanity and about humanity, that human beings in themselves (and not only in what they do) reflect the divine image.

On such matters, Karl Barth has proven particularly insightful.[22] For him, creation is the external basis of the covenant (which relationship itself grows out of God's own character), for in humanity God created for himself a counterpart, a covenant partner.

> For the meaning and purpose of God at his creation were as follows. God willed the existence of a being which in all its nondeity and therefore its differentiation can be a real partner; which is capable of action and responsibility in relation to him; to which his own divine form of life is not alien; which in a creaturely repetition, as a copy and imitation, can be a bearer of this form of life. Man [*sic*] was created as this being. But the divine form of life, repeated in the man created by him, consists in that which is the obvious aim of the "Let us." In God's own being and sphere there is a counterpart: a genuine but harmonious self-encounter and self-discovery; a free co-existence and co-operation; an open confrontation and reciprocity.[23]

Insofar as the Genesis language of "us" and "our" reflects a linguistic convention of self-address in Hebrew (cf. Gen. 11:7), Barth inappropriately found here a presaging of Christian trinitarian language,[24] but this does not detract substantively from his important insight that the uniqueness of human beings consists in their being God's counterparts. From this, human beings draw their affirmation of exalted worth and reason for being, their fundamental vocation. Thus, humanity is created in relationship to God and finds itself as a result of creation in covenant with God. And humanity is given the divine mandate to reflect God's own covenant love in relation with God, within the covenant community of all humanity, and with all that God has created. One looks in vain in the creation story for any attempt to portray human beings in a dualistic way—either as body and soul or as something other than "creature."

22. Karl Barth, *Church Dogmatics,* vol. 3: *The Doctrine of Creation,* part one (Edinburgh: T. & T. Clark, 1958), 176-213.
23. Barth, *Church Dogmatics,* 3.1:184-185.
24. See Brevard S. Childs, *Biblical Theology of the Old and New Testaments: Theological Reflection on the Christian Bible* (Minneapolis: Fortress, 1992), 568; cf. Westermann, *Genesis 1-11,* 144-145. This use of the first-person plural may have signified God's address to the heavenly court—so Gordon J. Wenham, *Genesis 1-15,* Word Biblical Commentary 1 (Waco, Tex.: Word, 1987), 27-28.

Creation "in the image of God" otherwise plays little role in the Old Testament, though it is mentioned in Deuterocanonical materials (e.g., Wis. 2:23-24; Sir. 17:1-13) and later texts from Hellenistic Judaism. In the New Testament, Paul's thought is closest to the interpretation of the *imago dei* expressed in Wisdom,[25] wherein the phrase is used with reference to the actual expression of the "image of God" in a human life rather than to human capacity or potential (as in Sirach). Hence, Paul develops the motif of Christ as the "image of God" (2 Cor. 4:4; Col. 1:15; cf. Phil. 2:6) and, as its corollary, the conformation of human beings into the "image of Christ" (Rom. 8:29; 1 Cor. 15:49; 2 Cor. 3:18). Accordingly, in Christ believers have access to the ultimate purpose of God for humanity set forth in the creation of human life. Through his creative and reconciling activity and in his ethical comportment, Christ both reveals the nature of God and manifests truly the human vocation (cf. Luke 6:35-36).

The affirmation of human beings as bearers of the divine image in Genesis, together with the interpretation of the *imago dei* tradition at the hands of Paul, points unquestionably to the uniqueness of humanity in comparison to all other creatures. It does not locate this singularity in the human possession of a "soul," however, but in the human capacity to relate to God as his partner in covenant, and to join in companionship within the human family and in relation to the whole cosmos in ways that reflect the covenant love of God. "Humanness," in this sense, is realized in and modeled by Jesus Christ.

The Human Person: Some Linguistic Considerations

If one cannot turn to the *imago dei* tradition for conceptualizations of a dichotomous or trichotomous portrait of human beings, neither can one turn to the anthropological vocabulary of the Hebrew Bible. The Hebrew term *nephĕš* is used with reference to the whole person as the seat of desires and emotions, not to the "inner soul" as though this were something separate from one's being. *Nephĕš* can be translated in many places as "person," or even by the personal pronoun (e.g., Lev. 2:1; 4:2; 7:20). It denotes the entire human being but can also be used with reference to animals (e.g., Gen. 1:12, 24; 2:7; 9:10). From time to time, the Hebrew term *basar* stands in parallel with but not in contrast to *nephĕš*—the one referring to the external being of the person, the other to the internal (e.g., Isa. 10:18). Indeed, although *basar* frequently refers to the fleshly aspect of a person (e.g., Ps. 119:73; Isa. 45:11-12), this term is also prominent as an expression of the spiritual. *Basar* and *nephĕš* ". . . are to be understood as

25. See Jerome Murphy-O'Connor, *Becoming Human Together: The Pastoral Anthropology of St. Paul,* Good News Studies 2 (Wilmington, Del.: Michael Glazier, 1982), 33-57; Murphy-O'Connor, however, thinks of the *imago dei* especially in terms of "creativity."

different aspects of man's [*sic*] existence as a twofold unity."[26] The related term, *gewiyya*, refers to the human being in her wholeness, though usually in a weakened condition; typically, it is used to denote the body of a human only in its state as a corpse or cadaver.[27] The Hebrew Bible employs other language, too, to speak of humans from the perspective of their varying functions—e.g., *leb*, with reference to human existence, sometimes in its totality (e.g., Gen. 18:5; Ezek. 13:22), sometimes with reference to the center of human affect (e.g., Prov. 14:30) or perception (Prov. 16:9);[28] and *ruah*, used with reference to the human from the perspective of his being imbued with life (e.g., Gen. 2:7; Job 12:10; Isa. 42:5). In spite of its cursory nature, this précis is enough to suggest with what lack of precision the anthropological vocabulary of the Hebrew Bible is utilized. Upon close examination, what becomes clear is that the Hebrew Bible provides no particularly "scriptural" vocabulary for anthropological analysis, but rather draws on the common terminology of the ancient near east in order to depict the human person as an integrated whole.[29]

Implications

It is axiomatic in Old Testament scholarship today that human beings must be understood in their fully integrated, embodied existence. Humans do not possess a body and soul, but are human only as body and soul. From the standpoint of our development of a biblical "portrait(s)" of the human person, moreover, we should add that the Old Testament is equally if not more insistent that human beings cannot be understood in their individuality. (Even those individuals that do gain prominence in the Old Testament have significance typically on account of their role among the people of God.) The proverb known to us from Libya, "We are, therefore I am," is at home in the Old Testament world in a way that Descartes' famous dictum, "I think, therefore I am," can never be.[30]

26. N. P. Bratsiotis, "בשׂר"in *Theological Dictionary of the Old Testament,* vol. 2, ed. G. Johannes Botterweck and Helmer Ringgren (Grand Rapids: Wm. B. Eerdmans, 1975), 313-332, at 326.

27. See H.-J. Fabry, "נדיה," in *Theological Dictionary of the Old Testament,* 2:433-438 (esp. 435-436).

28. See Heinz-Josef Fabry, "לב," in *Theological Dictionary of the Old Testament,* vol. 7, ed. G. Johannes Botterweck, Helmer Ringgren, and Heinz-Josef Fabry (Grand Rapids: Wm. B. Eerdmans, 1995) 399-437.

29. See Fabry, "לב," 412-413; Childs, *Biblical Theology,* 566, 571-572; Eduard Schweizer, "Body," in *The Anchor Bible Dictionary,* 6 vols., ed. David Noel Freedman (New York: Doubleday, 1992), 1:767-772 (esp. 768).

30. See Anton Wessels, *Images of Jesus: How Jesus Is Perceived and Portrayed in Non-European Cultures* (Grand Rapids: Wm. B. Eerdmans, 1990), 96.

Evidence from the Old Testament is important for our enterprise but is not conclusive in and of itself. Because of additional, including counter, influences on the earliest Christians and the New Testament writers, we cannot simply assume that Old Testament witnesses to an integrated anthropology will have been reproduced within the New Testament documents. Indeed, many early Christians did not even read what would become known as the Old Testament in its form as the Hebrew Bible and so would not have had direct access to the reflections summarized above; for them, the Scriptures of Israel were available in Greek translation. Hence, when turning to the New Testament it is important to grapple with the influence of the Greek world (Hellenism) as well as that of the Old Testament.

THE HUMAN PERSON AND HELLENISM

One reviewing the history of discussion regarding the contribution of the New Testament to our understanding of the human person would with justification imagine that the chief issue is whether the New Testament writers were influenced more by Greek or Hebrew thought. This presumed dichotomy, at least, has provided the terms of the debate for most concerned. Such a focus is wrongheaded on several accounts, however. First, an affirmation of the monism of the Old Testament is not itself proof that "Hebraic thought" disallows duality. Second, "Greek thought" cannot be reduced to a single viewpoint on our question. Third, in those cultural circles in which the New Testament documents were generated and preserved, "Judaism" itself was not monochromatic and, indeed, had intermingled with Hellenism for some three centuries. Even in Palestine, "Judaism" exists on a continuum, more or less Hellenized.[31] Fourth, we must therefore consider that the Old Testament would have been mediated to early Christianity via Hellenistic Jewish (and Hellenistic) readings.

By way of constructing further the framework of influence in relationship to which New Testament writers worked to portray the nature of the human person, we will, first, briefly remind ourselves of the diversity of Hellenistic views of the human person. Following this, we will summarize some of the ways in which the human person was understood within Hellenistic Judaism. Insofar as the New Testament materials are themselves representative of the diversity of Hellenistic Judaism, we will mention selected New Testament texts as well.

31. See Martin Hengel, *Judaism and Hellenism: Studies in Their Encounter in Palestine During the Early Hellenistic Period,* 2 vols. in 1 (Philadelphia: Fortress, 1974); idem, *The "Hellenization" of Judaea in the First Century after Christ* (London: SCM; Philadelphia: Trinity Press International, 1989).

Hellenistic Views

Nancey Murphy has already sketched some of the history of ancient philosophical views of the human person, so we need provide nothing more than summary comments.[32] By and large, the Greeks never took the path Descartes would take—namely, juxtaposing corporeal and incorporeal as if this were the same thing as juxtaposing material and immaterial (or physical/spiritual). Although belief in a form of body-soul duality was widespread in philosophical circles, most philosophers regarded the soul as composed of "stuff." Aristotle, for example, considered the soul, the basis of animate life, as part of nature, so that psychology and physics ("nature") could not be segregated. For him, "soul" was not immaterial; even if "soul" is not the same thing as body, neither is it "nonmatter" but can still occupy "space." Even Plato thought that the soul was constructed from elements of the world, though he argued for a radical distinction between body and soul. Within Epicureanism, mind and spirit were understood to be corporeal because they act on the body, and all entities that act or are acted upon are bodies. Borrowing in part from Aristotle, Stoicism taught that everything that exists is corporeal; accordingly, only nonexistent "somethings" (like imagined things) could be incorporeal.

Following the demise of the Platonic academy as an institution in the early first century B.C.E., neo-Platonism took many forms, especially as influenced by Stoicism. As Martin notes, "When we analyze the Platonism—or perhaps we should say the Platonisms—that were around [in the first century C.E.], we encounter self-styled Platonists whose ideas of body and soul look to us remarkably like the monisms of Aristotle and the Stoics."[33] When one departs the work of these philosophers and examines the views of ancient medical writers (who were, themselves, philosophers of a sort), one finds a keen emphasis on the inseparability of the internal processes of the body ("psychology," in modern parlance) and its external aspects ("physiology"). This is not because of tendencies to think in terms of "psychosomatic conditions" (to use concepts that are quite anachronistic), but because any differentiation between inner and outer was fluid and permeable. We have already had occasion to refer to the diversity of opinion concerning the question, what happens after we die? It may be useful, nonetheless, to refer to Cicero, who summarizes the two primary, competing views: either the body and soul are annihilated at death or the soul separates from the body.[34]

---

32. See Murphy, chapter 6, this volume. For a more full rendering of the discussion than is possible here, see the helpful survey in Martin, *Corinthian Body*, esp. 3–37.
33. Martin, *Corinthian Body*, 12.
34. Cicero, *Tusculan Disputations* 1.11.23–24.

In short, although some may find it useful to speak of a body-soul duality in the Greco-Roman world as a lowest common denominator in educated circles, this hardly relates the whole story. The Hellenism that would have occupied a prominent place on the horizon of early Christians and the New Testament writers cannot be reduced so easily to a common denominator on questions of body and soul. This means that one cannot solve the problem of the relationship between body and soul in earliest Christianity merely by referring to parallels of thought or cultural settings. Such parallels and settings are themselves too complex for such decisions, and the ingredients available to those early Christian writers were more diverse than usually thought.[35]

Hellenistic Judaism

Shaping the cultural map of the New Testament world in a far-reaching way were the innovations and upheavals in the Near East following in the wake of the military successes of Alexander the Great (356-323 B.C.E.) in the last half of the fourth century B.C.E. When Alexander died, he had opened up the near east to the migration of Greek language and cultural expressions. Closely boundaried, more parochial societies were gradually joined by increasing cultural intercourse symbolized above all by the spread of Attic Greek as the *lingua franca*. Hellenism thus refers to the spread and embrace of the Greek language, but also to the way of life, business, education, and ethos mediated through the spread and use of that language. Within Judaism, this led to the development of significant diversity, a corollary of the range of responses to the challenges of Hellenism.

One of the areas in which Hellenistic influence is notable is in the developing belief among the Jewish people, first, that humans have "souls" and, second, that these "souls" had a prior existence before taking up residence in material bodies. This way of thinking may have roots in the Hebrew Bible (e.g., Jer. 1:5), but it was under the influence of some strands of Greek philosophy that Jewish literature would exhibit this doctrine. In Wisdom 8:19-20, for example, we read, "As a child I was naturally gifted, and a good soul fell to my lot; or rather, being good, I entered an undefiled body" (NRSV). Written later, some think as early as the late first century C.E., *2 Enoch* notes that "all souls are prepared for eternity, before the composition of the earth" (23:5).[36]

---

35. The ease with which decisions of this sort have been made in this century derives in part from our failure to perceive the depth of Descartes' innovations. The Cartesian view of humanity was understood to have embraced ancient ways of thinking, with the result that few seemed to notice when Plato (for example) was conscripted to support Cartesian categories. Other Hellenistic writers, as well as the New Testament materials themselves, have similarly been read through Cartesian lenses.

36. This translation from the Slavonic is from Francis I. Andersen, "2 (Slavonic

Evidence of this doctrine also surfaces in the Gospel of John, where the disciples ask Jesus concerning a man born blind, "Rabbi, who sinned, this man or his parents, that he was born blind?" (9:2; my translation).

Evidence of a body-soul dualism in the New Testament may also be traced in a text like Matthew 10:28, "Do not fear those who put the body to death but are unable to kill the soul" (my translation). In this text, the Greek term *psyche* probably refers to the disembodied soul that lives on beyond physical death—a notion witnessed also in the *Testament of Job* (first century B.C.E. or first century C.E.), where we are informed that Satan was given authority over Job's body but not his soul (20:3).[37] The parallel in Luke 12:4, however, leaves open the possibility that we are to understand Jesus as saying no more than that those who are persecuted should take comfort in the fact that martyrdom is only the end of life in this world, not the end of one's human existence; in this case, *psyche* would refer not to "soul" but to "vitality."

Much less likely is the notion that Paul's benediction in 1 Thessalonians 5:23 provides testimony to a tripartite understanding of human nature (spirit, soul, and body). The parallelism of the two phrases—"May the God of peace himself sanctify you completely, and may your spirit and soul and body be preserved in entirety, free from blame . . ." (my translation)—signifies that Paul uses these three terms to repeat and expand on the idea of "completely"—that is, in order to emphasize the completeness of the sanctification for which he prays. This is not a list of "parts," then, but a reference to "your whole being."[38]

The Alexandrian Jew Philo provides a witness of a very different sort, however. A Hellenistic Jewish philosopher, Philo is one of our best-known examples of a first-century C.E. neo-Platonist. In his writings one finds the preservation of a body-soul duality, though the "soul" was not for him an "immaterial substance" in the Cartesian sense. The first-century Jewish historian Josephus also held to the independent existence of the soul, destined for immortality. Philo's writings are well-preserved because of their interest

---

Apocalypse of) Enoch: A New Translation and Introduction," in *The Old Testament Pseudepigrapha,* 2 vols., ed. James H. Charlesworth (Garden City, N.Y.: Doubleday, 1983), 1:91-213, at 140. The dating of *2 Enoch* in the late first century C.E. is an editorial gloss (91); in the text of his introduction, Andersen notes that any attempt to date the document is speculative.

37. Cf. *Martyrdom of Isaiah* 5:10.

38. See F. F. Bruce, *1 and 2 Thessalonians,* Word Biblical Commentary 45 (Waco, Tex.: Word, 1982), 129-130; Charles A. Wanamaker, *Commentary on 1 and 2 Thessalonians,* New International Greek Testament Commentary (Grand Rapids: Wm. B. Eerdmans; Exeter: Paternoster, 1990), 206-207.

among early Christians, as were Josephus's, but this is not to say that their views are representative. To the contrary, most Jews during this period would have rejected this form of anthropological duality in favor of a more "integrated" anthropology.[39]

HUMAN NATURE
IN LUKE

Usually regarded as the only Gentile author in the New Testament, and also one of the more Hellenized, Luke is responsible for having written more than one-fourth of what would become the New Testament. Although he never deals in a direct way with the nature of the human person, the major theme of his writing is "salvation," and it is through this emphasis that we are able to gain insight into how he understands human nature. That is, Luke's soteriology of necessity raises questions about "what needs to be saved" and "what saved existence would look like," and these point toward his understanding of authentic human existence. In order to gain our bearings, we will examine in sequence two Lukan passages—one concerned with healing as salvation, the other depicting the nature of eschatological existence.[40]

Healing as Salvation (Luke 8:42b-48)

The larger unit in which this text is set begins with Luke 8:40 and continues through verse 56, thus including Luke's narration of the raising of a dead girl. The most obvious and important structural feature of this larger unit is the intercalation of the two episodes: The narrative of the healing of the woman suffering from a hemorrhage (8:42b-48) has been embedded into the narrative of the raising of Jairus' daughter (8:40-42a, 49-56). The relationship between these two episodes transcends concerns of structure and includes numerous commonalities.[41]

Through the technique of intercalation, the Evangelist presents the simultaneous unfolding of these two narrative events. Moreover, the interruption of the one story of healing by the other heightens the drama of the first. The little

---

39. Wright, *People of God,* 254-255.

40. On what follows, see Joel B. Green, *The Gospel of Luke,* New International Commentary on the New Testament (Grand Rapids: Wm. B. Eerdmans, 1997).

41. Thus, for example, falling before Jesus (vv. 41, 47), daughter (vv. 42, 48, 49), twelve years (vv. 42, 43), desperate circumstances (vv. 42, 43, 49), the fact and immediacy of healing (vv. 44, 47, 55), touching (vv. 44, 45, 46, 47, 53), impurity (flow of blood—v. 43, corpse—vv. 53, 54), fear (vv. 45, 47, 50), and the inseparable connection between faith and salvation (vv. 48, 50).

girl is dying; does she not need immediate attention? Taken together, these two episodes document the sort of faith for which Jesus has been looking. Moreover, the completion of the one incident prepares for the finale of the other. After the abundance of healing power available in the case of the woman with a hemorrhage, might we not anticipate Jesus' ability to raise a dead girl to life?

The text we will consider reads as follows:

> As he went, the crowds pressed in on him. (43) Now there was a woman who had been suffering from hemorrhages for twelve years; and though she had spent all she had on physicians, no one could cure her. (44) She came up behind him and touched the fringe of his clothes, and immediately her hemorrhage stopped. (45) Then Jesus asked, "Who touched me?" When all denied it, Peter said, "Master, the crowds surround you and press in on you." (46) But Jesus said, "Someone touched me; for I noticed that power had gone out from me." (47) When the woman saw that she could not remain hidden, she came trembling; and falling down before him, she declared in the presence of all the people why she had touched him, and how she had been immediately healed. (48) He said to her, "Daughter, your faith has made you well; go in peace" (NRSV).

As Jesus makes his way to the home of Jairus, a woman appears, whose behavior redirects Jesus' attention away from the needs of Jairus and his daughter. The woman whom Luke introduces provides the Evangelist with yet another opportunity to define "the poor" to whom the good news is brought (4:18-19; 7:22; 8:1). The simple fact that she is a woman in Palestinian society already marks her as one of relatively low status. In addition to this, she is sick, and her sickness, while apparently not physically debilitating,[42] was socially devastating. Her hemorrhaging rendered her ritually unclean,[43] so that she lived in a perpetual state of impurity. Although her physical condition was not contagious, her ritual condition was, with the consequence that she had lived in isolation from her community these twelve years. Her prospects for renewed social intercourse had dropped to nil with her lack of help from the physicians. Whether her doctors had been the celebrated physicians whose exorbitant fees made them accessible only to the elite or the quacks that exploited members of a naive and needy public,[44] the outcome is the same.

---

42. After all, she has suffered with this problem, presumably uterine bleeding, for twelve years.

43. See Lev. 15:19-31; 11QTemple 48:14-17; *m. Niddah.*

44. See Howard Clark Kee, *Medicine, Miracle and Magic in New Testament Times,* Society of New Testament Studies Monograph Series 55 (Cambridge: Cambridge University Press, 1986), 64.

To her otherwise sorry condition is now added a further factor: her material impoverishment.[45]

Her degraded status vis-à-vis the larger crowd could hardly be more pronounced; the same, of course, could be said of her need, which has been depicted as indeed grave. Just as the Geresene demoniac had dwelled among the dead (Luke 8:27), so this woman exists outside the boundaries of the socially alive in her community. The press of the crowds guarantees that she will infect others with her impurity, and her aim to touch Jesus is a premeditated act that will pass her uncleanness on to him. What is it that motivates her to risk the rebuff of the crowds, of the synagogue ruler (who, we may presume, is walking with Jesus back to his home), and of Jesus on account of her social impropriety? This is the story of her resolution to cross the borders of legitimate behavior to gain access to divine power.[46]

The effect of touching Jesus' garment is immediate. Her bleeding stops, and so she experiences a reversal of her malady. As we shall see, however, though her physical problem may be cured, she is not yet healed.[47]

The significance of the woman's action is highlighted by the fourfold appearance of the verb "to touch" in verses 44-47. Its first importance is its ambiguity. Why did this unclean, disgraceful woman presume to touch one to whom even a synagogue ruler had bowed (v. 41)? Even when interpreted in the most obvious (and negative) way available within the narrative, the damage she has done is not irreversible; the law contained a remedy: rites of purification for Jesus, a reprimand for the woman. But Jesus does not adopt this reading; instead, he recognizes that her touch instigated a transfer of "power."

It is at this juncture that the real test of this woman begins, for Jesus calls upon her to acknowledge her actions to the whole crowd. In fact, at this point Luke's account is largely concerned with the movement of this woman from

45. In addition, given her condition it is difficult to imagine that this woman is married. In this case, it is possible that we are to imagine that she had inherited money on which to live, money that is now in the hands of her unsuccessful physicians.
46. See Gerd Theissen, *The Miracle Stories of the Early Christian Tradition,* Studies of the New Testament and Its World (Philadelphia: Fortress, 1983), 43-45, 74-80.
47. *Contra* numerous interpreters (e.g., Darrell L. Bock, *Luke,* 2 vols., Baker Exegetical Commentary on the New Testament 3 [Grand Rapids, Michigan: Baker, 1994/96], 1:795). Working at both explicit and implicit levels of this account is an understanding of human wholeness that cannot be equated with biomedical definitions of wellness (see Hahn, *Sickness and Healing;* also, e.g., Byron J. Good, *Medicine, Rationality, and Experience: An Anthropological Perspective,* The Lewis Henry Morgan Lectures 1990 [Cambridge: Cambridge University Press, 1994]). As we have suggested, this woman's debilitating problem is not physical but religious and social. Until the latter is resolved, she will not be "well."

seclusion—the isolation first of ritual impurity and now of denial—to public proclamation. The crowds are pressing in, ready to choke faith as it sprouts; will she give in to her fear or respond in faith? At this juncture, the narrative is emphatic: All (including this woman) denied having touched Jesus.

Why does she hide; and why, when she realizes that hiding is futile, does she let herself be known in "trembling"? It is important to remember that her touching Jesus was irregular and thus open to interpretation. How would the stifling crowds respond? How would the synagogue ruler? How would Jesus? Crossing the boundaries from the nonhuman world of socioreligious quarantine into the human world, and extending beyond the human world so as to access divine power is, on the one hand, a violation of the biblical purity code. On the other, it is an act of faith, or so it is interpreted by Jesus. In order for that faith to express itself fully, however, it must transverse the perimeters of the holiness code and overcome the stranglehold of social banishment. In actuality, given her social position, her hiding and trembling are expected behaviors.

What is unprecedented and unanticipated is her touching Jesus in the first place, and now, even more so, her public announcement. Luke spares her no potential embarrassment. Her proclamation is before *all* of the people. Note, too, the content of her declaration. She is concerned with *why* she touched him; that is, she is presented as a hermeneut and not simply as one who chronicles what had happened.

Only now, in response to her public testimony, does Jesus commend the woman and pronounce that she is whole. Her cure was realized in the privacy and anonymity afforded by the crowds, yet her real problem was a public one. Hence, he has her make a public declaration of her actions and her understanding of what she had done. Then, he confirms her story and verifies her healing, ruling out all possible interpretations of her unconventional behavior save one—namely, his view that it was an expression of her faith. Jesus' actions are calculated to signal, first, that her faith, tested by the boundaries of ritual purity legitimated by community sanctions, is genuine. Its authenticity is manifest in her willingness to cross the barriers of acceptable behavior in order to obtain salvation. Second, he signals that he is not content to leave her cured according to biomedical definitions only.[48] He embraces her in the family of God by referring to her as "daughter," thus extending kinship to her and restoring her to the larger community—not on the basis of her ancestry (cf. 3:7-9), but as a consequence of her active faith. Now she is not the only one who knows what God has done for her; so do the crowds gathered around

---

48. Note that only in v. 48 does the word *sozo* ("to save," "to heal") appear; in v. 47. *hiaomai* ("to heal") is used. Of the two, *sozo* has the more expansive range of meaning.

Jesus. Because he has pronounced her whole, they are to receive her as one restored to her community and to the people of God.

Eschatological Ambiguity (Luke 16:19-31)

> (19) There was a rich man who was dressed in purple and fine linen and who feasted sumptuously every day. (20) And at his gate was tossed[49] a poor man named Lazarus, covered with sores, (21) who longed to satisfy his hunger with what fell from the rich man's table; even the dogs would come and lick his sores. (22) The poor man died and was carried away by the angels to be with Abraham. The rich man also died and was buried. (23) In Hades, where he was being tormented, he looked up and saw Abraham far away with Lazarus by his side. (24) He called out, "Father Abraham, have mercy on me, and send Lazarus to dip the tip of his finger in water and cool my tongue; for I am in agony in these flames." (25) But Abraham said, "Child, remember that during your lifetime you received your good things, and Lazarus in like manner evil things; but now he is comforted here, and you are in agony. (26) Besides all this, between you and us a great chasm has been fixed, so that those who might want to pass from here to you cannot do so, and no one can cross from there to us." (27) He said, "Then, father, I beg you to send him to my father's house— (28) for I have five brothers—that he may bear witness to them,[50] so that they will not also come into this place of torment." (29) Abraham replied, "They have Moses and the prophets; they should listen to them." (30) He said, "No, father Abraham; but if someone goes to them from the dead, they will repent." (31) He said to him, "If they do not listen to Moses and the prophets, neither will they be convinced even if someone rises from the dead" (NRSV).

Within its narrative co-text, the parable of Luke 16:19-31 is told to Pharisees who have called into question Jesus' fidelity to the law. In this setting, the parable serves as a counterchallenge, indicating both his faithfulness before the law and Pharisaic duplicity. In one sense, the parable is concerned with wealth and its manifestations: a wealthy man engages in conspicuous consumption without regard for a poor man, in spite of the fact that this beggar who resides at his gate is quite literally his "neighbor" (vv. 19-21; cf. 10:29-37); and the rich and poor experience the eschatological reversal forecast in 6:20-24 (v. 25). In another sense, it is focused on the law (and, more broadly, the Scriptures) which, the parable informs us, is very much concerned with the state of the poor. In this case, a wealthy man comes to realize too late that he has ignored the words of Moses and the prophets concerning the poor.

49. NRSV: "lay."
50. NRSV: "warn them."

Our concerns here are more focused, however, on the eschatological picture painted by the parable—especially what it might say about an "intermediate state" and "individual eschatology."

The stage of Jesus' parable is set by the extravagant parallelism resident in the depictions of the two main characters. The social distance between the two is continued through to the end, symbolized first by the gate, then by the "distance" ("far away," v. 23) and the "great chasm" fixed between them (v. 26). The rich man is depicted in excessive, even outrageous terms, while Lazarus is numbered among society's "expendables," a man who had fallen prey to the ease with which, even in an advanced agrarian society, persons without secure land holdings might experience devastating downward mobility.

Jesus' comparison of these two characters in life continues in death. Both Lazarus and the wealthy man are apparently in Hades, though segregated from each other. Thus, while Lazarus is in a blissful state, numbered with Abraham, the wealthy man experiences Hades as torment and agony. This portrait has many analogues in contemporary Jewish literature, where Hades is represented as the universal destiny of all humans, sometimes with the expected outcome of the final judgment already mapped through the separation of persons into wicked or righteous categories.[51]

This parable is often taken as instruction on "the intermediate state,"[52] often with reference to the state of a disembodied soul; or as a manifestation of Luke's "individual eschatology."[53] Although this text probably assumes an intermediate state, (1) it does so largely in order to make use of the common motif of the "messenger to the living from the dead," only to deny the sending of a messenger;[54] (2) the notion of a disembodied soul must be read into the story since the characters in Hades act as human agents with a corporeal existence;[55] (3) *Testament of Abraham* 20:14—where the bosom of Abraham and

51. See *1 Enoch* 22; 4 Ezra 7:74-101; cf. the helpful summary in Richard J. Bauckham, "Hades, Hell," in *Anchor Bible Dictionary*, 3:14-15.

52. Cf. Cooper, *Body, Soul, and Life Everlasting*, 136-139. See the discussion in A. J. Mattill Jr., *Luke and the Last Things: A Perspective for the Understanding of Lukan Thought* (Dillsboro, N.C.: Western North Carolina University Press, 1979), 26-32; he notes that many readers of Luke have found evidence here for "the platonizing of Luke-Acts," but argues that this is not the case.

53. See Jacques Dupont, "Die individuelle Eschatologie im Lukasevangelium und in der Apostelgeschichte," in *Orientierung an Jesus: Zur Theologie der Synoptiker*, ed. Paul Hoffman (Freiburg: Herder, 1973), 37-47. *Contra* John T. Carroll, *Response to the End of History: Eschatology and Situation in Luke-Acts*, Society of Biblical Literature Dissertation Series 92 (Atlanta, Ga.: Scholars, 1988), 64-68.

54. See Richard J. Bauckham, "The Rich Man and Lazarus: The Parable and the Parallels," *New Testament Studies* 37 (1991): 225-246 (esp. 236-244).

55. Note, for example, that the rich man desires to drink water.

his descendants are already in paradise, yet Abraham is to be taken to paradise—bears witness to the lack of precision in statements about the afterlife; and (4) neither Luke nor other Christian writers (like Paul) seem to think that discussion of the fate of an individual negates a more thorough-going apocalyptic (corporate, future) eschatology.[56]

Portraits of Human Nature in Luke-Acts

Luke-Acts provides no direct testimony regarding the Lukan anthropology, but everywhere, not least in its soteriology, assumes an understanding of the human person. If we were able to pursue our interpretive agenda in detail throughout Luke-Acts, we would see that the indications we have already surfaced would be underscored again and again. Luke regularly depicts human beings with a need, often physical, that turns out to be set within a much more complex interrelationship with what it means to be human; repeatedly, then, Luke disallows, say, the physical to be distinguished from other aspects of human existence. As the preceding discussion portends, Luke has no concept of a disembodied soul, either in present or in eschatological existence, and yet apparently has no difficulty visualizing an "intermediate state." This undercuts the argument of some that belief in an intermediate state requires the divine provision of a "soul" that survives the decaying body. More central to Luke's thinking is the inseparability of humans in their embodied and communal existence, with the result that his soteriology is oriented radically around the restoration of old or provision of new relations in the community of God's people.[57]

HUMAN NATURE IN PAUL

Status at Corinth, and the Message of the Resurrection

We have already indicated something of the diversity of opinion within the Greco-Roman world vis-à-vis the nature of the human person and its relationship to what happens when we die. In his recent study of *The Corinthian Body*, Dale Martin correlates those differences with the disparity within the Corinthian community around issues of social stratification. Although Martin is hardly the first to see issues of social status as a key to the disunity among

---

56. This last point is made by Carroll, *End of History*, 64–68.
57. See further, Joel B. Green, *The Theology of the Gospel of Luke*, New Testament Theology (Cambridge: Cambridge University Press, 1995); *idem*, "'Salvation to the End of the Earth' (Acts 13:47): God as Savior in the Acts of the Apostles," in *Witness to the Gospel: The Theology of Acts*, ed. I. Howard Marshall and David Peterson (Grand Rapids: Wm. B. Eerdmans, 1996), 83–106.

the Corinthian believers,[58] he is the first to suggest a correlation between status and views of the afterlife. Noting that persons of high status in Corinth would likely have followed contemporary custom in extending hospitality to "household philosophers," he draws the corollary that these Corinthians would have been influenced by more sophisticated notions about the afterlife. Indeed, they would have heard in Paul's talk of "the waking of the dead" echoes of fables about the resuscitation of corpses, the stuff of popular myths. Taught to degrade the body,[59] they would have found Paul's teaching about the resurrection incomprehensible, even ridiculous. Those of low status, on the other hand, would have been incapable of welcoming itinerant philosophers into their homes and, thus, would have lived apart from their influence. They would have had closer contact with superstitions and popular myths, including those relating the resuscitation of corpses and the endowment of those corpses with immortality. Since Paul's primary objective in 1 Corinthians is to restore unity (1:10), according to the scenario as Martin has reconstructed it Paul's challenge is to represent the resurrection belief of early Christianity with enough sophistication to communicate effectively with those of high status while not alienating those of lower status.[60]

It is in 1 Corinthians 15:38-58 that Paul discusses the nature of the resurrection, and in doing so he affirms the following: (1) There is a profound continuity between present life in this world and life everlasting with God. For human beings, this continuity has to do with bodily existence. That is, Paul cannot think in terms of a free-floating soul separate from a body. (2) Present human existence, however, is marked by frailty, deterioration, weakness, and is therefore unsuited for eternal life. Therefore, in order for Christian believers to share in eternal life, their bodies must be transformed. Paul does not here think of "immortality of the soul." Neither does he proclaim a resuscitation of dead bodies that might serve as receptacles for souls that had escaped the body in death. Instead, he sets before his audience the promise of the transformation of their bodies into glorified bodies (cf. Phil. 3:21). (3) Paul's ideas are, in part, rooted in images from the natural world and, in part, related to the resurrection of Jesus Christ. As it was with Christ's body, Paul insists, so it will be with ours: the same, yet not the same; transformed for the new conditions of life with God forever. (4) Paul teaches that this change will take place when Christ

---

58. See Gerd Theissen, *The Social Setting of Pauline Christianity: Essays on Corinth* (Philadelphia: Fortress, 1982).

59. Even those who believed in a body-soul duality, however, were not Cartesian in their anthropology, since they did not work with matter/nonmatter or physical/spiritual dichotomies.

60. Martin, *Corinthian Body,* 1-136.

returns. At that moment, both the living and the dead will be transformed. (5) For Paul, this has important meaning for the nature of Christian life in the present. For example, this message underscores the significance of life in this world—a fact that many Christians at Corinth had not taken seriously. We should not imagine that our bodies are unimportant, then, or that what we do to our bodies or with our bodies is somehow unrelated to eternal life (cf. Col. 1:24). The idea of eternal life is not "escapism." Rather, it provides the Christian both with hope as well as with a vision of what is important to God; as a result, we may look forward to the future while also allowing this vision of the future to help determine the nature of our lives in the present.

A "Naked Soul" in 2 Corinthians 5:1-10?

Undoubtedly, the most pressing evidence in Paul for a body-soul dualism is found in 2 Corinthians 5:1-10, and especially vv. 2-3, translated in the NRSV as follows: "For in this tent we groan, longing to be clothed with our heavenly dwelling—if indeed, when we have taken it off we will not be found naked." According to many interpreters, Paul presents here a thanatology concerned with the freeing of the soul from the body for a higher destiny. As one recent study puts it, "Paul speaks of three states: the present condition in the tent-like frame, the intermediate state of nakedness, which he does not find desirable, and the future condition in which a further frame will have been put on, hopefully, over the present one." "The earthly body is a tent-like existence, a temporary shelter. Paul seems to believe that believers' resurrection bodies are already prepared in heaven, in heavenly cold storage so to speak."[61] This is a possible reading, but it is not the only one. In fact, if Paul is concerned here with thanatology, which this view requires, then he has digressed rather dramatically from the focus of this larger section on apostolic suffering (4:7—5:10). Moreover, it involves Paul in a discussion the focus of which would be uncharacteristically subjective and individualistic.

Victor Furnish has offered an alternative reading that takes with greater seriousness the place of this passage in Paul's larger argument. In this case, what is on center stage is the frailty of human existence and the concomitant possibility of denying that one has been clothed in Christ if one suffers as Paul has suffered. Paul, then, would be speaking of his having been clothed with Christ at his baptism, a well-known metaphor, *and* longing for the completion of his salvation (i.e., his being "clothed over" and therefore not found naked in the

---

61. Ben Witherington III, *Conflict and Community in Corinth: A Socio-Rhetorical Commentary on 1 and 2 Corinthians* (Grand Rapids: Wm. B. Eerdmans; Carlisle: Paternoster, 1995), 391. Yet, earlier, Witherington seems not to think that Paul endorsed "the Greek idea of the immortal soul or of the body as the prison of the soul" (389).

final judgment).[62] As is typical of Pauline thought, the duality here would be eschatological, focused on the tension between the now and not–yet, not anthropological.

Paul and the Eschatological Body

In an essay of this brevity, it is impossible to cover the full range of Paul's "portrait of human nature," and we have had to be content with examining two specimens concerned with the relationship between human existence and the afterlife. Even though Paul's language may not be consistent in all cases, it is nevertheless clear that, for Paul, embodied existence is the norm; "there is no human existence without a body and it is inseparable from life."[63] Had we been able to pursue his line of thinking further, we would have seen the degree to which "body" is also for Paul an ecclesiological term, thus underscoring the notion that humans live out their divine vocation always in relation to God and within the community of the people of God.

HUMAN NATURE AND THE BIBLE: IMPLICATIONS AND DISCUSSION POINTS

Because our discussion has ranged across cultures and centuries it may be surprising to see the degree of concord among the biblical witnesses we have examined. We have seen that the Old Testament does not locate human uniqueness in a doctrine of a (potentially disembodied) soul, but emphasizes instead the character of humanity as God's covenant partner, his counterpart in relationship. The *imago dei* tradition highlights the location of human beings within the larger human family, emphasizes the human's covenantal relationships with other humans, and situates the human family in meaningful relationship with the whole cosmos.

We have also seen that the traditions informing the New Testament writers are more variegated than normally thought, but that, on the question of anthropological monism or dualism, there is greater accord between the traditions represented in the Hebrew Bible and some strands of Greek thought than is usually allowed. Accordingly, the question of a New Testament portrait(s) of human nature cannot be resolved simply with recourse to a supposed line of influence. One must speak always of diverse influences, and this underscores both the importance of attending to New Testament voices set within

62. See the discussion in Victor Paul Furnish, *II Corinthians: Translated with Introduction, Notes, and Commentary,* Anchor Bible 32A (Garden City, New York: Doubleday, 1984), 292–295.
63. Childs, *Biblical Theology,* 580.

their own contexts and sometimes ad hoc modes of argumentation and of identifying where the New Testament writers have articulated with and/or over against other cultural voices. By exploring key texts from two major New Testament writers, Luke and Paul, we have been able to suggest that (1) the New Testament is not as dualistic as the traditions of Christian theology and biblical interpretation have taught us to think, though enough conceptual glossolalia exists among New Testament witnesses for us to see how a dualist reading of human nature has developed among Christians; (2) nonetheless, the dominant view of the human person in the New Testament is that of ontological monism, with such notions as "escape from the body" or "disembodied soul" falling outside the parameters of New Testament thought; (3) New Testament writers insist on the concept of soteriological wholism and in their portraits of human nature place a premium on one's relatedness to God and to others; and (4) the emphasis on anthropological monism in the New Testament underscores the cosmic repercussions of reconciliation, highlighting the notion that the fate of the human family cannot be dissociated from that of the cosmos.[64]

64. In the end, these results can only be provisional since we have examined small portions of representative biblical materials. As references to other scholars indicate (see the notes, above), however, the prevailing view in the *scholarly* study of Scripture is that the Old and New Testaments support a monistic rendering of the human person. This has not been true in more *popular* circles, perhaps due in large part to the influence of Cartesian categories in Christian hymnody and in medicine.

Chapter Eight

On Being Human:
The Spiritual Saga of a Creaturely Soul

Ray S. Anderson

The ancient teacher of wisdom in Israel, who called himself Koheleth, was a keen observer of the human condition. As he pondered and probed, he discovered more questions than answers. In a tone that betrayed both relentless cynicism and restless hope, he asked: "Who knows whether the human spirit goes upward and the spirit of animals goes downward to the earth?" (Eccles. 3:21).

Who knows indeed! In former times, we might account for such ignorance as due to lack of scientific knowledge and philosophical precision. But how then would we account for the fact that today, some form of the same question tantalizes our scientists and torments our philosophers? Whether we call it spirit or soul, the question remains: what is it that makes humans both precious and perverse? What gives rise to our deepest religious insights but can also plunge us into the depths of guilt and despair?

Has the concept of a human soul disappeared in the presence of molecular biology, clinical psychology, and computer driven brain scans? Is the disappearance of the soul a consequence of our world "come of age" or is it we who are lost and our souls doing the searching? Perhaps one indication that humans have a soul is that they appear to be the only creatures on earth that are thinking about it! The words of Thomas Moore express this malaise dramatically:

> The great malady of the twentieth century, implicated in all of our troubles and affecting us individually and socially, is "loss of soul." When soul is neglected, it doesn't just go away; it appears symptomatically in obsessions, addictions, violence, and loss of meaning. Our temptation is to isolate these

symptoms or to try to eradicate them one by one; but the root problem is that we have lost our wisdom about the soul, even our interest in it.[1]

The word "soul" appears almost daily in our newspapers and on the lips of the pundits who peer into the psyche of our modern culture. Those who lament the loss of core values in our society warn us that we must recover the "soul" of our people or perish. Strategists who seek to turn their political party back to fundamental principles explain that they are attempting to "recover the soul" of their party. In certain sections of North America the people eat "soul food" and ethnic cultures sing "soul music." The news report of a plane crash reads: "There were 132 souls on board, and all were lost."

This may be why, as a recent survey demonstrated, theologians by and large have abandoned the concept of the "soul" in favor of the "spirit" as the essential core of human subjectivity.[2] Contemporary theologians have become uncomfortable with the concept of an abstract body/soul dualism that has its modern roots in the thought of René Descartes (1596-1650).[3] As a result, many have rejected the concept of the soul as a specific entity residing in the person distinct from the body.[4] Theologians often use the word "spirit" as a vir-

---

1. Thomas Moore, *Care of the Soul: A Guide for Cultivating Depth and Sacredness in Everyday Life* (New York: HarperCollins, 1992), xi.

2. Jeffrey H. Boyd, "The Soul as Seen through Evangelical Eyes, Part II: Mental Health Professionals and the 'Soul,'" in *Journal of Psychology and Theology* 23, no. 3 (1995), 161-170.

3. Descartes' concept of the soul as an independent constituent of humans, controlling the body which it animates, was called the "ghost in the machine" by Gilbert Ryle, *The Concept of the Mind* (London: Hutchinson, 1949). Commenting on this, Edmund Hill says, "Meanwhile the ordinary Christian, with some reason, will think that he cannot do without the concept of 'soul.' But now it has, most unfortunately and inconveniently and to a large extent through the fault of a Platonized Christianity, become a *religious* concept, something you believe in or something you don't, like God. And when it comes to making rational sense of the concept the Christian remains stymied, transfixed, paralysed, mesmerized, fascinated, dumbfounded and dogged by that magisterial sneer—'the ghost in the machine.'" *Being Human: A Biblical Perspective* (London: Geoffrey Chapman, 1984), 96-97.

4. For example, in G. C. Berkouwer, *Man: The Image of God* (Grand Rapids: Wm. B. Eerdmans, 1962), 203: "Scripture never pictures man as a dualistic, or pluralistic being, but . . . in all its varied expressions the whole man comes to the fore. . . . The discussion has especially turned on this point, whether the term 'soul' as used in Scripture has some special religious emphasis in the sense that we must deduce at least some sort of dichotomy. And this is more and more denied by theologians." So also, Karl Barth, *Church Dogmatics,* III/2 (Edinburgh: T. & T. Clark, 1960): "We do not a body here and the soul there, but man himself as soul of his body is subject and object, active and passive. . . ." (429); Krister Stendahl, "Immortality Is Too Little and Too Much,"

tual synonym for "soul" but without the implication, or embarrassment, of having to define or locate the "soul" as a component of human nature.

Can we recover the concept of the soul as an essential aspect of the human person while, at the same time, accepting the discoveries of science as to the apparent correlation of mental activity with brain functioning? Or, to put it more specifically in the framework of the discussion of this book, can we accept a nondualistic, nonreductive physicalist definition of human nature and still use the word "soul" as a distinctive *aspect* of the human person? The aim of this chapter is to argue that we can, provided certain qualifications are made.

In this chapter I will first sketch some portraits of human nature based on biblical terms and texts that point toward the uniqueness of persons as created in the divine image. Second, I will trace briefly some of the developments in theologies of human nature emerging out of the first century and leading up to the modern period. Third, I will discuss some of the contemporary issues raised by the biblical material as viewed by some representative Christian theologians and philosophers. Finally, I will look at issues pertaining to self-identity through death and resurrection in light of the argument that humans do not possess an immortal, indestructible soul. I do not advocate dropping the word "soul" from our theological and faith vocabulary, but wish to present a case for the uniqueness of human nature consistent with the nonreductive physicalist and non-dualist view presented in earlier chapters in this book.

My task as a theologian is to speak to the deeper yearnings and struggles of human existence as much as to bring to those existential human concerns some insights from the Word of God. It is for these reasons that I will use the term "soul" in this discussion with carefully nuanced and qualified meaning. I use the term "soul" to denote the inner core of the whole person, including the body. By "soul" I mean the personal and spiritual dimension of the self. Thus, the phrase "body and soul" is not intended to suggest that the soul is something that is merely "in" the body, or separate from the body, but the whole person with both an interior and an exterior life in the world.

BIBLICAL PORTRAITS OF HUMAN NATURE— TERMS AND IMAGES

Body, Soul, Spirit
Joel Green has reminded us in his chapter on the use of biblical terms regarding body, soul, and spirit that the Hebrew Bible provides no particularly scrip-

---

Meanings: The Bible as Document and Guide (Philadelphia: Fortress Press, 1984), 196: "The whole world that comes to us through the Bible, Old Testament and New Testament, is not interested in the immortality of the soul. And if you think it is, it is because you have read this into the material" (196).

tural vocabulary for anthropological analysis. Furthermore, he rightly warns us against contrasting Greek thought with Hebrew thought so as to attribute dualism to the Greeks and monism to the authors of the Bible. Not only do the Greek concepts of persons provide a variety of views, the Judaism of the first century had been intermingled with Hellenistic thought for some three centuries. The kind of dualism which I seek to challenge in this chapter is not primarily Hellenistic, rather, it can be attributed both to the rise of gnosticism in the first century and to the sixteenth-century Cartesian dichotomy between body and soul. These movements led to a dualism that continues to plague much of our contemporary theological anthropology.

When we look at the biblical terms translated into English it quickly becomes apparent that there is little to be gained by attempting to construct a single portrait of human nature based on tracing the English words "soul," "spirit," "heart," and "body" back to the original languages. The most we can say is that it would be wrong to conclude that the biblical terms lead to any kind of dualism between the physical and nonphysical dimension of the person. The biblical terms, *nephesh* and *psyche* (soul), and *ruach* or *pneuma* (spirit) are primarily functional. They do not denote discrete substances or entities. Thus, while there are some distinctive patterns of use, the words used in the Bible to denote aspects of human life are not analytical and precise in a philosophical or semantical sense.[5]

The word "soul" *(nephesh)* is never used to refer to something external to a person. The soul refers to either the whole person or to some aspect of the person, such as what we would call thoughts, feelings, energy, spirituality, the subjective viewpoint, mind, personality, psychology, or breath. The soul could never exist outside of a person. When the Bible says that a person's soul departed, it could be translated, "the person's life departed," or, more simply "she died" (Gen. 35:18). Soul is the life of the person, says Karl Barth. "To call man [*sic*] "soul" is simply to say in the first place that he is the life which is essentially necessary for his body."[6]

The Old Testament theologian, Hans Walter Wolff, says that the soul *(nephesh)* of a person is "never given the meaning of an indestructible core of being, in contradistinction to the physical life, and even capable of living when cut off from that life." Where there is mention of a "departing" of the soul from a person (Gen. 35:18), or its "return" (Lam. 1:11), the basic idea is that of ceasing or restoration of breathing.[7]

---

5. Jeffrey H. Boyd, "The Soul as Seen Through Evangelical Eyes," 151–160, esp. 155.
6. Barth, *Church Dogmatics*, III/2, 350.
7. Hans Walter Wolff, *Anthropology of the Old Testament* (Philadelphia: Fortress, 1974), 20.

The concept of an immortal soul is thus without clear biblical support. The saying of Jesus in Matthew 10:28 should not be construed as teaching the immortality of the soul: "Do not fear those who kill the body but cannot kill the soul; rather fear him who can destroy both soul and body in hell." This does not say that the soul cannot be killed, Barth reminds us, "but only that no man can kill it, while God has the power to cause both soul and body to pass away and be destroyed in the nether world. Hence we do not have here a doctrine of the immortality of the soul."[8]

The Image and Likeness of God

Human beings, as Thomas Torrance has said, can be viewed as the "focal point in the interrelations between God and the universe."[9] The self's existence as a personal, social, and spiritual being constitutes what the Bible calls the "image and likeness of God." While references to this divine image and likeness are rare in the Bible, the theme runs throughout Scripture (cf. Ps. 8:5; Heb. 2:5-9). Humans are of "more value" than earth creatures (Matt. 6:26; 10:31; 12:9-12; Luke 12:24), and are the object of God's special concern (Heb. 2:14-18).[10]

8. Barth, *Church Dogmatics,* III/2, 379. This also raises the question as to how a person acquires a "soul." The traditional Roman Catholic teaching, as well as Reformed theology, rejected "traducianism," the theory that one inherits a soul through biological procreation, in favor of "creationism," the theory that each person's soul is created by God out of nothing. "We don't owe our souls, says this teaching, to our parents but immediately to God; only our bodies are derived from our parents." Edmund Hill, *Being Human: A Biblical Perspective* (London: Geoffrey Chapman, 1984), 32. While Hill is uncomfortable with this teaching, he accepts the basic intention of the formulation as holding that humans have a direct orientation to God that cannot be predicated of other creatures. Hill suggests abandoning the use of the word "soul" as leading to an unfortunate kind of dualism between God's activity and human activity in the procreative process. Though he does not provide a very satisfactory alternative. Ibid., 36–37. James Reichmann, on the other hand, also a Roman Catholic theologian, dismisses the problems raised by Hill and concludes that the creationist view of the origin of the human soul "realistically accounts for the singular dignity of the human person, while at the same time providing the basis for a reasonable explanation of the phenomenon of religious experience common to humans of all cultures and ages." *Philosophy of the Human Person* (Chicago: Loyola University Press, 1985), 252. Karl Barth dismisses the relevance of this debate when he says, "none of the various attempted solutions, each of which outdoes the other in abstruseness, leads us even the slightest step forward" (*Church Dogmatics,* III/2, 573). What is relevant, Barth says, is the question of the future destiny of the body/soul existence, because it has no existence beyond its existence in time other than that willed and determined for it by God.
9. Thomas F. Torrance, *Divine and Contingent Order* (Oxford: Oxford University Press, 1981), 129.
10. W. Eichrodt reflects on Ps. 8:4 as follows: "Ultimately, therefore it is a spiritual factor which determines the value Man sets upon himself, namely his consciousness of

The Distinctive Quality of Being Human. What distinguishes the human from all other creatures is a spiritual orientation to and personal relation with God as Creator. One way of pointing to this distinctive is to recall that the texts that speak of the "image and likeness of God" (Gen. 1:26-27; 5:1; 9:6) refer only to humans and not to nonhuman creatures. While it is true that animals also were created as "living souls" (Gen. 1:20, 21, 24), and there is reference to the "spirit" *(ruach)* of beasts (Eccles. 3:21), there is no reference in Scripture to animals being created in the divine image and likeness. Similarly, in the second creation account, the human emerges from the dust of the ground, at which point God "breathed into his nostrils the breath of life" (Gen. 2:7). Nowhere in Scripture is this said of the animals.[11] Humans are not described in Scripture as having a different earthly origin than animals; rather, their origination as *human* creatures is qualitatively marked off from nonhuman creatures by the endowment of the divine image and the divine inbreathing.

The Relational Character of the Image. In the second creation account the divine image is not completed in the single individual: "it is not good that the man should be alone" (Gen. 2:18). Only when the man and the woman exist as complementary forms of human being is there a sense of completeness: "This at last is bone of my bones and flesh of my flesh" (Gen. 2:23). On the basis of this passage, some contemporary theologians view the image and likeness more in relational terms than as a static attribute or rational/spiritual capacity. It is in relationship with other persons as well as with God that the divine image is expressed.[12] This "ecological" relation among the various aspects of the human self, between one human and another, is positively determined by this divine endowment and is subject to disorder, destructiveness and death when humans fall out of relationship with God through sin.

"The individual personal spirit lives solely by virtue of sociality," wrote Dietrich Bonhoeffer. "It is only in interaction with other spirits that self-conscious thinking and willing are possible and meaningful."[13] Structural

---

partnership with God, a privilege of which no other creation is considered worthy." *Theology of the Old Testament,* 2 vols. (Philadelphia: Westminster Press, 1975), 2:120-121.

11. "For Man to be created in the likeness of God's image can only mean that on him, too, personhood is bestowed as the definitive characteristic of his nature. . . . This quality of personhood shapes the totality of his psycho-physical existence; it is this which comprises the essentially human, and distinguishes him from all other creatures" Eichrodt, *Theology of the Old Testament,* 2:126.

12. See Berkouwer, *Man the Image of God,* 87ff., 179, 197–198; Barth, *Church Dogmatics,* III/2, 196.

13. Dietrich Bonhoeffer, *The Communion of Saints* (New York: Harper and Row, 1963), 45-46, 49.

openness to other persons, said Bonhoeffer, is not only necessary for the development of one's self-identity, but is also the basis for our own spiritual identity. Spirituality is thus contingent upon social being as prior to and the foundation for religious instincts and experiences.[14]

Following this line of thought we can say that the human spirit that is expressed through the body/soul unity must function in two dimensions or directions. This is reflected in the two great commandments expressed in the Old Testament and reiterated by Jesus: "'You shall love the Lord your God with all your heart, and with all your soul, and with all your mind.' This is the greatest and first commandment. And a second is like it: 'You shall love your neighbor as yourself'" (Matt. 22:37–39; cf. Deut. 6:5; Lev. 19:18). The human spirit, as empowered by the Divine Spirit, opens up in love toward God as the source of life. True religion, as the Scriptures say, must be grounded in the spiritual integrity of one's relation to the other person as well as to God (cf. Micah 6:6–8; James 1:27).

The Effects of Sin and the Fall. The original humans are depicted as being in a state of innocence, under divine command and preservation, though subject to temptation. Sin emerged as an act of self-determination in disobedience to the divine command (Gen. 3). Humans were not first of all free moral agents, having the capacity to know good from evil. The knowledge of good and evil as an autonomous moral agency was specifically prohibited according to the biblical account. "You may freely eat of every tree of the garden; but of the tree of the knowledge of good and evil you shall not eat, for in the day that you eat of it you shall die" (Gen. 2:16–17). Humans were created in a spiritual relation to God, not only as moral agents. Breaking of a moral law leads to guilt, while severing a spiritual relationship leads to death. That there were moral consequences to the sin that severed the spiritual relation between God and the humans themselves, is obvious. The point to be made here is that the essential distinctive of human being in the image of God is the spiritual dimension of relationship with God as the basis for all other relations. Physical death, while not occurring instantly as a result of sin, was an inevitable consequence of spiritual separation from God, as the entire person as body/soul unity is mortal and subject to death apart from the Spirit of God. Sin did not result in the loss of immortality as an intrinsic characteristic of the soul, but rather, caused the person as a body/soul unity to be subject to the natural mortality of creaturely life. Humans were created out of the dust of the ground with a physical body, which, by nature alone, would return to the dust, that is, die. Sin did not cause physical death but separated the human creature from the life-giving and

14. See Brown, chapter 5, this volume.

sustaining spiritual relation with God the Creator. We can then account for physical death as a consequence of the fall, but not introduced as a possibility until only after the fall. Had the fall not occurred, one could argue that a transformation of the human person from temporal (mortal) to eternal life would still have been necessary.[15]

The holistic and relational nature of the soul/body unity as depicted in Scripture is also reflected in the effects of sin. The effects of sin produced disunity and disorder at the physical, social, psychological, and spiritual core of human life such that the original unity of personal well-being as embodied soul and besouled body became disrupted and subject to dissolution and death. The image of God as social, spiritual, and moral health was corrupted and became the source of pride, jealousy, hatred, and violence against others. The ecology of human life in terms of relationship with the earth, other humans, and with God was thrown out of balance so that injustice, oppression, poverty, and war permeated all of human society.

In a Christian anthropology, sin is understood as a failure to live humanly in every area of life as social, personal, sexual, and spiritual. Salvation from sin thus entails the recovery of true humanity in each of these aspects of life. The tendency of some to view salvation as "saving souls" without regard to the total life of the person as a physical, social, and psychological being is not a Christian one. From the perspective of a Christian anthropology, salvation touches each area of a person's embodied life, though not with equal effect short of the resurrection of the body.

POINTS OF CLARIFICATION
WITH SUGGESTED CONCLUSIONS

1. The use of the term "soul" in this chapter is not intended to refer to a substance or entity residing in the body, but to represent the whole person, especially the inner core of human personal life as created and upheld by God.

2. The biblical terms, "body," "soul," and "spirit" are not susceptible to an analytical depiction of human nature and do not denote discrete entities or substances that comprise the human person. Rather, these terms overlap in their meaning and are used more or less in a functional way to describe the phenomena of human existence.

3. Nonetheless, I have argued that human life is experienced as an inner life expressed through embodied relation to other persons and the cosmos itself.

15. For a discussion of the concept of human mortality, see my book, *Theology, Death and Dying* (Oxford: Basil Blackwell, 1986), 37-63.

4. While humans share with nonhuman creatures a "life soul" *(nephesh)*, and a common origin with regard to a physical/temporal life form, humans have an orientation and destiny contingent upon relation with the Spirit of God as the source of their earthly life.

5. The uniqueness of human life as contrasted with nonhuman creatures can be understood to be the result of the endowment of the divine image and likeness (Gen. 1:26-27), and a divine "inbreathing" (Gen. 2:7). Both of these point to the same quality of spiritual life as a calling and task to serve God and to have dominion over the earth and its creatures (Gen. 1:28).

6. Humans were created as mortal beings with a spiritual life contingent upon relation to God's Spirit, and thus subject to mortality and non-existence, apart from the divine intention and determination of God as creator and sustainer of human life. There is no warrant in Scripture for asserting that human nature bears some immortal, indestructible soul that has a natural capacity to survive death.

7. Sin as rebellion against God results in a severing of human spiritual life from God. This, in turn, results in physical death as the natural consequence of the mortality of human nature but is also a divine judgment against humans as spiritual beings.

8. A holistic account of salvation points toward the restoration of ecological, social, psychological, and spiritual health experienced partially in this lifetime and completely in the life to come. Salvation from sin involves not only pardon for personal guilt but the restoration of the possibility of eternal life through resurrection of the same person through a sovereign act of God's power and Spirit.

THEOLOGICAL PORTRAITS OF HUMAN NATURE— OLD AND NEW

The Greek Fathers of the first three centuries of the Common Era (C.E.) drew upon various traditions within the Greco-Roman world from as early as Plato and Aristotle in formulating their language and concepts of the human person. The original Greek concept of person was ontological, that is, having to do with a cosmic monism in which humans were caught up in a necessary rational harmony, without discrete individual and existential attributes.

The gnostic movement that emerged in the first-century church viewed the flesh (physical human nature) as the source of corruption and defilement. Gnosticism, derived from the Greek word for knowledge *(gnosis)*, was a philosophical and religious movement that influenced the Mediterranean world from the first century B.C.E. to the third century C.E. It expressed itself in a variety of pagan, Jewish, and Christian forms. A pervasive dualism underlay much of gnostic thought. Good and evil, light and darkness, truth and falsehood, spirit and matter were viewed as opposed to one another in human experience. The created universe and human experience were characterized by a radical disjunction between the spiritual, which was pure, and the physical, which was corrupt. Renunciation of physical desires and strict asceticism, combined with mystical rites of initiation and purification, were thought to liberate the immortal souls of believers from the prison of physical existence. The true self of the person was viewed as derived from the world of light, from above: only through *gnosis,* which is brought to the self from above, can the self be freed and receive salvation.[16]

The second-century theologian, Irenaeus, Bishop of Lyon, wrote a polemic against this teaching, arguing that original humans were created immature, not imperfect, and being created in a bodily condition, would reach the perfection of bodily existence in the resurrection. He was one of the first theologians in the Common Era to develop a holistic view of human persons.[17]

The fifth-century North African theologian Augustine was the first to teach that, though the human body like every other creature bears a *trace* of the Trinity, the human soul alone bears its *image.* For Augustine, the soul as the origin of self-knowledge and self-love is called "memory," that is, the soul's abiding psychic life, which distinguishes it from mortal corporeal things.[18]

Thomas Aquinas (1225-1274 C.E.) accepted the Aristotelian theory of the human soul as the substantial form of the human body. Even though he held that the soul as the intellectual power of the body is a substance distinct from the body, he taught that the soul separated from the body is not a human person and requires union with its own body at the resurrection to become again a fully human person.[19] Paul Jewett suggests that "Thomas's treatment of the

16. For a discussion of gnosticism and its influence in the early church, see Helmut Koester, *Introduction to the New Testament,* 2d ed., vol. 1 (New York: Walter de Gruyter, 1995).

17. Irenaeus, *Against Heresies,* 2 vols., Ante-Nicene Christian Library, eds. A. Roberts and J. Donaldson (Edinburgh: T. & T. Clark, 1868). For a discussion of early gnosticism, see J. Patout Burns, trans. and ed., *Theological Anthropology: Sources of Early Christian Thought* (Philadelphia: Fortress Press, 1981), 3ff. See also, J. T. Nielsen, *Adam and Christ in the Theology of Irenaeus of Lyons* (Assen, The Netherlands: Van Gorcum, 1968), 2ff.

18. Benedict M. Ashley, O.P., *Theologies of the Body: Humanist and Christian* (Braintree, Mass.: Pope John Center, 1985), 128–29.

19. Ibid., 54. Ashley notes that Thomas argued that "the union of body and soul is certainly a natural one, and any separation of soul from body goes against its nature and is imposed on it. So if soul is deprived of body it will exist imperfectly as long as that situation lasts. Now how can a normal situation in accord with nature come to an end,

body/soul relation (*Summa Theologiae,* pt. 1. q.76), is much more plausible than nineteenth-century theories of preestablished harmony, psychophysical parallelism, and the like." He goes on to say that with Thomas, the view that the soul is the *form* of the body is much closer to Christian thought than to view the soul as the *function* of the body (materialism).[20]

René Descartes (1596-1650 c.e.) obliterated what remained of the Aristotelian tradition and substituted for it a simplified Platonic view of the soul as a pure mental state independent of the body. This subject/object dichotomy became the basis for much of the philosophic tradition in Western thought up to the early part of this present century.[21] The influence of Cartesian dualism upon views of human nature is pervasive, both in philosophical and theological anthropology. Philosophical concepts of human nature tend to split the physical from the mental, leading to a body/mind dualism. Theologians, seeking to preserve the spiritual value of persons, turned to the soul as a concept of personal being that constituted the true identity of the self, even surviving the death of the body.[22]

THEOLOGICAL ISSUES AND PERSPECTIVES

Contemporary theologian Wolfhart Pannenberg says that one cannot speak of the soul as a component of the person along with the body:

> The soul *(nephesh)* is not another component part of a human being over and above the body, as in Cartesian or Platonic dualism. It is simply the bodily being as living. . . . But insofar as the soul is the life of its body it is an effect

---

having lasted no time at all, and a situation imposed against nature then last for ever! But this is what must happen if the soul is to go on existing without its body forever. . . . What human beings desire by nature is their own well-being. But soul is not the whole human being, only part of one: My Soul Is Not Me. . . ." See Thomas Aquinas, *Selected Philosophical Writings,* selected and trans. T. McDermott (Oxford: Oxford University Press, 1993), 192.

20. Paul K. Jewett, *Who We Are: Our Dignity as Human* (Grand Rapids: Wm. B. Eerdmans, 1996), 42. Jewett adds: "The difficulty with Thomas's argument, as we see it, is that the Scriptures have little interest in his subject; hence they throw virtually no light on it. Theologians can do no better than to settle for the commonsense view found by a tacit consent throughout Scripture. This commonsense view simply assumes that there is a constant interplay, a mutual influence, between body and soul. When the design of the wallpaper and the print on the page begin to assume a democratic likeness, the soul of the theology student preparing for an exam is being overcome with the fatigue of the body" (ibid.).

21. Ashley, *Theologies of the Body,* 154–155.

22. See Murphy, chapter 1, this volume.

` of the life giving spirit. The divine creative spirit causes human beings to
have life within them, and to that extent the spirit is internally present to
them, although it does not on that account become a "part" of them.[23]

From this perspective it is not quite correct to say that a person "has a
soul." Rather, one might better say that a "person *is* soul."

Paul Jewett rejects the notion that the soul can be thought of as a substance,
even though it be a nonmaterial substance, existing along with and in the
body. At the same time he says that the soul is not simply a concept of thought:
"It has objective reality, though not the reality of a material object." However,
in having said that, he follows with the statement that in his judgment, even
that is an inadequate way to speak of the soul.

> For one thing, it tends to invite questions that the Scriptures do not ask—
> and the theologian cannot answer—such as, Where is the soul located and
> how is it related to the body? It is better, therefore, to think of the soul in
> personal categories. While there is an ineluctable relationship between soul
> and body, the soul is not some spiritual substance "in" the body as a fetus is
> "in" the womb. Nor is it a spiritual substance diffused through the body as
> blood "through" the veins. Rather, the soul is just the personal self, the "I,"
> animating the body and manifest in a bodily way.[24]

As an alternative to the dualism/monism dichotomy, Karl Barth suggests
what might be called "contingent monism." The body and soul, argues Barth,
are clearly differentiated *aspects* of the unique and singular *experience* of each
human person. While Barth himself will call this "concrete monism," as
opposed to "abstract dualism," I believe that the phrase, "contingent monism"
better expresses what he means.[25] "Contingent monism" means that the unity
of human personal life is contingent upon relation to God. When humans are
viewed in abstraction from their spiritual "life support" system as determined
by the Spirit of God, body and soul tend to be seen as opposed to each other

---

23. Wolfhart Pannenberg, *Anthropology in Theological Perspective*, trans. Matthew J.
O'Connell (Philadelphia: Westminster, 1985), 523.

24. Jewett, *Who We Are,* 42.

25. Karl Barth, *Church Dogmatics*, "It is to this concrete monism that we find ourselves
guided by the biblical view and the biblical concept of the 'soul.' The abstract dualism
of the Greek and the traditional Christian doctrine, and the equally abstract materialist and spiritualist monism, are from this standpoint a thoroughgoing and interconnected deviation." (III/2, 393). What maintains the unity of the body/soul duality of
the person, says Barth, is Spirit, i.e., the immediate action of God himself "which
grounds, constitutes and maintains man as soul of his body. It is thus the Spirit that unifies him and holds him together as soul and body" (ibid.).

in some form of dualism. In attempting to overcome this dualism, some have opted for a reductionist view of humans, where a portrait of human nature is drawn solely from physical properties.

As suggested earlier, many contemporary theologians have substituted the word "spirit" for the "soul." However, this creates a new dichotomy between the secular and the spiritual aspect of life. While the older dualism between body and soul became troublesome for both philosophy and science, the dichotomy between the secular and the spiritual life created serious ethical and practical problems for the theologian. When the life of the spirit becomes detached from one's embodied existence, spirituality lacks ethical content with respect to how one views the body, with all of its needs, instincts, drives, and potentialities. This is a point well made by Stephen Post in his contribution to this book. James shows the fallacy of this kind of thinking. "If a brother or sister is naked and lacks daily food, and one of you says to them, 'Go in peace; keep warm and eat your fill,' and yet you do not supply their bodily needs, what is the good of that? So faith by itself, if it has no works, is dead" (James 2:15-17).

It was not only a body/soul dualism that led to the evangelistic slogan of "saving souls," but the dichotomy between the spiritual and the secular. This same dichotomy can be found in the more recent "anti-psychology" literature, where spiritual truths as found in the Bible are taken to be the remedy for (secular) psychological needs and problems.[26]

When theologians refer to the spiritual dimension of human persons they ordinarily mean something more than that which philosophers call mind and what scientists call brain. For this reason, the abandonment of a theory of mind/brain or a body/soul dualism does not entail the reduction of the spiritual life of persons into mere physical phenomena.

When I speak of the soul, this dimension of the self calls for more than merely an "extension" of the brain as a physical organism. To reduce self-consciousness, intentionality, personality, intuition, imagination, spiritual awareness, among other aspects of the self, to epiphenomena of a physicalist or natural explanation of persons goes beyond what is warranted by a careful study of the biblical texts.[27]

---

26. For example, see Jay Adams, *More than Redemption: A Theology of Christian Counseling* (Grand Rapids: Baker, 1979); Martin and Diedre Bobgan, *Prophets of Psychoheresy II* (Santa Barbara, Calif.: Eastgate, 1990).

27. Robert Corrington suggests that the human spirit emerges out of nature through an evolutionary process. "All children of the spirit are children of nature and derive their healing energies from the grace of the spirit, itself an eject of nature." Suffering a primal "self-fissuring," humans experience an "ontological wound" that creates an ecstatic openness to the self that goes beyond finite melancholy in search of the "lost object" in an infinite, post-temporal order. Human spirit, he argues, is a product of

Human nature itself may be understood in a scientific way that does not exclude the operation of a divine reality that impinges upon human persons and which produces effects that are coterminous with physical phenomena but not totally explained by physical causation. It is in this sense that one could say that the essence of the human self as spiritual being is contingent upon a spiritual order or, more specifically, upon the Spirit of God.[28]

Physicality sets limits to our personal existence and, at the same time, produces the phenomena we recognize as manifestations of the soul. In other words, there is no manifestation of the soul that is not produced through the brain even though the brain is not the sole effective cause. Therefore we should not be surprised and should indeed expect that the firing of selected brain cells affects what we might call spiritual impulses, attitudes, and actions. However, spiritual self-identity as used theologically and on biblical grounds, is contingent upon the Spirit of God both as to its formation and its growth. The existence of brain cells is a necessary but insufficient condition for the expression of the life of the soul as personal and spiritual being.

SELF-IDENTITY, MORTALITY, RESURRECTION OF THE BODY

Human life is the spiritual saga of the creaturely soul; limited, but also expressed through physical embodiment; distressed, but also inspired through the power of spirit; mortal, but also graced with the promise of immortality through the promise of God.

The critical issue with regard to the human soul becomes more narrowly focused in the discussion of continuity of human self-identity through the death and resurrection experience as depicted in Scripture.

"ecstatic naturalism." See *Nature's Self: Our Journey from Origin to Spirit* (Lanham, Md.: Rowman and Littlefield Publishers, Inc. 1996), 144-145, 160. Corrington's view is similar to that of the evangelical scientist, Richard Bube, "The soul is ... a reality which is produced as an emergent property of the living system of a human being. As life is produced as an emergent property of a non-living system by the appropriate patterned interaction of non-living subsystems, so soul is produced as an emergent property of non-soul subsystems when they interact according to the appropriate pattern." "Other Options?" *Journal of the American Scientific Affiliation* 24 (March 1972): 14-15.

28. The concept of contingence is not unknown to modern scientific methodology and is quite familiar to the science of theology. T. F. Torrance, for example, speaks of a "social coefficient" of knowledge whereby one breaks out of the isolation of selfhood and experiences an external reality as the capacity of the subject to be affected and modified by what it knows independent of itself. See *Theology and Science at the Frontiers of Science* (Edinburgh: Scottish Academic Press, 1985), 103.

What Happens to the Soul When People Die?

The issue can be put this way. If one assumes that death does not annihilate individual human life as determined by God, then what insures that the uniqueness and individuality of a person survives the death experience? *Crucial*

Human persons as personal, embodied, mortal creatures are created by God. The human soul is not an immortal substance encased in a mortal body. The life of the person (soul) emerges simultaneously with the bodily form of human existence. Human life has no existence independent of a body.

In a Christian anthropology, human nature is not defined ultimately by tracing humanity back to its origins, nor by explaining humanity in terms of its existence under the conditions of sin. Rather, human nature is life experienced as a personal body/soul unity, inspired and empowered by the Spirit of God. Self-identity is both determined by the Spirit of God within each person and acquired by the person through experience and interaction with the physical, social, and spiritual environment of life.

In this sense, one could say that each person has an identity that is more or less dependent upon the subjective life of the self, as well as an identity that is projected upon the person from and by the Spirit of God. Even in our mother's womb, the psalmist says, we were given personal identity by God:

> For it was you who formed my inward parts; you knit me together in my mother's womb. I praise you, for I am fearfully and wonderfully made. Wonderful are your works; that I know very well. My frame was not hidden from you, when I was being made in secret, intricately woven in the depths of the earth. Your eyes beheld my unformed substance. In your book were written all the days that were formed for me, when none of them as yet existed. (Ps. 139:13-16)

For the Israelite, even the prospect of death and descent into the earth does not extinguish self-identity, for "if I make my bed in Sheol, you are there" (Ps. 139:8). Self-identity arises as the subjective life (soul) of the body and is grounded in the existence of the whole person as a unity.

What happens to the person when life (soul) has expired? The identity of the self as a body/soul unity is now dependent upon a source and power beyond its own capacity for survival. Even as the "person" was present in the unborn state through divine perception and determination (Ps. 139), so the person can survive death by that same divine knowledge and power.

"Do not let your hearts be troubled," Jesus told his disciples, "Believe in God, believe also in me. In my Father's house there are many dwelling places. If it were not so, would I have told you that I go to prepare a place for you? And if I go and prepare a place for you, I will come again and will take you to myself, so that where I am, there you may be also" (John 14:1-3). Surely Jesus

intended that his disciples understand that this was a guarantee of the continuation of their individual and personal self-identity beyond death. The question then arises, what really happens to the person when death occurs?

What Happens to the Person when Life Expires?

Paul's discussion of the state of the person through the process of death points
to the issue of continuity of self-identity as a personal reality (2 Cor. 5:1-10).
When he contemplates his own death, Paul does not flinch at the prospect of
the death of the body, for he considers that "being unclothed," while a necessary letting go of the earthly form of his body, will be followed by being "further clothed" in the resurrection. The certainty of this is assured because God
"has given us the Spirit as a guarantee" (2 Cor. 5:2-5). We notice that Paul did
not base his assurance on the indestructible nature of the soul, but on the
Spirit of God as a guarantee. It is clear from the context, as Joel Green has
reminded us in his earlier chapter, that Paul is not here responding to a question or problem with regard to life after death. Rather, in defending his suffering as an apostle he argues that even though he should perish, he nonetheless has an eschatological hope based on his relationship with the risen Christ.

Being "away from the body" (5:8) is not to be taken as the freeing of the
soul from the body itself, but as having the "mortal" body "swallowed up by
life" (5:4). To be "away from the body and at home with the Lord" is viewed
by Paul as preferable, though not a present necessity (5:8). When Paul says that
he does not "wish to be unclothed" (5:4), it is doubtful that he is contemplat-
ing an "intermediate state" during which he will exist as a disembodied soul.

New Testament scholar Murray Harris argues persuasively that the issue of
"what part of the person survives death" is irrelevant, as there is no suggestion
in Paul's thought that a "soul" survives death as a disembodied substance awaiting a "spiritual body." "In Pauline thought it is not the soul but 'this mortal
body' *(to thnenton touto)* that is destined to put on immortality, to become
immortal through a somatic resurrection (1 Cor. 15:53-54); it is not by birth,
but by grace, and through resurrection, that immortality is gained."[29]

In fact, Paul had already answered some questions concerning the nature of
the resurrection body put to him by the church in Corinth in his earlier let-
ter (1 Cor. 15). There is no question in his mind about the continuity of self-
identity even though the "mortal body" must "put on immortality" (15:53).

---

29. Murray J. Harris, *Raised Immortal—Resurrection and Immortality in the New Testament*
(Grand Rapids: Wm. B. Eerdmans, 1983), 140, 237. See also his later book, *From the
Grave to Glory: Resurrection in the New Testament* (Grand Rapids: Zondervan, 1990),
210ff.; and L. Cerfeaux, *The Christian in the Theology of St. Paul* (London: Chapman,
1967), 190ff.

The physical body is "sown in weakness" and raised in glory. It is sown a physical body and raised a spiritual body. If there is a physical body, he asserts, there will also be a spiritual body (15:42-43). We note in Paul's discussion no reference to a "spiritual" soul that would replace the creaturely soul in somewhat the same way as the "spiritual" body replaces the "physical" body. There could be two reasons for this.

First, if humans do not have a soul that can have an independent existence apart from the body, the primary concern of those who sought some answers from Paul would be for the life of the body. The assumption would be that even as life (soul) emerges with the body as the subjective life of the person, so it will emerge simultaneously with the "spiritual" body. For a body without life (soul) would not be a body. With the death of the body, the life (soul) of the body also disappears. With the resurrection of the body, the life (soul) of the body reappears. If this is the case, then questions concerning the effect of death upon a human soul would not naturally arise.

Alternatively, one could assume that Paul *did* have a theory of a human soul that ruled the mortal body and that is indestructible and survives death, awaiting a new "spiritual" body. The absence of any comment by Paul on the status of the soul as distinct from the body in discussing the nature of the resurrection body might be taken as support for the view that the soul is indestructible and survives death as the bearer of personal self-identity. If this were the case, then questions concerning the effect of death upon the soul would not naturally arise. The problem with this view is that there are no scriptural grounds for supporting such a view, and certainly not in the writing of Paul.

Instead of providing a solution to the exegetical problem as formulated above, Paul shifts the emphasis from anthropology to Christology. It is not human nature itself that provides the answer, but the nature of Jesus Christ. Paul compares Adam as representative of all who are "from the dust." "The first man was from the earth, a man of dust; the second man is from heaven. As was the man of dust, so are those who are of the dust; and as is the man of heaven, so are those who are of heaven. Just as we have borne the image of the man of dust, we will also bear the image of the man of heaven" (1 Cor. 15:47-49). What provides assurance of continuity of the self through death and resurrection is not an immortal soul but the granting of immortality to the mortal human person as a body/soul unity, as having already taken place on our behalf through the resurrection of Christ.

The Continuity of Self-Identity through Death and Resurrection

"If mortals die, will they live again?" is a question older than Job (14:14) but asked by every new generation. Not content with vague, impersonal generalities, Job persisted: "After my skin has been thus destroyed, then in my flesh I shall see God, . . .and my eyes shall behold, and *not another*" (19:27, emphasis added).

The concept of resurrection cannot be put in the mind of Job from this passage, but he clearly expresses the desire that his very own self (soul) survives the destruction of his flesh so that he, in his body, should stand before God. It is his own self-identity—and *not another*—that must survive, not merely as an extension of his present life, but that he could finally confront God. It was not death itself that tormented Job, but the loss of God's presence and affirmation.

The majority of persons who believe in some form of life after death assume the existence of some form of a nonphysical personal entity that survives, whether it is called soul or spirit. Biblical revelation supports the belief that personal self-identity continues after death but that this is solely due to God's sovereign determination, not due to an immortal soul or mind residing in the human person. What is at stake is not the belief that there is life after death but whether that life is due to something resident in human nature or whether it is due to God's power and Spirit.

Death affects the soul as it does the body, says Barth, "The ostensibly all-powerful soul becomes completely impotent in death because it becomes bodiless. . . .The difference and antithesis between soul and body is as great in death as it can possibly be within the created world."[30]

Where Scripture does affirm the stability and continuity of the self through death and resurrection, the basis is not that of an indestructible soul but the guarantee of the Spirit of God (2 Cor. 5:5). The assurance that self-identity will survive death is not based on some nonphysical aspect of the person but on the bond between the risen Jesus Christ and the believer through the Holy Spirit.

---

30. Karl Barth, *Church Dogmatics,* III/2, 370. "Man as such, therefore, has no beyond. Nor does he need one, for God is his beyond. . . . Man as such, however, belongs to this world. He is thus finite and mortal. One day he will only have been, as once he was not. His divinely given promise and hope and confidence in the confrontation with God is that even as this one who has been he will share the eternal life of God Himself" (ibid., 632-633). One should read this carefully! The key is Barth's phrase "man as such." It is not that persons do not have hope of eternal life, but this hope is not based on some intrinsic power or character of humanity *as such.* When Barth is understood in this way, both Pannenberg and Moltmann can be found in agreement. See Pannenberg, *Anthropology in Theological Perspective,* 322; Moltmann, *God in Creation,* 263-264. Dietrich Bonhoeffer also asserts that both body and soul are mortal: "In the Christian person body and soul are bound together in an indissoluble unity. Real community is possible only through man's being equipped with a body, so we must think of body and soul as being essentially connected. We assume that with the body the sinful soul also dies, and that in the resurrection God, with the soul, also creates a new body, and that this new spiritual body is a warrant and condition for the eternal communion of personal spirits" *Communion of Saints* (New York: Harper and Row, 1963), 201.

"If the Spirit of him who raised Jesus from the dead dwells in you, he who raised Christ from the dead will give life to your mortal bodies also through his Spirit that dwells in you" (Rom. 8:11; cf. 1 Thess. 4:13-15).

We must admit that the Bible does not provide an answer as to how personal self-identity continues through the death and resurrection process in such a way that it is the very *same* person who dies with a corruptible body and is raised with an incorruptible body, as Paul seems to indicate is the case. Paul's argument in 1 Corinthians 15 rests on the fact that the same Christ who died was raised again; and if this is true, then those who die "in Christ" will also be raised. The testimony of the disciples to the fact that it was the same Jesus who died who presented himself to them alive supports Paul's argument even though he probably only had access to this information through their oral report. The written report that came after Paul's death confirms this truth (cf. John 20:19-29).

In advancing this thesis, we must admit that there can be shown no mechanism whereby the Spirit of God directly causes, empowers, and sustains the body and soul as a unit of self-identity. The evidences of spiritual causation upon a person's physical life can be observed, though not explained, through both natural and behavioral science. Positive effects of prayer and religious faith have been noted through double-blind, controlled research studies.[31] Similarly, the actual process by which human mortal life becomes immortal is hidden from us.

With reference to the biblical writings, I have suggested that body and soul are essentially indivisible. At the same time, a portrait of the human nature faithful to the biblical texts appears to allow a *conceptual* differentiation between body and soul in order to avoid a reductive physicalist explanation of persons. In this case, as with many others, it may be well to remember that theology may quickly become mythology when it attempts to answer questions that the Bible does not ask!

In this chapter I have defined the human soul as that which represents the whole person as a physical, personal, and spiritual being, especially the inner core of an individual's life as created and upheld by God. I have argued that the uniqueness of human persons as contrasted with nonhuman creatures is solely due to the encounter, relation, and destiny of humans contingent upon relation with the Spirit of God as the source of earthly life and the possibility of

31. "A 1995 study at Dartmouth-Hitchcock Medical Center found that one of the best predictors of survival among 232 heart-surgery patients was the degree to which the patients said they drew comfort and strength from religious faith. Those who did not had more than three times the death rate of those who did." See "Faith & Healing," by Claudia Wallis, *Time Magazine,* 147, no. 26 (pp. 59–62) (June 24, 1996).

eternal life. I have presented biblical evidence for the view that death is the end of human life in its totality, except for the sovereign power and determination of God, and that only through the death and resurrection of Jesus Christ do we have assurance of our own resurrection and continuing identity following death.

Concern for the "soul" as expressed by Thomas Moore at the beginning of this chapter, then, does not necessitate a view of the soul as a separate mental or spiritual entity alongside or within the body. Rather, concern for the soul is concern for the quality of human life at the deepest core of our existential life, at the center of the ecology of our physical life as life in the cosmos, in the manifestation of the divine image in our manifold social relations, and as the spiritual beings that we are by the breath of God's Spirit.

Chapter Nine

A Moral Case for Nonreductive Physicalism

Stephen G. Post

IS SOUL ESSENTIAL?

Nonreductive physicalism is one form of "monism," the view in metaphysics and ontology that stresses the oneness or unity of reality in its essential aspects. A physicalist monism postulates that this reality is substantive (rather than the mere projection of mind), and that there is nothing in nature or human nature beyond what is presented—that is, an undivided reality perceivable by the five senses. The nonreductive form of physicalism claims that the human capacities for moral life and relations with God, both essential in Christianity, are not compromised by the rejection of dualisms and may even be enhanced. While much Christian thought on human nature has been influenced by a Platonic "substance" dualism, often positing a natural (inferior, visible) body and a supernatural (superior, invisible) soul, preceding chapters have indicated that this view is increasingly untenable in the light of the neurosciences. Human capacities once attributed to a nonmaterial soul are now carefully mapped in various sections of the neurological substrate.

Nonreductive physicalism understands the human as "a physical organism whose complex functioning, both in society and in relation to God, gives rise to 'higher' human capacities such as emotion, morality, and spirituality."[1] This view, then, does not include an immortal, immaterial soul. But as Etienne Gilson wrote in his 1931–32 Gifford Lectures, the idea of an immortal soul is not as essential to Christianity as might be assumed:

> It would probably surprise a good many modern Christians to learn that in certain of the earliest Fathers the belief in the immortality of the soul is

1. See Murphy, chapter 1, this volume.

vague almost to non-existence. This, nevertheless, is a fact, and a fact to be noted, because it casts so strong a light on the point on which Christian anthropology turns and on the course of its historical development. A Christianity without the immortality of the soul is not, in the long run, absolutely inconceivable, and the proof of it is that it has been conceived. What really would be absolutely inconceivable would be a Christianity without the resurrection of the Man.[2]

Gilson, the twentieth century's leading interpreter of medieval theology and of the thought of Thomas Aquinas in particular, asserts the immortality of the soul, but only with ambivalence. He does not consider the nonmaterial soul to be a requirement of Christian belief. Aquinas, influenced by Aristotle, resisted much of Platonic dualism, emphasized the unity of human nature, and developed strained arguments for the soul's immortality.[3]

Thus, the history of Christian thought on the nature of the human being is quite complex and varied. Ignorance of this variation, however, has resulted in the uninformed pitting of the monistic, physicalist, and naturalist tradition against religion (supernature) in general and Christianity in particular. The utilitarian philosopher Jeremy Bentham (d. 1832), for example, denied the existence of an immortal soul and considered this justification for the castigation of Christianity. Yet as this book contends, Christianity is compatible with a nonreductive physicalism that allows a neurological grounding for human existence, while allowing for an account of God's actions upon the human being.

My task in this chapter is narrowed to the question of what might be the practical moral results of a theological anthropology that excludes an invisible soul. What is at stake, if anything, for Christian ethics in the rise of neuroscientific physicalism, in which attributes of the soul are explained in terms of neurological function?

While dualism has arguably provided certain limited benefits in Christian ethics, it has also created monumental burdens. Indeed, as a general trend, many Christian ethicists have moved away from dualism in recent years. But in fairness to dualism, I begin with a section on its purported benefits before turning to its adverse consequences. A major benefit of dualism has been the argument that the presence of a soul confers equal moral worth on all humans. Some may worry that this sort of moral inclusiveness will be lost if a physicalist account of the person is adopted. Therefore, I conclude with a brief statement on the influence of the Christian story on an inclusive *agape,* which, I argue,

2. Etienne Gilson, *The Spirit of Medieval Philosophy,* trans. A. H. C. Downes (New York: Charles Scribner's Sons, 1936), 172.
3. See Murphy, chapter 1, this volume.

affords equal moral standing even to those who are severely neurologically incapacitated.

THE PURPORTED MORAL ACHIEVEMENTS OF DUALISM

Radical dualism (the soul or mind is separable from the body, and the person is identified with the former) purportedly confers a protective canopy over those imperiled and vulnerable people at the very margins of human mental capacity. The most severe cases of retardation or advanced irreversible progressive dementia (e.g., Alzheimer's disease) only hinder the expression of the invisible soul, which in fact still exists in all its eternal value under the veneer of confusion. Therefore (so the argument would go) caregivers need never think that their loved one is no longer present, that they have before them only a "shell" or "husk" or "half-empty" glass. Indeed, the glass is still full because the soul is still there, even if camouflaged by neurological devastation. Such lives are worthy of all the moral consideration and standing that we would ordinarily bestow upon those of us who are neurologically more intact.

One of the best-known advocates for people with retardation, Wolf Wolfensberger, describes the threat of "deathmaking" through the denial of life-saving treatment or euthanasia. This threat, he contends, builds on "modernistic values," which include various elements, the most prominent being materialism: "The first element of modernism is a materialistic worldview which denies the existence (or at least the relevance) of any immaterial, spiritual dimensions to reality and life, and instead embraces a materialistic, mechanistic, reductionistic way of relating to reality, including human beings."[4] This materialism "views the human as a mere body, without a soul, and certainly not made in the image and likeness of God. Therefore, there resides no absolute transcendent value in the individual human."[5] One might disagree with such a statement for its radical dualism but nevertheless appreciate the inclusion of the most imperiled among us under the protective umbrella of the principle of nonmaleficence.

In a remarkable and important theological study of Alzheimer's disease as manifested in his mother's long illness, theologian David Keck describes his personal experience as a caregiver. Keck points out that although his mother no longer functions cognitively in the same purposeful ways that she once did,

4. Wolf Wolfensberger, "The Growing Threat to the Lives of Handicapped People in the Context of Modernistic Values," *Disability & Society* 9, no. 3 (1994): 395–413, 396.
5. Ibid., 400.

she nevertheless seems to retain an aesthetic sensibility that allows her to appreciate the beauty of nature and enjoy wandering along a wooded path. Keck also believes that his mother can have "spiritual" experiences in church, stimulated by beautiful music, deeply learned hymns, and litanies fixed in her mind since childhood. Then Keck turns to a lengthy analysis of the soul, reviewing the various alternative monisms and dualisms that concern this book (see Murphy, chapter 1). He asks, with all the passion of a good caregiver, whether his mother is still there, despite her growing incapacitation. What has become of her memories, of her self-identity achieved over the journey of life? Keck then asserts a form of substance dualism. It may appear that his mother is now "gone," all the experiences of a lifetime peeled away. But in fact she is actually "still with us"; her soul retains all that she was and all that she is. This confidence in the presence of his mother, despite the appearance of a loss of all her temporal glue between past, present, and future, encourages the author in his laudable commitment and remarkable love.[6]

The nineteenth-century historian, W. E. H. Lecky, would have concurred with Wolfensberger and Keck. The early Christian tradition, he argued, with its Platonic dualistic image of the self, deepened the sense of the sanctity of human life, for every self has an invisible soul that is the seat of equality. Lecky's *History of European Morals* describes the discountenancing of infanticide by the Christian church, which thereby broke decisively with the conventional morality of the Roman empire. Lecky juxtaposed the Christian ethics of *agape* (universal love especially concerned with the vulnerable) with Rome in these pointed terms:

> Whatever mistakes may have been made, the entire movement I have traced displays an anxiety not only for the life, but also for the moral well-being, of the castaways of society, such as the most humane nations of antiquity had never reached. This minute and scrupulous care for human life and human virtue in the humblest forms, in the slave, the gladiator, the savage, or the infant, was indeed wholly foreign to the genius of Paganism. It was produced by the Christian doctrine of the *inestimable value of each immortal soul.*[7]

"Considered as immortal beings" and as "sacred beings," from this notion "grew up the eminently Christian idea of the sanctity of all human life."[8] Infant life, although undeveloped and in this sense less significant than adult life, nevertheless possessed a fearful significance because the soul is destined

6. David Keck, *Forgetting Whose We Are* (Nashville: Abingdon Press, 1996).
7. William E. H. Lecky, *The History of European Morals from Augustus to Charlemagne,* vol. 2 (New York: George Braziller, 1955 [original 1869]), 34. Emphasis is mine.
8. Ibid., 18.

for hell unless saved by baptism. Those with deranged or demented minds too have a sanctity equal to those whose capacities are spared, for they are still ensouled.

But should we uncritically accept Lecky's statement that this "scrupulous care for human life" was the result of "the inestimable value of each immortal soul"? After all, infanticide was widely accepted in Plato's Athens, and specifically defended as a method of population control in his *Republic,* despite the dominant dualistic images of human nature. This single fact suffices to suggest that the Christian affirmation of the moral considerability (significance or standing) of newborns such that their killing was condemned may be the fruit of the New Testament narratives (perhaps the special concern Jesus showed for children, e.g., Mark 10:14-16) and the related ritual of infant baptism. If so, the assertion that Christian inclusivity is nothing other than the archaic vestige of an outdated dualism need not be taken seriously.[9] Inclusivity may have had nothing to do with images of human nature either dualistic or monistic, but may instead have been firmly grounded in *agape* coupled with the *imitatio Christi* (the imitation of Christ). The classical Christian prohibition of infanticide, never fully influential in Europe, cannot be summarily dismissed as dualistic poppycock.[10]

But in fairness to the argument that substance dualism is a source of moral protection, I shall bracket suspicions until later. It is certainly the case that caregivers construe substance dualism as protective, as in the case of David Keck referred to above.

Mount Vernon. To exemplify this construal, I begin with a brief story about my encounter with a Hindu psychologist. In August 1996 an emeritus neurologist and friend, Joseph M. Foley, M.D., invited me to Mount Vernon, Ohio's state institution reserved for those with the most severe forms of retardation and the characteristic accompanying dementing seizures, uncontrollable by drugs lest the patient become stuporous. Once inside the units, I admit to feeling considerable anxiety. I, a "normal" human being, was surrounded by patients, most of them incontinent, incapable of speech, malformed of limb, and in various ways horrifying to behold. But each patient was beautifully cared for by a devoted staff. At lunch in nearby Kenyon, I asked the institution's most experienced psychologist—a Hindu—why she seemed so joyful in her work.

9. Earl E. Shelp, *Born to Die? Deciding the Fate of the Critically Ill Newborn* (New York: Free Press, 1986), 37.
10. Helga Kuhse and Peter Singer, *Should the Baby Live: The Problem of Handicapped Infants* (New York: Oxford University Press, 1985).

"Well you see," she answered, "I believe that each of these patients has an eternal soul, and this requires that they be honored just like us." "So the soul is the great equalizer?" I asked. "Of course, and their souls are expressed in their personalities, which they truly do have once you get to know them. They all have likes and dislikes." This psychologist presumed the existence of a nonmaterial substance underlying the chaos of severe retardation, and this radical dualism inspired her.

In Mount Vernon, I could understand for fleeting moments Friedrich Nietzsche's diatribes against Christian ethics for its foolish commitments to the weakest among human beings.[11] According to the ethics of substance dualism, I am to tell myself that each of these people is a child of a caring Lord *because* within each one is a nonmaterial soul that creates a sphere of categorical equality and inviolability. I am to feel a sense of reluctant awe before even the most debilitated of them.

Still Alive to Me. Another story points out that the idea of an invisible soul can be protective—and even too much so. One of my colleagues in ethics discussions is an orthodox Jewish neurologist who is frequently asked to make in-patient determinations of death by whole brain criteria—that is, irreversible cessation of all functions of the entire brain, including the brain stem. There are many, including myself, who believe this definition of death to be overly conservative, instead opting for a higher brain definition (the irreversible cessation of all cognitive function).[12] Setting aside such controversies—often acrimonious because those who are dead are not afforded the same moral considerability as those who are living—the sensible reality is that even the patient who is dead by whole brain criteria remains warm to the touch with heart beating and lungs filled by ventilator support.

But my orthodox friend will not remove the ventilator from this "dead" human being. "Why?" I queried. "Don't you understand," he responded, his voice getting more emphatic, "according to my faith the patient still has a soul!" I asked the obvious, "Well, when doesn't the patient have a soul?" The response, "Only when there is no more breath." So my friend lets others who do not share his view of the soul remove the mechanical ventilator.

To these others, there is no invisible entity in the patient—no soul—alien to thought and unassimilable by it, nothing that resists inclusion in one real-

11. Friedrich Nietzsche, *Twilight of the Idols/The Anti-Christ,* trans. R. J. Hollingdale (New York: Penguin Books, 1968, [original 1870]).
12. Jeffrey R. Botkin and Stephen G. Post, "Confusion in the Determination of Death: Distinguishing Philosophy from Physiology," *Perspectives in Biology and Medicine,* 16, no. 1 (1992): 129-138.

ity. The brain is dead and no soul hovers unseen under the veneer of neuro-physiology. To them, the idea of applying valuable medical resources to a patient whose neurological activity has entirely ceased is appalling, and the defense of this in the name of an invisible soul can only be seen as archaic. The life-preserving canopy of the soul may benefit people with retardation or demen-tia, but most would not apply it to those who are already legally dead, born with no higher brain (anencephalic), or perhaps in the persistent vegetative state.

Dementia with Bluebird. It has been several years since I visited Mrs. G. She came from an old family of distinction. I visited her in the Alzheimer wing of a good-quality nursing home. She carried an old book under one arm as she walked slowly down the corridor. I greeted Mrs. G. but she said nothing. However, she showed a picture to me and seemed to smile, but I was not quite certain of this. It was a James Audubon print book. They told me she always has it open to the same page and points to the same picture, a bluebird. I guided Mrs. G. to a table and we sat. I asked her how her children were. She did not respond, although she again appeared to smile. She seemed to say "sky," but who knows?

She had a certain graceful charm and a slight smile. They say that habitual mannerisms and demeanor are so ingrained that they are the last things to go. Are these graces just the simulacrum of the self, a kind of deception that sug-gests more of Mrs. G. is there than meets the eye? Slowly Mrs. G. arose and walked away, a little tear in her eye. She seemed to have emotions left, and emo-tions are a part of well-being. The ability to experience emotions has not been lost, and in this sense Mrs. G. was as fully human as anyone else, or even more so. Some people like Mrs. G. who are "written off" as hopelessly demented may, given proper environmental and social cooperation, demonstrate a degree of temporary reversal, and perhaps with the proper creative activities the dete-rioration can be somewhat slowed.[13]

Dementia is both a decline from a previous mental state and a terrible breaking off from the values of dominant culture. The moral task is always to enhance the person with dementia. What cues seem to elicit memory? What music or activity seems to add to well-being? How can capacities still intact be creatively drawn out? How can modalities of touch and voice convey love to the person? Rather than think of people with dementia as out of reach because of forgetfulness, or as unworthy because of cognitive disability, the moral task is to bring them into discourse in creative ways.

But in asserting the moral considerability of the deeply forgetful, I do not rest my case on dualism, but rather on a commitment to the Christian ethic

13. Tom Kitwood, "Towards a Theory of Dementia Care: The Interpersonal Process," *Aging & Society* 13 (1993): 51-67.

of *agape* that makes resurrection-of-a-sort possible through "being with" rather than "doing to."[14] Richard Tarnas summed up the Christian transformation of Western ethics as bringing about "a vital concern for every human soul, no matter what level of intelligence or culture was brought to the spiritual enterprise, and without regard to physical strength or beauty or social status."[15] This is a fair summarization. But arguably this transformation followed from the ethos of bestowed love and from the narrative images of Jesus among the most vulnerable (so beautifully captured in the sketches of Rembrandt), rather than from substance dualism per se.

Overview

In this section, I have attempted to explain how the notion of a nonmaterial soul has been thought to encourage moral inclusivity within the Christian tradition (the idea of the nonmaterial soul creates an aura of mystery that surrounds even the most severely imperiled, from very young to very old, at the edges of life). Yet it is necessary to suggest that the source of this moral idealism and quickening of beneficence may be simply the parable of the good Samaritan, or perhaps the passage "I was sick and you took care of me ... just as you did it to one of the least of these who are members of my family, you did it to me" (Matt. 25).

In summary, the purported moral significance of having an immaterial immortal soul is that it ensures the moral commitment of a good society to protect all human beings, based not on their varied and unreliable capacities but on the basis of a basic human equality. Such equality in moral standing and consideration is easily broken by the power of the cognitively privileged as they demand additional privileges in what I have called a "hypercognitive society."[16] The privileged are prone to create excessively rationalistic criteria for moral inclusion under the protective umbrella of "do no harm," and are confounded by loyalty to those whose minds have faded. If the idea of a nonmaterial soul has contributed to the course of Western moral life, as has been suggested, there are many examples of its contribution, as well, to all that must be considered discriminatory and exclusionary.

14. G. D. Weaver, "Senile Dementia and Resurrection Theology," *Theology Today* 42, no. 4 (1986): 444-456.
15. Richard Tarnas, *The Passion of the Western Mind: Understanding the Ideas That Have Shaped Our World View* (New York: Ballantine Books, 1991), 116.
16. Stephen G. Post, *The Moral Challenge of Alzheimer Disease* (Baltimore: John Hopkins University Press, 1995).

ADVERSE MORAL CONSEQUENCES OF
NONMATERIAL SOULS

The dualism of Plato is not that of Descartes, and certainly not that of Aristotle, Thomas Aquinas, and the scholastic tradition, for which the soul is the substantial form of the body rather than a separate entity or substance. The dualism that I most associate here with adverse moral consequences can plausibly be derived from Plato and Descartes, but not from Aristotle and Aquinas.[17]

Is substance dualism the cause of patriarchy, slavery, the debasement of sex and body, and callous speciesism? Or is it the other way around? My claim is not for a clearly causal relationship between substance dualism and these regrettable realities, for surely history is more complex in the etiology of wrongfulness. It suffices here to note a certain affinity between ideas and social practices.

Whether or not substance dualism has been a seedbed of oppression, Christian inclusivity has certainly been undermined in some instances by use of the analogy of dualism and the dualistic account of human nature to distinguish between superior (soul, male, free) and inferior human beings (body, women, slave). Substance dualism has served as an ideological support for the exclusionary inclination ("might makes right") to place categories of human beings outside of ordinary restraints on wanton infliction of harm and on coercion.

Such limits are necessary for people to live together in peace, avoiding what one philosopher dubbed "the war of all against all." Within the contractarian tradition of ethics, simply stated, people agree to adhere to limits on harm because this is to everyone's enlightened self-interest.[18] All religious ethical systems assert the wrongness of harm with the help of a morally minimalist negative golden rule: Do not do unto others as you would not have them do unto you. Such a rule does not require any moral idealism (beneficence); instead it prescribes a restraining of our destructive tendencies.

The negative version of the golden rule is purely formal and only exists in the context of particular moral systems that include or exclude certain categories of human beings. The principle of nonmaleficence provides a protective moral umbrella that is only as inclusive as a culture permits. Religion at its best encourages all-inclusive regard for the neighbor; at its worst, it passionately divides "them" from "us."

The width and depth of that protection is shaped by some theory of the human self that affords (or diminishes) moral considerability. No contingency

17. See Murphy, chapter 1.
18. Bernard Gert, *Morality: A New Justification of the Moral Rules* (New York: Oxford University Press, 1988).

of principle is involved (i.e., nonmaleficence appears universal), but "contingency of value" based on an interpretation of the worth of a self-appraised positively or negatively. The moral agent cannot escape interpretation: scientists interpret data, literary critics provide interpretations of texts, human beings interpret one another's remarks. Interpretation is "perhaps the most basic act of human thinking; indeed, existing itself may be said to be a constant process of interpretation."[19]

In interpreting the moral considerability or worth of the other, metaphors often have a powerful effect on the listener, for people tend to remember striking analogies. New analogies expose what has not been considered and uproot dogmatic mind-sets. New analogies, as much as old ones, require evaluation and must be scrutinized, for an analogy can lead to adverse consequences. Human beings think and behave in accordance with tacit or hidden analogies and metaphors. Worldview and metaphor become intertwined and are reflections of each other. It is generally easier to scrutinize the metaphors and analogies of cultures other than our own because they leap out at us as odd.[20] But we must equally scrutinize our own metaphors and analogies, because these define our interpretation of the world and of people in it. Few analogies have been more forceful in shaping Western moral history than that of physical body and nonmaterial soul.

Slavery

A major justification for slavery emerged from a substance-dualistic conception of the human person. Plato, for example, likened the body to the slave of the soul. The relationship of body and soul informed a political apologetic for slavery.[21] The master-slave relationship was couched in a cosmology perceived as a similar dualism (intelligent divine primary cause and irrational mechanical cause). Thus, slavery was supported by an appeal to natural law—that is, because the soul has total dominion over the body, the master should have total dominion over the slave.[22] Aristotle, despite his departure from Plato's substance dualism, still followed Plato in rationalizing slavery by showing its consistency with the order of being.

Suffice it to say that Christianity, with its various forms of dualism, did not condemn slavery until well into the nineteenth century, when Quaker reform-

---

19. R. E. Palmer, *Hermeneutics* (Chicago: Northwestern University Press, 1969), 15.
20. Wayne C. Booth, *The Company We Keep: An Ethics of Fiction* (Chicago: University of Chicago Press, 1988).
21. Gregory Vlastos, "Slavery in Plato's Republic," *The Philosophical Review* 50 (1941): 289–304.
22. David Brion Davis, *The Problem of Slavery in Western Culture* (Ithaca, N.Y.: Cornell University Press, 1966), 69.

ers began to assert the egalitarian social implications of a common inner light within all people.[23] Again, this is not a causal assertion. Arguably, substance dualism was merely the ideological "superstructure" that resulted from the force of "foundational" economic oppression. This perhaps explains why Aristotle, who rejected substance dualism, nevertheless was willing in strained manner to continue the analogy of soul-body and master-slave. It is enough to state the "elective affinity" (Max Weber's term) between a slave economy and a substance dualistic view of the human; together, they undermined the agapic inclusivity of Christian ethics.

Denying the Pleasure Principle

A leading Roman Catholic Christian ethicist, Lisa Sowle Cahill, has recently described the relation of dualism to the denial of pleasure and intimacy as values in married love.[24]

Cahill begins with a cautionary note: the beneficial affirmation of companionship and pleasure in contemporary sexual ethics should not forget the moral meaning of parenthood and kinship, despite suspicions of a historical emphasis in early Christianity on procreation as the sole good of marriage.

The notion that sex is not to be associated with pleasure emerged most forcefully with Augustine, who in defending marriage against Gnostic denunciation could ultimately only defend the sex act as a demeaning and irrational necessity for the sake of continuing the species. Throughout Augustine's influential writings, a neo-Platonic substance dualism encourages the notion that the body is a mere hindrance to the spiritual contemplation of God. Cahill repudiates dualism, then, for its denial of the value of pleasure in physical intimacy; human flourishing depends on the values of the legitimacy of pleasure and intimacy in sexual relations. This certainly was the ethos of the Old Testament.

But in Christianity, pleasure and intimacy in sexual relations were associated with the irrational and subservient body, with which women, too, were particularly associated. For example, the *Malleus Maleficarum* (or "Hammer against Witches"), a handbook of late medieval inquisitors that resulted in the torture of many women, states that only women could be witches because their irrational and unruly passions led them to physical intimacies with the devil.[25] In essence, the devil attacks through the door of the body to defile the soul,

23. Ibid., chapter 7.
24. Lisa Sowle Cahill, *Sex, Gender, and Christian Ethics* (Cambridge: Cambridge University Press, 1996).
25. See Elizabeth Clark and Herbert Richardson, eds., *Women and Religion* (New York: Harper and Row, 1977).

and it is women who make this possible. Seduced by the devil in fornication, they in turn seduce spiritual men.[26] The irrationality of women associated analogically with their bodiliness—in contrast to the spirituality of males—has its modern ideological place in Freudian thought, which understood women to be especially prone to hysteria, mental illness, and irrationality.

The analogy to soul and body is, then, complicit in the sexual alienation of early Christianity. As a harsh critic of this alienation, James B. Nelson, points out:

> The historical roots of this sexual alienation are not difficult to find. They emerged as two intertwining dualisms. Spiritualistic dualism (spirit over body, mind over matter) emerged with power in late Hellenistic Greece and made a lasting impact upon the Christian church. Championed by Neoplatonists, the dualism viewed the immortal spirit as a temporary prisoner in a mortal, corruptible body. The good life and, indeed, salvation itself required escape from flesh into spirit.[27]

The patriarchal dualism of man over woman "became inextricably intertwined as men assumed to themselves superiority in spirit and reason while identifying woman with body, earthiness, irrationality, and instability."[28] Nelson encourages a greater appreciation for the incarnation of Christ and the divine gift of sexuality. The impact of dualism has been an unduly morbid assessment of the divine good of sexuality, issuing in celibacy and various extreme ascetic tendencies. Yet Nelson departs from traditional Christian ethics when he indicates that in some cases marital fidelity is fully consistent with nonexclusive sexual intimacies.

It is remarkable that any appreciation of marriage and embodiment has managed to survive in the dualistic tradition. The early church was highly ambivalent about marriage—a suboptimal state of being when compared with celibacy—and even went so far as to counsel the remarkable phenomenon of celibate marriages. Marriage was interpreted as a good by Augustine, but sex was always, at best, morally ambiguous. Given the tension between the affirmation of marriage and the degradation of sex, the celibate marriage was perhaps an inevitable ideal.

26. Susan Moller Okin, *Women in Western Political Thought* (Princeton, N.J.: Princeton University Press, 1979).

27. James B. Nelson, *Between Two Gardens: Reflections on Sexuality and Religious Experience* (New York: Pilgrim Press, 1983), 6.

28. Ibid., 7.

Patriarchy and Marriage

Cahill also emphasizes that human flourishing depends on the equality of the sexes, male and female. Christian ethics, she contends, demands a reordering of relationships of dominance. She turns to the oppressive nature of purity laws and of gender hierarchy within the ancient patriarchal family. The early Christians were engaged in conflict with the Roman family, especially with the unlimited legal power of the husband and father over wife and children *(patria potestas)*. For this reason, Christianity downplayed "not only procreation but family ties in any form (Mark 3:31, Luke 19:29 and 8:21)."[29] It also "mildly" advocated equality in marriage. Its idealization of celibacy was driven then by "commitment to communal solidarity and a rejection of the hierarchical and state-controlled functions of the patriarchal family."[30] What of parenthood? It is given little or no attention in early Christianity because in the patriarchal family it perpetuated dominion. Abstinence meant freedom of the soul; but this was achieved at "the denigration of sex, marriage, and parenthood."[31] Cahill indicates that Roman Catholicism's current dualistic liability is its lack of "demonstrated commitment to the equality and well-being of women."[32]

Over and over again the Western Christian justification for patriarchal dominance appeals analogically to substance dualism. Christian ethicists have over the last two decades begun the effort to rescue from dualism the gospel ideal of marriages of true equality, true faithfulness, and *agape*.[33]

In a nonconfessional and impartial summary of the trajectory of Christian tradition, historian of religions Geoffrey Parrinder has written that, "Every religion has some distinctive characteristics and Christianity is the only major religion which from the outset has seemed to insist upon monogamy."[34] He points out that Jesus' teachings on marriage, relying on Genesis, provide a "high but difficult morality, and much has been made of these verses in the later Church's rigorous attitudes toward divorce."[35] This rigor is demanding, "but in this instance Jesus seems to have been looking to the purpose of creation, and he took the divine pattern of the creation of man and woman in singleness and unity. In such a context, for a married man or woman to take

29. Cahill, *Sex, Gender and Christian Ethics,* 151.
30. Ibid., 152.
31. Ibid., 172.
32. Ibid., 256.
33. Stephen G. Post, *Spheres of Love: Toward a New Ethic of the Family* (Dallas: Southern Methodist University Press, 1994).
34. Geoffrey Parrinder, *Sex in the World's Religions* (New York: Oxford University Press, 1980), 202.
35. Ibid., 208.

another partner would be against the unity of their creation."[36] To deter the violation of this unity, even the wayward imagination must be controlled. Parrinder concludes, "The unity of man and wife in 'one flesh,' commanded by Jesus and referred back to the original action of God at creation, seems to require a single lifelong union. Paul repeated this doctrine. . . ."[37] While this was true of Judaism as well, argues Parrinder, polygamy was nevertheless tolerated until the eleventh century C.E.

Few passages have been more influential on the history of Western marriage than Genesis 2:24, which decrees that a man shall leave father and mother to cleave to his wife that they might become "one flesh." In the New Testament, the appeal to this passage is definitive (see Matt. 19:3-9; Mark 10:3-9; Eph. 5:31). Jesus appears to have found in Gen. 2:24 an authoritative basis for monogamous marriage. Thus marriage circumscribes the command to procreate in Genesis 1:28.

The firmness of Jesus' appeal suggests significance consistent with his concern for the well-being of children, so evident in his blessing of them despite the protest of his adult followers (Mark 10:14-16), and with his concern for women, long subjected to the patriarchal double standard and arbitrary divorce.

Regrettably, Paul's eschatological ambivalence about the responsibilities of marriage and family was misinterpreted by the early church and used to defend dualism. As David G. Hunter writes, it was "read by later Christians in a context no longer troubled by the impending eschaton. Shorn of their apocalyptic significance, Paul's views took on a rather different meaning: marriage itself came to be regarded as a state inferior to that of celibacy."[38] This misinterpretation of Paul is surprising because later New Testament writings continued Paul's resistance to the demands of ascetic Christians by providing a detailed marriage ethic modeled after patriarchal Roman household codes (Col. 3:18—4:1; 1 Peter 2:17—3:9; 1 Tim. 2:8-15; 6:1-10; Titus 2:1-10).

Dualists tended to deny the value of marriage because of its embodied quality. Occasionally a former ascetic would embrace the ideal of marriage in enthusiastic terms. In 390 C.E. Jovinian, for example, argued against the exaltation of virginity. He drew on Genesis 1-3 and the statements of Jesus confirming these passages. The opposition from the arch-dualist Jerome was fierce and immediate. But even Jerome's *Against Jovinian*, for all its exaltation of virginity and negative images of married women, does not utterly condemn

36. Ibid., 208.
37. Ibid., 215.
38. David G. Hunter, "Introduction," in *Marriage in the Early Church*, trans. and ed. Hunter (Minneapolis: Fortress Press, 1992), 5.

marriage.[39] The late historian John Boswell ignores many of the theological sources affirming marriage, but he does capture the impact of dualism that resulted in early and medieval Christianity being "overwhelmingly ambivalent" about marriage.[40] Space does not permit a full exploration of the tension between dualism and the Christian faith with respect to both the goodness of marriage, and the goodness of equality within marriage. It has taken nearly 2,000 years to cut these Gordian knots.

The Moral Meaning of Deconstruction

In this section I have pointed to some negative consequences of dualism. The fact that a tradition with a dualistic theory of human nature has a paradoxical moral legacy, one radically egalitarian and inclusive, the other radically aristocratic and exclusive, suggests that dualism contains no single moral message. Instead, it is used to justify antithetical moral and sociopolitical constructs; its "meaning is in its use" (Ludwig Wittgenstein's phrase). By now the reader begins to see that a theory of human nature can be exceedingly controversial and easily manipulated. This leads me to the following broader discussion of ethics, power, and portrait painting.

Theories of human nature are politically powerful because they inform our understanding of relations with nature, human nature, each other, and God. We move from a description of that which is essential to human nature to a prescription about what human beings ought to do. The caution is that theorists read into a portrait of human nature just those elements that they desire in order to rationalize a particular social order. Usually, theories of human nature are value-laden. Prominent in such theories is a normative or evaluative component imposed on a description of human nature. For example, it is no accident that Plato's dualism was articulated in a polis that condoned slavery.

In reaction to the political origins of such theories, modern scholars ask whether it is possible to find qualities that characterize human beings universally. Postmodern deconstructionist writers such as Jacques Derrida and Michel Foucault reject any essentialist theory of human nature because they believe that such theories are typically propounded by those with their own political agenda. He or she who paints the portrait wins the language game and achieves dominion. Better, they insist, for the purposes of freedom against dominance, to acknowledge the impossibility of a universally valid portrait.

---

39. Jerome, "Against Jovinian," in Clark and Richardson, eds, *Women and Religion* 61–68, 61.

40. John Boswell, *Same-Sex Unions in Premodern Europe* (New York: Vintage Books, 1994), 111.

Animal welfarists point with a similar suspicion at Descartes, whose view of souls (active, immaterial, and immortal) and bodies (unthinking, passive, mechanical, and finite), each coincident with a distinct sphere of reality, led him to see animals as mere stimulus-response mechanisms. This justifies the exclusion of animals from moral consideration. Later Cartesians defended vivisection, equating the howling of cut dogs to the squeaking of machinery.

Certainly racism and sexism, and for some speciesism, are evils justified by (if not caused by) an appeal to dualist human nature in and of itself. It should come as no surprise that as these "isms" are rejected, so is their dualistic underpinning.

The substance dualistic view may fade quickly not just because it has such an ambiguous moral history, but because it makes it difficult to take seriously the information produced by behavioral genetics. If, following Descartes, the body and soul are two distinct entities and substances, then the soul cannot be influenced by genetic factors. But if the behaviors commonly associated with the soul are in fact a function of the body and of genetics, then it is an error to think that altering said behaviors is beyond scientific reach.[41]

Then the immediate question is whether such genetic-monistic views threaten human equality, since some individuals have different and perhaps "better" genes than others. Genetic elitism has often been successfully countered by appeals to that which is entirely beyond gene and body, thereby assuring a radical equality merely camouflaged by external differences in everything from intelligence to height. However, "criticizing bodiless conceptions of equality does not mean abandoning equal respect."[42] Christians can be outraged at social injustice and inequality based on the belief that every human being is equally the beloved child of God while recognizing that every person is also genetically unique.

ENVOI: CHRISTIAN ETHICS IN
NONREDUCTIVE PHYSICALISM

In the final analysis, it seems doubtful that the setting aside of dualism poses any significant threat to Christian ethics, and such a move may even allow Christian ethics to be more Christian. Presumably nondualist theologians have and can remain within the domain of Christian moral thought. Even the most incapacitated human being deserves our full consideration not because he or she has a nonmaterial soul, but because of a common Christian narrative that bids us to love even the most devastated and imperiled neighbor.

41. Erik Parens, "Taking Behavioral Genetics Seriously," *Hastings Center Report* 26, no. 4 (July–August 1996): 13-18.
42. Ibid., 17.

The radical inclusivity of Christian neighbor love is the fruit of scriptural narrative and community. While the Greek ideal of friendship constituted an aristocratic closed circle, friendship within the context of the New Testament narrative was opened to outsiders. Paul J. Wadell makes this point eloquently:

> What friendship sets out is one thing if the friends aim to secure excellence in Athens, another thing if they aim for the Kingdom of God. Part of the reason philia is so often overruled by agape is that it is interpreted apart from the narrative that allows it to be integral to the Christian life. . . . Friendship both born from and seeking the Kingdom may be exactly the kind of love which enables us ultimately to be friends of the world. In that case, we do not leave preferential love behind, we extend its domain.[43]

Agape, universal and fully inclusive love, presses concentric circles of preferential love to an ever-widening scope. Partiality is universalized so as to become impartial. This movement outward to the neighbor is shaped by stories of Jesus caring for the outcast.

In other words, it is not a view of the nonmaterial soul that shapes and drives Christian ethics. Instead, the image of Christ's love properly appreciated will hopefully permeate any anthropology with the power of its insistence on radical inclusivity. Dualist views of human nature have proved particularly difficult for Christian inclusivity, for the love of Christ must struggle against the sealed circles of moral considerability created by the dualist's analogical imagination. It is the story of Christianity that strongly demands solicitude for all, including those with retardation and dementia.[44]

Sacred Equality. A nonreductive physicalism can sustain the Christian moral norm of the sanctity of life because each human being is equally a child of God and the recipient of the Lord's love and grace. The worth of the person is still to be defined in terms of a graced relation to God, and is therefore not subject to the vicissitudes of utilitarian calculations (person A is only of worth based on social contribution Y to the greatest happiness of the greatest number). The transcendent and eternal value of each individual remains utterly equal. The "point of contact" between the person and God is in no way compromised if grounded in neurological substrate rather than nonmaterial spirit. Further, even in those with severely diminished capacity, we can never falsify the claim that a graceful God remains present with them to the very end.

43. Paul J. Wadell, *Friendship and the Moral Life* (Notre Dame, Ind.: University of Notre Dame Press, 1989), 73.
44. See Stanley Hauerwas, *Suffering Presence: Theological Reflections on Medicine, the Mentally Handicapped, and the Church* (Notre Dame, Ind.: University of Notre Dame Press, 1986).

Agape. Neither does a nonreductive physicalism compromise the loyal stead-fast love that Christians call *agape.* This love is one of bestowal rather than of appraisal. In an appraisive love, the person is loved based on the possession of certain attractive qualities; in the love of bestowal, the person is loved simply because he or she is loved by God.

This love is manifested in solicitude (anxious concern) for the welfare of self and others, and usually in a delight in the presence of the other. Love is the abrogation of the self-centered tendency. Many partial descriptions of *agape* can be combined to suggest that, building on a foundation of solicitude, love includes joy, compassion, commitment, and respect; love rejoices in the exis-tence, growth, and presence of the other; love responds supportively to suffer-ing, although present in the absence of suffering; love is loyal and patient; love honors the other's freedom, integrity, and individuality while encouraging the other's good.

Ultimately this love is sustained by the conviction that at the center of the universe there exists a caring God, revealed in the love of Jesus toward even the least among us. The power of this love is in no way limited by our efforts to paint a portrait of the human that leaves aside the nonmaterial.

Chapter Ten

Conclusion: Reconciling Scientific and Biblical Portraits of Human Nature

Warren S. Brown

SCIENCE AND FAITH

Integrating and reconciling the truth claims made by Christian theology with new theories in science is always challenging. If viewed as mutually exclusive alternative explanations of similar phenomena, the situation is irreconcilable. But even when viewed as complementary and potentially reconcilable realms of description, discussions often become discordant. Competitive claims of authority and a certain lack of humility regarding the limits of disciplines prevent dialogue that might be mutually informative. Both sides tend to escalate arguments by overestimating what is at stake. Those who would defend Christian doctrine exaggerate the impact that a scientific discovery or theory might have on the central tenets of the faith. Similarly those who argue the side of science are frequently too quick to presume the irrevocable damage that particular scientific data might do to a religious perspective, feeding the defensiveness of those of faith. However, never have the central and important tenets of the Christian faith been damaged, disproved, or significantly changed by looking honestly, humbly, and intently at new advances in science, without dodging their meaning or blushing at their veracity.[1]

An example of the discordant dance of faith and science can be found in the conflict between medieval dogma regarding the correct geography of the

---

1. David C. Lindberg and Ronald L. Numbers, eds., *God and Nature: Historical Essays on the Encounter between Christianity and Science* (Berkeley and Los Angeles: University of California Press, 1986).

world and advances of Renaissance geography and cartography. Substantial progress in the understanding of geography had been made by the ancients. Greek scholars of the fifth century B.C.E. had already determined that the world must be a sphere, and Eratosthenes had calculated its circumference with reasonable accuracy. Unfortunately, all of this was forgotten in the "Europe-wide phenomenon of scholarly amnesia"[2] that afflicted Western culture during the Middle Ages. Medieval world maps were flat "wheel maps," also called "O-T" maps. These maps presented the world as a flat disk (an "O"), with Jerusalem at the center. The Mediterranean was set on the vertical diagonal of the disk that formed the upright part of a "T" (or cross). The Danube and Nile rivers were depicted as flowing in a straight line and forming the arms. Around the edges was the "Ocean Sea." Within these maps where located many non-geographic places that were of theological significance, such as the kingdoms of Gog and Magog, the Garden of Eden, and Paradise. "Designed to express what orthodox Christians were expected to *believe,* they were not so much maps of knowledge as maps of Scriptural dogma. The very simplicity that offends the geographer testifies to the simple clarity of Christian belief."[3]

Although these medieval maps were geographical caricatures, they symbolized important aspects of Christian faith. Thus, these maps were not without a measure of truth, but the truth was primarily theological, not geographical. However, in the Renaissance, the geography of the ancients was rediscovered, confirmed, and extended by the explorers of the fifteenth and sixteenth centuries. Development of a better geography of the world and increasingly better methods for accurate cartography challenged the medieval O-T maps with new data. When theological constraints on the form and content of maps were eventually lifted, previously imagined negative consequences to the central tenets of faith failed to materialize. There was no inherent incompatibility between a science of geography and a Christian understanding of the nature of the physical world. Thus, the church ran no real risk in looking openly and clearly at the amassing information about world geography. Nothing critical or fundamental was lost, many things were better understood.

This book has attempted to examine, as openly and clearly as possible, the portraits of human nature painted by the rapidly accumulating data in the human biological and social sciences, and to consider this information in the light of a Christian view of philosophy, theology, sacred Scriptures, and ethics. Such an open and encompassing view of the scientific data suggests that our "map" of human nature may need some modification and adjustment, but in

2. Daniel Boorstin, *The Discoverers: A History of Man's Search to Know His World and Himself* (New York: Vintage, 1985), 100.
3. Ibid., 101.

ways that (as we believe these essays have demonstrated) will do no damage to the tenets of faith. Christians run no real risk to their faith by looking with unguarded, but discerning, eyes at a modern biological and social science account of human nature. Indeed, theological benefits may accrue from a hard look at the scientific data if, in the process, we discern more clearly the critical and the not-so-critical aspects of our Christian anthropological dogma.

The authors of this book have attempted to present a consistent picture at least as regards nonreductive physicalism (i.e., seeing the person as a unitary physical entity without a separate nonphysical soul, but not reducible to "nothing but" the physiology of cells or the chemistry of molecules). Our descriptions of scientific progress in understanding human nature have attempted to demonstrate that a physicalist mapping of human nature need not contradict fundamental truths of Christian faith and theology. With regard to philosophy, theology, biblical studies, and ethics, we have attempted to demonstrate that physicalism can be sustained without contradicting the central doctrines and beliefs of the Christian faith. In many cases, we have found physicalism to be more compatible with biblical faith than dualism.

NONREDUCTIVE HUMAN SCIENCE

One contribution of these essays has been to present a nonreductive view of the current state of the scientific portrait of human nature from several critical fields. The sciences of human nature generally have advanced by the demonstration that a higher-level, more complex capacity depends in some specifiable way upon lower-level, more general physical (biological) processes. However, we have attempted to demonstrate that embodiment of a human ability or function within a biological, neurological, or cognitive process does not imply that higher-level explanations can be replaced entirely by accounts in terms of lower-level phenomena. For example, the dependence of human mental activity on underlying neurobiological processes does not imply that the processes of our thinking and deciding are epiphenomenal illusions without real causal efficacy. The important role in human behavior of such phenomena as free will, conscious agency, and personal responsibility are not diminished or altered by the recognition of the neurobiological substrates of consciousness and thought. A physicalist view of human nature does not lead inevitably to the conclusion that people are nothing but the product of organic chemistry and, ultimately, molecular physics.

Debate over reductionism is currently raging within science itself.[4] Those in favor of reductionism point out how fruitful this form of research and

4. Nigel Williams, "Biologists Cut Reductionist Approach Down to Size," *Science* 227 (1997): 476-477.

thinking has been over the past several hundred years. Those who argue in favor of a nonreductionist point of view would contend that either or both of the following are true:

1. The fruitfulness of reductionism is limited since the human mind will not be able to grasp the ultimate physical/molecular explanation of any complex phenomenon, particularly those involving the human mind.
2. New principles of explanation emerge at higher, more complex levels of organization that are not evident in the laws governing more molecular phenomena.[5]

For example, new principles emerge in neural networks that are not relevant to an understanding of single nerve cells. Complex learned motor behavior, involving the interaction of large numbers of neural networks, demands explanatory concepts not available in an understanding of individual neural networks. Understanding human language and complex thought demands principles not apparent in an understanding of complex motor behavior, and so on. Thus, a nonreductionist view of science such as we have taken in this book is not just a convenient position marketed by those who wish to defend a religious point of view in a scientific age, but increasingly seems to be demanded by science itself.

Evolution—Biology and Human Culture

The viewpoint of physicalism raises the issue of phylogenetic relationships and evolutionary processes in the creation of humankind. Ayala summarized the evolutionary process as it is currently understood, emphasizing the fact that the development in modern humans of a large and complex brain allowed for a process of cultural evolution, which can be considered to have transcended biological evolution in shaping human nature. Ayala argued that the capacity for ethics, for example, is dependent on an ability to anticipate the consequences of one's behavior, the ability to make value judgments, and the ability to choose alternate behaviors. Ayala would part ways with much of sociobiology by maintaining that the norms of ethics and morality are not themselves a product of biology but emerge in cultural development.

Here can be seen an example of a nonreductive theory of the origins of human traits within the science of evolutionary biology. A relatively small but critical change in physiology (i.e., the development of a large and complex cerebral cortex) resulted in the emergence of rather massive differences in human behavior that are evident in the development of culture (language, lit-

5. Thomas Nagel, as quoted in ibid., 277, 476.

erature, art, science, technology, moral/ethical sensitivities, and religion). However, the processes of cultural development have so transcended the neurobiological evolution that allowed them that it becomes impossible to imagine human culture to be nothing but neurobiology and genetics. Human culture is subserved by the enhanced functions of the physical brain, but it cannot be reduced to the operation of these physical processes.

The question then arises as to how and why culture developed the specific norms, ethics, morals and religious perspectives that exist. Here the Christian sees the role of God's progressive revelation to humankind as constantly influencing the development of human culture and community such as to engender a perspective that understands events from his perspective. The biblical view of cultural evolution would be that God, as creator, participates in the events of human history such as to influence the direction of ethical, moral, and religious development. God-in-dialogue— that is, God in personal relatedness—participates in directing (and redeeming) the human process of cultural development, just as he directed and works to redeem physical and biological evolution.

To many Christians, a nonreductionist evolutionary explanation of human origins may still sound "godless" and incompatible with the Genesis account: "Then God said, 'Let us make man in our own image, after our likeness' . . . so God created man in his own image." How can two such different accounts of the origins of human nature, the evolutionary and the biblical, be simultaneously true? As both a Christian and a scientist working in human neuropsychology, I am helped by two concepts. One important concept is that of differences in space-time perspectives. Evolution speaks about processes and causal chains of event apparent within space and time, while creation describes what has been revealed about the causes and meanings of events from the perspective of God who is not limited to our cosmological space and time. A second helpful concept is that of the supervenience of higher-level explanations over lower-level ones.[6] While physical or biological explanations may be complete at their own level of analysis and understanding, they do not capture all of the relationships, causes, and meanings of events that can be represented by higher-level explanations. Thus, explanations offered at a higher level may supervene over lower-level descriptions without the lower-level explanations being considered false, irrelevant, or unimportant.

When considering both differences in perspective and supervenience, one sees that there is confusion and misconceptions on both sides of the evolution-creationism debate. The biblical fundamentalist is correct in understanding the Genesis account as a description of God's work in the creation of humankind

---

6. See Murphy, chapter 6 of this volume, section entitled, "Defeating Causal Reductionism."

as seen from a perspective outside of space and time (but revealed by the creator to his creatures), and thus, as a supervenient explanation. However, the biblical fundamentalist is misguided in presuming that such truth is necessarily contradictory to scientific statements about the processes of creation within our space and time. Similarly, the evolutionary fundamentalists may (or may not) have their facts relatively straight regarding the physical processes of biological evolution. Nevertheless, they would be misguided and confused in presuming that such scientific theory and data are in any way contradictory to statements made about the work of a creator as seen from a perspective outside of the space-time events of the physical and biological universe. While the "fundamentalist" label has typically been reserved for the creationist, statements such as those quoted in a recent issue of *Science* illustrate the existence of similarly misguided scientific fundamentalism. "Study of something as simple as a chicken's egg can topple 'every church or temple in the world'" (Denis Diderot, 1769). "The space available for God appears to be shrinking" (Leon Lederman). Or, "Only the scientifically illiterate accept the 'why' question where living creatures are concerned" (Richard Dawkins). [7]

Genetics and Determinism

The role of genetic influences in the determination of the physical and psychological makeup of each person is an issue of current public concern. We regularly read in scholarly journals or hear in the news that another physical or mental trait or disorder has been "linked to" a particular gene. In the realm of human behavior, various forms of psychosis, a tendency for violent behavior, alcoholism and addiction disorders, and sexual preference (to name but a few) have all been suggested to be genetically "determined." Elving Anderson discussed the implications of such statements. He pointed out that genes themselves are subject to regulatory processes and thus the pathway from gene to human trait is more complex and less predictable than has been assumed. Genes do not rigidly define a trait, but define a "reaction range" of probabilities of traits or behaviors developing. In fact, the primary information about the likelihood of a genetic influence on a behavioral trait is never an absolute one-to-one correspondence but rather a somewhat greater-than-chance probability of the trait or behavior occurring given the same (or similar) genetic makeup. There is always variability in outcome that is not accounted for even by the combination of the same genetic endowment and the same environmental influences. In a review of twin studies, Thomas Bouchard has written, "The results of twin studies, I believe, refute biological and environmental

7. Gregg Easterbrook, "Science and God: A Warming Trend?" *Science* 277 (1997): 890-893.

determinism. They do not negate the effect of the environment on behavior, nor do they over-glorify the role of genetics. They account for the uniqueness of each of us and remind us that we are an integral part of a complex biological world and not apart from it."[8]

The recent success in cloning animals raises certain issues of the genetics of humanness. Would cloning of a human entail continuation of the person from whom the genetic material originated? Certainly not—no more so than identical twins could ever be considered the same person. "In spite of the unconscious urgings of their identical genomes, in spite of being raised together and schooled together, identical twins still respond differently to many items on our [personality] questionnaires. And those differences are only the tip of the iceberg. Beneath them flow shadowy memories and feelings, experiences and dreams that no investigator can sound, much less reproduce. Selves, unlike cells, can never be cloned."[9]

Therefore, genetics cannot be seen to provide much grist for the determinist/reductionist mill. Genetic codes set a *range* of *probable* physical or behavioral expression; the genes themselves, as well as the behaviors and traits they influence, are subject to regulation and modulation by the environment and by events of personal history, including the top-down influences of personal choice. For example, imagine an individual who chooses to try a potentially addictive drug. Further imagine that the drug use results in a change in the pattern of expression of genetic information within the neurobiology of the individual, resulting in expression of previously dormant genetic tendencies to addiction. In this case, an explanation for the behavior cannot be entirely genetic (i.e., cannot be said to be nothing but genetics), but must include the top-down influences of personal choice. Although genetics plays some role in human behavior, and the events of personal choice are subserved by a neurobiological system, when focus is on behavioral outcome, reduction of explanations to the level of the genetic cannot be either adequate or entirely complete.

Brain Damage and the Mind
Over the past 150 or so years, evidence for the tight coupling between brain function and human behavior has come from increasing knowledge regarding the behavioral outcomes of focal brain damage. The past decade has seen a dramatic acceleration of this knowledge based upon the new technology of functional imaging of brain processes during specific cognitive states or behavioral activities. Jeeves reviewed this ever-tightening link that is being established between brain function and complex human thought and behavior.

8. Thomas Bouchard, "Whenever the Twain Shall Meet," *The Sciences* 37 (1997): 57.
9. Ibid., 54.

The unity of the body-mind-soul is clear in clinical neuropsychological phenomena such as the moral and religious breakdown in some individuals with Alzheimer's disease, or the hyperreligiosity of some individuals with temporal lobe epilepsy, or spiritual depression secondary to physical disorders. Thus, the subjective experiences of soul and spirit rest deeply in the functions of the physical brain, which abides by physical/biological laws.

Does this make our behavior determined? Are our deciding, intending, willing, and even religious believing merely an illusion? As with genetics, changes in brain function associated with neurological damage or disease can only be said to influence the range of potential behaviors available to the individual. While remembering may become more difficult, some memories survive. Although planning of behavior may be deficient, behavior is seldom totally chaotic. While brain damage or dysfunction may enhance or diminish the probability of various religious or moral behaviors, there remains a strong influence of the person's premorbid religious life influencing what is said and done. Though increasingly severe brain damage may progressively restrict the range of behavioral possibilities such as to make the person appear strongly "determined," only in the most severely brain damaged (i.e., nearly comatose) does one find a sense of inevitability in the patient's behavior.

In fact, there is a serious logical flaw in the presumption that a mechanistic brain presumes complete determinism of thought and behavior. Donald MacKay reminds us that consideration of a prediction regarding the future state of one's own brain significantly changes the very mechanism about which the prediction was made. Therefore, even if our brains were as determined as clockwork, when faced with a prediction regarding our future, logically we would be equally correct to either believe or to disbelieve any such deterministic predictions. Deterministic predictions of our future behavior hold no claim to truth until such time as we make up our mind. Our future is logically up to us to decide.[10] MacKay's argument is consistent with what is currently being appreciated regarding top-down causation in neuropsychology.

The interpretations of the results of modern behavioral and cognitive neurobiology have ranged widely. Nobel laureate neurophysiologist John Eccles favored dualism since he could not see any other alternative explanation for mind other than the postulation of a nonmaterial mind or soul. Radical reductionism and determinism were espoused by physiologist and Nobel laureate Francis Crick for whom mind was definitely nothing but the phenomena of molecular biology. The emergentist view of neurophysiologist Roger Sperry (also a Nobel prize winner) is positioned somewhere in the middle. Jeeves argues for physicalism (monism) with a necessary *dualism of aspect*. Although it

10. Donald M. MacKay, *Behind the Eye* (Oxford: Basil Blackwell, 1991).

is unnecessary to posit the existence of a nonphysical mind or soul, two views of mental phenomena must be maintained and kept distinct—one is a view of the neurobiology of the physical system; the other, a view of an efficacious subjective mental life. Any mixture or attempt to interchange descriptors from these two views of cognitive events only serves to obscure the meaning of the respective data and diminish understanding. Both Jeeves and MacKay consider the aspect of subjective experience to be "ontologically prior" in that it is the thing we know about first and most inescapably.

Human Intelligence and Relatedness
If the line between the physical and the spiritual is not drawn between humans and lower animals, but between humans and God, what has become of the soul? In what ways might a neurobiologically embodied center of consciousness be considered spiritual? How do we understand the "soul" language of Scripture and Christian tradition? I attempted in my chapter to take the argument of nonreductive physicalism somewhat further by proposing that soul is a capacity for a particular realm of experience rather than a nonphysical essence inhabiting the body. Working backward from the phenomena generally associated with soul, I have suggested that a critical element in soulishness is the capacity for, and experience of, personal relatedness. It is further argued that the capacity for deep and meaningful personal relatedness emerges from the operation of an interactive web of core cognitive abilities, each of which are present in lower primates, but markedly more developed in humans. Soul is the music made by an orchestra of cognitive players performing in the context of interpersonal (or intrapersonal) dialogue. Played out in relationship to God who chooses to be in dialogue with his human creatures, the cognitive capacity for personal relatedness embodies spirituality.

The particular cognitive abilities described were not meant to be exhaustive, but rather were chosen to suggest how areas of cognitive ability subserve relatedness and how these capacities compare between humans and our nearest primate relatives. Each of the cognitive abilities discussed was shown not to be unique, but substantially enhanced in humans relative to apes. Even if the quantitative increase in level of each ability does not amount to a qualitative human uniqueness, certainly the level of personal relatedness emerging as these abilities function in concert amounts to unique dimensions of relatedness in humans.

A view of the soul as emerging from the experience of personal relatedness is attractive in that it rescues the concept of soul from the individualism that is deeply ingrained in modern Western culture. Soul is not something that stands for our individuality, but something that links us to other individuals and to our community, and to God. Most particularly, soul is the product of grace as God chooses to enter into dialogue with his creatures. The chapters by Green, Ray Anderson, and Post carried forward this theme of an embodied soul existing as a product of the capacities and experiences of personal relatedness.

Escape from Reductionism

Murphy has dealt with some of the knotty philosophical problems raised by a physicalist approach to the brain-mind-soul problem. Is physicalism inherently reductionistic? Is an explanation at a lower, more biological level always more adequate and complete than an explanation at the level of human consciousness and will? Here Murphy argues that descriptions and explanations formulated at a higher level (e.g., human consciousness) can be seen as supervening on lower-level explanations, even though they presume the necessity of the operation of processes at a lower level. This philosophical argument is consistent with two ideas that have currency in modern cognitive neuroscience.[11] First is the concept of top-down causation, and second is the idea of emergence of new capacities at higher levels of complexity that cannot be predicted or adequately explained on the basis of the operation of lower-level processes. If higher-level explanations can be shown to supervene on explanations based on lower-level phenomena, then the concept of supervenience allows an escape from the seemingly inevitable tendency for physicalism to become reductionistic.

Important to Murphy's argument for supervenience was the idea that supervenient explanations of phenomena must be contextually specific. That is, particular higher-level explanations that may supervene over lower-level explanations often do so under one set of circumstances but not another. Thus, to fruitfully apply a higher-level explanation, one must represent contextual constraints within the explanation. Particular mental or spiritual explanations of behavior would supervene on specific neurobiological explanations only as they meet certain contextual, circumstantial criteria, while similar behavioral or neurobiological phenomena might be given differing supervenient interpretations when occurring in other contexts.

This concept of contextual conditioning of supervenient explanations recognizes that higher-level phenomena often represent significantly greater degrees of complexity of interacting phenomena. The movement from lower to higher levels of observation and explanation necessarily involves considering the complex interactive contributions of a wider array of phenomena. The importance of a particular array of interactive events to the explanation of the phenomenon of interest cannot be captured at lower levels and without concepts resident at the higher levels. The rationale or meaning of a men-

11. Discussed in Jeeves, chapter 4; and Brown, chapter 5, this volume.

tal state or behavior can only be complete when it includes the explanatory language of higher supervenient levels.

As an important illustration of supervenience, let us return to the topic of evolutionist versus creationist accounts of human origins. It could be said that under certain contexts, the concept of creation supervenes the explanation of evolution. Thus, the claim that life is *created* would supervene on the claim that life *evolved* under a particular circumstance, namely, the circumstance of the evolutionary process achieving God's creative intentions. Or, to put the case more formally, something's having evolved constitutes its having been created by God only under a particular circumstance, that is, that the evolutionary process was God's intended manner of creating.[12] This formulation of the relationships between the concepts of creation and evolution helps in understanding the relationship between biological and religious descriptions of the events described in the geologic, fossil, and anthropologic records. The theological account supervenes on, but does not replace, evolutionary theory.[13]

Scientific Status of the Soul

The essays on neurobiological science and the philosophy of science have not attempted to present fatal arguments against a dualist viewpoint or prove that a substantive soul does not exist. The presence or absence of a nonphysical entity such as a human soul or spirit cannot be proven scientifically. Nor have these chapters contended that a nonreductive physicalist viewpoint is the only position consistent with either science or religious faith. Rather we have attempted to demonstrate that little of what has been presumed to be true and important about humans based upon belief in an incorporeal soul, need disappear on account of the scientific data when viewed from the perspective of nonreductive physicalism.

PHYSICALIST THEOLOGY

In order for the portrait of human nature suggested in these essays to be credible we need to have not only a nonreductive science of human nature, but a physicalist theology. By this I mean a biblical and theological anthropology that can sustain a physicalist view of humans without loss or degradation of biblical teachings, theological substance, or critical Christian doctrines. Our goal in

12. See Murphy, chapter 6, this volume, section entitled "Defeating Causal Reductionism."
13. Here "evolutionary theory" is not meant to include those statements that extend beyond the data regarding evolutionary progression into metaphysical statements regarding ultimate causes.

these essays has been to explore the "look and feel" of a portrait of human nature that is nondualist, particularly in light of the embodiment of so many critical aspects of personhood suggested by modern neurobiology. Is any significant aspect of Christian faith lost or hidden when viewed from this perspective? Is it possible to give a physicalist account of religious experience? Is it possible accurately to exegete critical biblical passages (Green), construct a reasonable systematic theology (R. Anderson), or articulate a viable ethic (Post) from a physicalist viewpoint? Is there interdisciplinary coherence in this position? Are there aspects of a biblical account of human nature that are better understood from a physicalist position than from a dualist one?

Biblical View of Soul

From the perspective of biblical exegesis, Green has helped us deal with three important aspects of our portrait of human nature: (1) the nature of the image of God, (2) the status of an ontologically separable soul within Scripture, and (3) the important role of community (the people of God) within a biblical understanding of human nature.

While scriptural teachings regarding the image of God do not address directly the dualism–physicalism distinction, there is nothing in these teachings that would necessitate belief in an ontologically distinct soul. However, what is clear in Scripture is that the image of God is relational, that is, it implies the capacity to enter into covenant relationships with God and with other humans. Humans are considered unique from the rest of God's creation primarily due to the capacity for covenantal relationships.

Green describes it as "axiomatic" that the Hebrew Scriptures view the human person as an integrated and embodied whole. The different words used in the Hebrew Scriptures to refer to various aspects of a human being do not imply separate entities. More apparent support for dualism can perhaps be found within the New Testament. However, even here it is unclear whether any of the critical passages are meant to imply that the soul is a separable, nonmaterial essence. New Testament teachings may well be expressed within first-century habits of language and thought, which were strongly influenced by a Hellenized view of human nature, without the teachings themselves being committed to a dualist view.

Green argued strongly that a biblical portrait of humankind is dominated by a view of the person in relationship to the community—that is, the biblical portrait of humans is uniquely relational. Theologian Jürgen Moltmann took a similar point of view regarding the image of God. Moltmann suggests that there is a distinction between the idea of an individual (an indivisible element) and a person. A person is defined by the potential for communication. Individuals become persons in relationship to God; thus personhood (the image of God) is based in relatedness and communication. The soul is discovered, according to Moltmann, by going outside of oneself.

> The modern understanding of the dignity of each and every human being derives from the biblical traditions and from the history of their influence in the Western world. They are concerned, however, not with the individual human being as an "individual," but rather as a "person." An individual, like an atom, is literally that ultimate element of indivisibility. An ultimate element of indivisibility, however, has no relationships, and also cannot communicate. Hence, Goethe is quite correct in his dictum: "*Individuum est ineffabile.*" If an individual has no relationships, then he also has no characteristics and no name. He is unrecognizable, and does not even know himself. By contrast, a person is the individual human being in the resonance field of the relationships of I-you-we, I-myself, I-it. Within this network of relationships, the person becomes the subject of giving and taking, hearing and doing, experiencing and touching, perceiving and responding. . . . The "person" emerges through the call of God.[14]

Thus, soul is manifest in the potentialities, characteristics, or attributes that allow humans to be related to others, to the self, and to God. These potentialities and characteristics would be, from the point of view of physicalism, embodied capacities not properties of a separate nonphysical entity.

The scientific (Ayala, E. Anderson, Brown, and Jeeves) and philosophical (Murphy) portraits of human nature offered in this book are thus compatible with the essence humanness from a biblical point of view. It is cultural (community, interpersonal, etc.) development, not physical evolution or genetic endowment, that most uniquely describes *Homo sapiens*. It is the higher brain capacities that subserve the richness of interpersonal relationships that emerge as cognitively most distinct in humans. Loss of those neurocognitive capacities that are most necessary for personal relatedness results in the most significant impact on qualities of personhood.

Theology of Embodiment and Relatedness

In order to accept within Christian theology a physicalist account of human nature, one must "touch all of the theological bases." It must be possible to maintain this position consistently and systematically while answering basic theological questions in a way that is consistent with Scripture. Ray Anderson considered a number of critical theological questions: What is the soul? What is spirituality? What is the "image of God"? What is sin? How are death, resurrection, and immortality to be understood?

14. Jürgen Moltmann, "Christianity and the Values of Modernity and the Western World," lecture presented at Fuller Theological Seminary (April 1996).

The concept of soul as the embodied capacities and experiences of personal relatedness, is central to the theological treatise of Anderson. The commandments to love God and love our neighbor, essential requirements of the Christian life, indicate the critical role of personal relatedness in Christian spirituality. To be spiritual is to be in relationship with God who is spirit. This then forms our understanding of the nature of the image of God. As Green also pointed out, God's image is to be found in the capacity for covenantal relatedness, that is, in the capacity to love God and neighbor. Sin is therefore that which destroys or disrupts relatedness to God, as well as that which damages our relatedness to others.

Particularly problematic for a physicalist account of human nature is the Christian doctrine of life after death. If our self-identity and soulishness are embodied in a physical and mortal body, how can these survive death? Understanding eternal life in terms of resurrection of the body is the original biblical concept and allows for the continuance of self-identity within a physicalist understanding of human nature. Anderson further points out that, while continued self-identity is guaranteed by Scripture, it is always promised in the context of the activity of God's creative work. Immortality is not an endemic quality of humanity but is granted by God in the context of our relatedness to him. Continuance of self-identity after death is, thus, entirely a product of the activity of a sovereign and omnipotent God.

Christian Ethics without Dualism

Ideas regarding the nature of persons ultimately affect the way we treat one another. Our understanding of human nature inevitably impacts our ethics. Therefore, it is important to consider what might be the consequences of a physicalist view of human nature. Would such a view start us down a slippery slope of ethical decline?

Post suggests in his chapter that dualism—the view that the distinctive attribute of human nature is the possession of a spiritual soul—has had both negative and positive impact on ethics in the past. Dualist views have sustained a sense of caution regarding what can appropriately be done to the besouled body of another individual. If an immortal soul is present, does this not force one to continue to honor and love the seriously mentally deficient or the demented? But, does not this view also result in an irrational inability to withdraw or withhold heroic medical treatments from an individual with no hope of sustaining life in anything but a vegetative state? Dualism has played a protective role within ethical systems, at times to a fault.

But do Christian ethics necessarily require dualism, or are they more rightly understood as resting on other grounds? Post suggests that the fundamental biblical motive for the care of those who have little ability to reciprocate (psychologically or functionally) is not to be found in a dualist consideration of the soul of the other. Rather, it emerges from "the ethos of bestowed love and from the narrative of Jesus among the most vulnerable." A narrative of love and consideration to helpless, dying, or deficient persons is sufficient motive, and perhaps a more purely biblical motive, than the consideration of a separate substantial soul.

Dualism has also tended to foster various forms of asceticism and gnosticism, where anything that is associated with the physical is viewed as inherently evil, or at least "nonspiritual" and therefore not of value.[15] While extremes of this view are not difficult to find in the history of religious cult movements, more subtle forms easily become a part of broader religious perspectives. For example, we not uncommonly encounter attitudes that denigrate sexual intimacy as basically nonspiritual, or view physical health as spiritually irrelevant ("Your sickness or psychological distress is not important so long as your soul is OK."). The opposite of asceticism has at times resulted from dualist thinking (i.e., "It matters not what I do to or with my body, only my soul matters").

Alternatively, a physicalist view suggests that one cannot separate the physical, mental, and spiritual. Distress in one area has impact on the others. It is important to my mental and spiritual life what I eat or drink, how I express my sexuality, or whether I am healthy or sick. My mental state can be expected to affect me physically and spiritually. As a Christian, I need to be as concerned about the physical and mental health of others, as much as I am about their spiritual well-being.

THE PRACTICAL VALUE OF NONREDUCTIVE PHYSICALISM

Probably nothing in the known universe is as complex as human nature. On the physical side, Owen Flanagan describes well the dimensionality of the human nervous system. Given 100 billion neurons each with an average of around 3,000 connections, each human being has something like 100 trillion (10^{14}) synaptic switches. If each of these synapses can assume 1 of 10 conductive levels we have $10^{100,000,000,000,000}$ potentially distinct brain states. If one assumes that 99.9 percent of these make no functional difference, we are still left with $10^{99,999,999,999,997}$ functionally unique states. If you further assume that 99.9 percent of these are unconscious, $10^{99,999,999,999,994}$ distinct conscious states are possible. By comparison, there is estimated to be something on the

15. See R. Anderson, chapter 8, this volume.

order of 10^{87} elementary particles in the universe.[16] What laws and influences are at work within the brain to select and establish particular conscious states from such a vast array of possibilities? Next, consider the infinite variety of possibilities of environmental and sociocultural influences within the life history of an individual. When you couple this physical and environmental complexity with the difficulty of a creature trapped in space and time comprehending the mind of the Creator and his relationship with humankind, the problem of comprehending human nature appears, at the very least, formidable.

In this very challenging task of comprehending human nature, the authors of this volume believe that nonreductive physicalism has some practical advantages. First, humans are what you see; that is, there is not another invisible, nonmaterial part of the individual that must be factored into the formula of understanding. The person is he or she who physically stands before you. Second, this position allows one to accept and profit from both scientific and theological accounts of humankind since the supervenience of higher-level explanations on lower-lever explanations is allowed. Finally, and most importantly, a nonreductive physicalist point of view forces one to attempt to reconcile theological and scientific accounts. If the human being is not divided into parts, such as body and soul, then explanations given by different disciplines and from difference perspectives must ultimately be seen as noncontradictory. A complete understanding of human nature remains a grandiose objective. However, when human beings are viewed as whole and undivided, the project is at least theoretically possible. No part of human behavior or experience is prima facie excepted as nonmaterial and thus unobservable in principle.

N.C. basketball player shot 600 buckets in an effort to break old pattern & establish a new one. what does that say re: ethics + morality?

---

16. Owen Flanagan, *Consciousness Reconsidered* (Cambridge, Mass.: MIT Press, 1992), 35–37.

Bibliography

Adams, Jay. *More than Redemption: A Theology of Christian Counseling*. Grand Rapids: Baker Book House, 1979.

Andersen, Francis I. "2 (Slavonic Apocalypse of) Enoch: A New Translation and Introduction." In *The Old Testament Pseudepigrapha*, 2 vols., ed. James H. Charlesworth, Garden City, N.Y.: Doubleday, 1983, 1:91-213 (140).

Anderson, H. Elving. "Resisting Reductionism by Restoring the Context." In *Genetic Ethics: Do the Ends Justify the Genes?* ed. Kilner, John F., Pentz, Rebecca D. and Young, Frank E., Grand Rapids: William B. Eerdmans, 1997.

Anderson, Ray S. *Theology, Death and Dying*. Oxford: Basil Blackwell Ltd, 1986.

Anderson, W. French. "Genetic Engineering and Our Humanness." *Human Gene Therapy* 5 (1994): 758-759.

Arolt, Volker, et al. "Eye Tracking Dysfunction Is a Putative Phenotypic Susceptibility Marker of Schizophrenia and Maps to a Locus on Chromosome 6p in Families with Multiple Occurrence of the Disease." *American Journal of Medical Genetics* (Neuropsychiatric Genetics) 67 (1996): 564-579.

Aquinas, Thomas. *Selected Philosophical Writings*. Selected and trans. T. McDermott, Oxford: Oxford University Press, 1993.

Ashkenas, John. "Williams Syndrome Starts Making Sense." *American Journal of Human Genetics* 59 (1996): 756-761.

Ashley, Benedict M., O.P. *Theologies of the Body: Humanist and Christian*. Braintree, Mass.: Pope John Center, 1985.

Ayala, F. J. "The Biological Roots of Morality." *Biology and Philosophy* 2 (1987): 235-252.

Ayala, F. J. "The Difference of Being Human: Ethical Behavior as an Evolutionary Byproduct." In *Biology, Ethics and the Origin of Life*, ed. Rolston III, H., Boston and London: Jones and Bartlett, 1995.

Ayala, F. J. "The Evolutionary Concept of Progress." In *Progress and Its Discontents*, ed. G. A. Almond et al., Berkeley: University of California Press, 1982.

Ayala, F. J. "The Myth of Eve: Molecular Biology and Human Origins." *Science* 270 (1995): 1930-1936.

Ayala, F. J., and Dobzhansky, T., ed. *Studies in the Philosophy of Biology: Reduction and Related Issues*. Berkeley: University of California Press, 1974.

Baddeley, D. *Working Memory*. Oxford: Oxford University Press, 1986.

Badham, Paul. *Christian Beliefs about Life after Death*. London: Macmillan, 1976.

Barbour, Ian. *Issues in Science and Religion*. San Francisco: Harper & Row, 1966.

Barbour, Ian. *Religion in an Age of Science: The Gifford Lectures, Volume One*. San Francisco: Harper and Row, 1990.

Baron-Cohen, S. "The Autistic Child's Theory of Mind: A Case of Specific Developmental Delay." *Journal of Child Psychology and Psychiatry* 30 (1989): 285-297.

Barth, Karl. *Church Dogmatics* III/2. Edinburgh: T & T Clark, 1960.

Bastian, Jarvis. "Primate Signaling Systems and Human Language." In *Primate Behavior: Field Studies in Monkeys and Apes,* ed. Irven DeVore, New York: Holt, Rinehart and Winston, 1965.

Bauckham, Richard J. "The Rich Man and Lazarus: The Parable and the Parallels." *New Testament Studies* 37 (1991): 225-246.

Bear, M. and Fedio, P. "Quantitative Analysis of Intercital Behaviour in Temporal Lobe Epilepsy." *Archives of Neurology* 34 (1977): 454-467.

Beckermann, A., Flohr, H., and Kim, J., eds. *Emergence or Reduction? Prospects for Nonreductive Physicalism.* Berlin: New York: deGruyter, 1992.

Bellah, Robert N., Madsen, Richard, Sullivan, William M., Swidler, Ann, and Tipton, Steve M. *Habits of the Heart: Individualism and Commitment in American Life.* Berkeley: University of California, 1985.

Berkouwer, G. C. *Man: The Image of God.* Grand Rapids: Eerdmans Publishing Company, 1962.

Bickerton, Derek, *Language and Species.* Chicago: University of Chicago Press, 1990.

Bobgan, Martin and Diedre. *Prophets of Psychoheresy II.* Santa Barbara, Calif.: Eastgate, 1990.

Bock, Darrell L. *Luke,* 2 vols., Baker Exegetical Commentary on the New Testament 3, Grand Rapids: Baker, 1994/96.

Bonhoeffer, Dietrich. *The Communion of Saints.* New York: Harper and Row, 1963.

Boorstin, D. J. *The Discoverers: A History of Man's Search to Know His World and Himself.* New York: Vintage, 1985.

Booth, Wayne C. *The Company We Keep: An Ethics of Fiction.* Chicago: University of Chicago Press, 1988.

Boswell, John. *Same-Sex Unions in Premodern Europe.* New York: Vintage Books, 1994.

Botkin, Jeffrey R. and Post, Stephen G. "Confusion in the Determination of Death: Distinguishing Philosophy from Physiology." *Perspectives in Biology and Medicine,* 36, No. 1, 129-138.

Bouchard, Thomas. "Whenever the Twain Shall Meet." *The Sciences* 37 (1997): 52-57.

Bouchard Jr., Thomas J., Lykken, David T., McGue, Matthew, Segal, Nancy L., and Tellegen, Auke. "Sources of Human Psychological Differences: The Minnesota Study of Twins Reared Apart." *Science* 250 (1990) 1498.

Bowler, Dermont M. "'Theory of Mind' in Asperger's Syndrome." *Journal of Child Psychology and Psychiatry* 33 (1992): 877-893.

Boyd, Jeffrey H. "The Soul as Seen through Evangelical Eyes. Part I. Mental Health Professionals and the 'Soul.'" In *Journal of Psychology and Theology* 23, no. 3 (1995): 151-160.

Boyd, Jeffrey H. "The Soul as Seen through Evangelical Eyes, Part II: Mental Health Professionals and the 'Soul.'" In *Journal of Psychology and Theology* 23, no. 3 (1995), 161-170.

Brown, G. Gillian and Yule, George. *Discourse Analysis.* Cambridge Textbooks in Linguistics, Cambridge: Cambridge University, 1982.

Brown, Warren S. "MacKay's View of Conscious Agents in Dialogue: Speculations on the Embodiment of Soul." *Journal of Philosophy and Psychology* 4 (1997): 497-505.

Bruce, F. F. *1 and 2 Thessalonians.* Word Biblical Commentary 45, Waco, Texas: Word, 1982.

Brunner, H. G., Nelen, M., Breakefield, X.O., et al. "Abnormal Behavior Associated with a Point Mutation in the Structural Gene for Monoamine Oxidase A." *Science* 262 (1993): 578-580.

Brunner, H. G., Nelen, M. R., van Zandvoort, P., et al. "X-Linked Borderline Mental Retardation with Prominent Behavioral Disturbance: Phenotype, Genetic Localization, and Evidence for Disturbed Monoamine Metabolism." *American Journal of Human* Genetics 52 (1993): 1032-1039.

Byrne, Richard. *The Thinking Ape: Evolutionary Origins of Intelligence.* Oxford: Oxford University Press, 1995.

Byrne, Richard and Whiten, A. *Machiavellian Intelligence: Social Expertise and the Evolution of Intellect in Monkeys, Apes and Humans.* Oxford: Clarendon Press, 1988.

Bube, Richard. "Other Options?" *Journal of the American Scientific Affiliation* 24 (March 1972): 14-15.

Bultmann, Rudolf. *Theology of the New Testament.* 2 vols., New York: Charles Scribner's Sons, 1951/55, 1:192-203.

Burns, J. Patout, translator and editor. *Theological Anthropology: Sources of Early Christian Thought.* Philadelphia: Fortress Press, 1981.

Cahill, Lisa Sowle. *Sex, Gender, and Christian Ethics.* Cambridge: Cambridge University Press, 1996.

Cairns, Robert S. "Aggression from a Developmental Perspective: Genes, Environments and Interactions." In *Genetics of Criminal and Antisocial Behavior,* Ciba Foundation Symposium 194, Chichester: Wiley, 1995.

Campbell, Donald. "'Downward Causation' in Hierarchically Organized Systems." In *Studies in the Philosophy of Biology,* ed. F. J. Ayala and T. Dobzhansky, Berkeley: University of California Press, 1974.

Carroll, John T. *Response to the End of History: Eschatology and Situation in Luke-Acts.* Society of Biblical Literature Dissertation Series 92, Atlanta, Georgia: Scholars, 1988.

Cases, Oliver, and others. "Aggressive Behavior and Altered Amounts of Brain Serotonin and Norepinephri-ne in Mice Lacking MAOA." *Science* 268 (1995): 1763-1766.

Cerfeaux, L., *The Christian in the Theology of St. Paul.* London: Chapman, 1967.

Chalmers, David J. *The Conscious Mind: In Search of a Fundamental Theory.* New York: Oxford University Press, 1996.

Chamblin, J. Knox. "Psychology." In *Dictionary of Paul and His Letters.* ed. Gerald F. Hawthorne, Ralph P. Martin, and Daniel G. Reid, Downers Grove, Ill.: InterVarsity, 1993, 765-75.

Childs, Brevard S. *Biblical Theology of the Old and New Testaments: Theological Reflection on the Christian Bible.* Minneapolis: Fortress, 1992.

Churchland, Patricia Smith. "A Perspective on Mind-Brain Research." *Journal of Philosophy* 77 (1980): 185-207.

Churchland, Paul M. "Eliminative Materialism and Propositional Attitudes." *Journal of Philosophy* 78 (1981): 67-90.

Churchland, Paul. *The Engine of Reason, the Seat of the Soul: A Philosophical Journey into the Brain.* Cambridge, Mass.: MIT Press, 1995.

Clark, Elizabeth and Richardson, Herbert, editors. *Women and Religion.* New York: Harper & Row, 1977.

Cohen, Jon. "Does Nature Drive Nurture?" *Science* 273 (1996): 578-579.

Cole, R. David. "The Molecular Biology of Transcending the Gene." In *Religion and Science: History, Method, Dialogue,* edited by W. Mark Richardson and Wesley J. Wildman. New York: Routledge, 1996.

Cole-Turner, Ronald, editor. *Human Cloning. Religious Responses.* Louisville: Westminster John Knox Press, 1997.

Cole-Turner, Ronald. *The New Genesis: Theology and the Genetic Revolution.* Louisville: Westminster John Knox Press, 1993.

Cooper, John W. *Body, Soul, and Life Everlasting: Biblical Anthropology and the Monism-Dualism Debate.* Grand Rapids: Wm. B. Eerdmans, 1989.

Corrington, Robert. *Nature's Self: Our Journey from Origin to Spirit.* Lanham, Md.: Rowman and Littlefield Publishers, Inc. 1996.

Cranor, Carl F. *Are Genes Us? The Social Consequences of the New Genetics.* New Brunswick, N.J.: Rutgers University Press, 1994.

Crick, F.H. *The Astonishing Hypothesis: The Scientific Search for a Soul.* London: Simon and Schuster, 1994.

Cruchfield, J.P. et al. "Chaos." *Scientific American* 225 (1986): 38-49.

Cullmann, Oscar. "Immortality of the Soul or Resurrection of the Dead?" In *Immortality and Resurrection,* edited by Krister Stendahl, 9-53. New York: Macmillan, 1958.

Damasio, A. *Descartes' Error: Emotion, Reason and the Human Brain.* New York: Grosset/Putnam, 1994.

Damasio, A. "Mechanisms of Face Recognition." In *Handbook of Research on Face Processing,* edited by A. W. Young and H. D. Ellis. New York: Elsevier, 1989.

Davis, Carolyn Franks. *The Evidential Force of Religious Experience.* Oxford: Clarendon Press, 1989.

Davis, David Brion. *The Problem of Slavery in Western Culture.* Ithaca, N.Y.: Cornell University Press, 1966.

Dawkins, Richard. *The Selfish Gene.* Oxford: Oxford University Press, 1989.

Delacour, J. "The Biology and Neuropsychology of Consciousness." *Neuropsychologia* 33, no. 9 (1995): 1061-1192.

Dole, J., et al. "Contemporary Perspectives in Chance, Providence and Free Will: A Critique of Some Modern Authors." *Science and Christian Belief* 7 (1995): 117-139.

Dupont, Jacques. "Die individuelle Eschatologie im Lukasevangelium und in der Apostelgeschichte." In *Orientierung an Jesus: Zur Theologie der Synoptiker,* edited by Paul Hoffman. Freiburg: Herder, 1973.

Dyrness, William A. *Let the Earth Rejoice! A Biblical Theology of Holistic Mission.* Westchester, Ill.: Crossways, 1983.

Easterbrook, Gregg. "Science and God: A Warming Trend?" *Science* 277 (1997): 890-893.

Eaves, L. J., Eysenck, H. J., and Martin, N. G. *Genes, Culture and Personality: An Empirical Approach.* New York: Academic Press, 1989.

Eaves, Lindon. "Behavioral Genetics, or What's Missing from Theological Anthropology?" In *Beginning with the End: God, Science, and Wolfhart Pannenberg,* edited by Carol Rausch Albright and Joel Haugen, 344-345. Chicago: Open Court, 1997.

Eaves, Lindon. "Spirit, Method, and Content in Science and Religion: The Theological Perspective of a Geneticist." *Zygon* 24, no. 2 (June 1989), 193.

Eaves, Lindon, and Gross, Lora. "Exploring the Concept of Spirit as a Model for the God-World Relationship in the Age of Genetics." *Zygon* 27 (1992): 269.

Eccles, J. C., editor. *Brain and Conscious Experience.* Berlin: Springer-Verlag, 1966.

Edelman, Gerald M. *Bright Air, Brilliant Fire: On the Matter of the Mind.* New York: Basic Books, 1992.

Eichrodt, W. *Theology of the Old Testament.* Philadelphia: Westminster Press, 1975.

Ettlinger, G. "Humans, Apes and Monkeys: The Changing Neuropsychological Viewpoint." *Neuropsychologia* 22, no. 8 (1984): 685-696.

Ewart, Amanda K., et al. "Hemizygosity at the Elastin Locus in a Developmental Disorder, Williams Syndrome." *Nature Genetics* 5 (1993): 11-16.

Flanagan, Owen. *Consciousness Reconsidered.* Cambridge, Mass.: MIT Press, 1992.

Flanagan, Owen. *Self Expressions: Mind, Morals, and the Meaning of Life.* New York: Oxford University Press, 1996.

Flanagan, Owen. *The Science of Mind,* 2d ed. Cambridge, Mass.: MIT Press, 1991.

Flavell, J. H., Green, F. L., and Flavell, E. R. "Young Children's Knowledge about Thinking." *Monographs of the Society for Research in Child Development* 60 No. 1 (1996): 1–96.

Fleishaker, Gary Raney. "Three Models of a Minimal Cell." in *Prebiotic Self Organization of Matter,* edited by C. Ponnamperuma and F .R. Erlich. n.p.p.: A. Deepak Publishing, 1990.

Freedman, Nancy. *Joshua: Son of None.* New York: Dell Publishing Company, 1973.

Furnish, Victor Paul. *II Corinthians: Translated with Introduction, Notes, and Commentary.* Anchor Bible 32A. Garden City, New York: Doubleday, 1984.

Fuster, J. *The Prefrontal Cortex: Anatomy, Physiology, and Neuropsychology of the Frontal Lobe.* New York: Raven Press, 1980.

Gert, Bernard. *Morality: A New Justification of the Moral Rules.* New York: Oxford University Press, 1988.

Gilson, Etienne. *The Spirit of Medieval Philosophy.* Translated by A. H. C. Downes. New York: Charles Scribner's Sons, 1936.

Good, Byron J. *Medicine, Rationality, and Experience: An Anthropological Perspective.* The Lewis Henry Morgan Lectures 1990. Cambridge: Cambridge University, 1994.

Goodglass, H. and Kaplan, E. *The Assessment of Aphasia and Related Disorders.* Philadelphia: Lea and Tebiger, 1972.

Gottesman, Irving L. "Origins of Schizophrenia: Past as Prologue." In *Nature, Nurture, and Psychology,* edited by Robert Plomin and Gerald E. McClearn. American Psychological Association: Washington, D.C. (1993).

Gould, S. J. *Full House. The Spread of Excellence from Plato to Darwin.* New York: Harmony Books, 1996.

Green, Joel B. *The Gospel of Luke.* New International Commentary on the New Testament. Grand Rapids: Wm. B. Eerdmans, forthcoming.

Green, Joel B. "Proclaiming Repentance and Forgiveness of Sins to All Nations: A Biblical Perspective on the Church's Mission." In *The World Is My Parish: The Mission of the Church in Methodist Perspective,* edited by Alan G. Padgett, Studies in the History of Missions 10. Lewiston, N.Y.: Edwin Mellen, 1992.

Greenblatt, Stephen. "Culture." In *Critical Terms for Literary Study,* edited by Frank Lentricchia and Thomas McLaughlin. Chicago: University of Chicago, 1990.

Grigorenko, E. L., et al. "Susceptibility Loci for Distinct Components of Developmental Dyslexia on Chromosomes 6 and 15." *American Journal of Human Genetics* 60 (1997): 27-39.

Gundry, Robert H. *Soma in Biblical Theology: With Emphasis on Pauline Anthropology.* Grand Rapids: Zondervan, 1987.

Gustafson, James M. "A Christian Perspective on Genetic Engineering." *Human Gene Therapy* 5 (1994): 747-754.

Gustafson, James M. "Where Theologians and Geneticists Meet." *Dialog* 33, no. 1 (Winter 1994): 7-16.

Hahn, Robert A. *Sickness and Health: An Anthropological Perspective.* New Haven, Conn.: Yale University, 1995.

Hare, R. *Without Conscience: The Disturbing World of the Psychopaths among Us.* Pocket Books, 1993.

Hare, Richard M. *The Language of Morals.* Oxford: Clarendon Press, 1952.

Harris, Murray J. *From the Grave to Glory: Resurrection in the New Testament.* Grand Rapids: Zondervan, 1990.

Harris, Murray J. *Raised Immortal—Resurrection and Immortality in the New Testament.* Grand Rapids: Eerdmans Publishing Company, 1983.

Hauerwas, Stanley. *Suffering Presence: Theological Reflections on Medicine, the Mentally Handicapped, and the Church.* Notre Dame, Ind.: University of Notre Dame Press, 1986.

Hauerwas, Stanley. *Vision and Virtue: Essays in Christian Ethical Reflection.* Notre Dame, Ind.: Fides Publishers, Inc., 1974.

Heil, John. *The Nature of True Minds.* Cambridge: Cambridge University Press, 1992.

Hengel, Martin. *Judaism and Hellenism: Studies in Their Encounter in Palestine during the Early Hellenistic Period.* Philadelphia: Fortress, 1974.

Hill, Edmund. *Being Human: A Biblical Perspective.* London: Geoffrey Chapman, 1984.

Holdrege, Craig. *Genetics and the Manipulation of Life: The Forgotten Factor of Context.* Hudson, N.Y.: Lindisfarne Press, 1996.

Horgan, Terence E. "Supervenience." In *The Cambridge Dictionary of Philosophy,* edited by Robert Audi, 778-779. Cambridge: Cambridge University Press, 1995.

Hume, D. *Treatise of Human Nature.* Oxford: Oxford University Press, 1978 [original 1740].

Hunter, David G. "Introduction." In *Marriage in the Early Church,* translated by and edited by David G. Hunter. Minneapolis: Fortress Press, 1992.

Huxley, T. H., and Huxley, J. S. *Touchstone for Ethics.* New York: Harper, 1947.

Irenaeus. *Against Heresies 2 vols.* Ante-Nicene Christian Library, edited by A. Roberts and J. Donaldson. Edinburgh: T & T Clark, 1868.

Jenkins, W. M., Merzenich, M. M., and Recanzone, G. "Neocortical Representational Dynamics in Adult Primates: Implications for Neuropsychology." *Neuropsychologia* 28 (1990): 573-584.

Jeeves, Malcolm A. *Human Nature at the Millennium: Reflections on the Integration of Psychology and Christianity.* Grand Rapids: Baker Books, 1997.

Jerome. "Against Jovinian." in *Women and Religion.* Elizabeth Clark and Herbert Richardson, editors. New York: Harper & Row, 1977.

Jewett, Paul K. *Who We Are: Our Dignity as Human.* Grand Rapids: Eerdmans Publishing Company, 1996.

Jewett, Robert. *Paul's Anthropological Terms: A Study of Their Use in Conflict Settings.* Arbeiten zur Geschichte des antiken Judentums und das Urchristentums 10. Leiden: E.J. Brill, 1971.

Kee, Howard Clark. *Medicine, Miracle and Magic in New Testament Times.* Society of New Testament Studies Monograph Series 55. Cambridge: Cambridge University, 1986.

Keck, David. *Forgetting Whose We Are.* Nashville: Abingdon Press, 1996.

Kim, Jaegwon. *Supervenience and Mind: Selected Philosophical Essays.* Cambridge: Cambridge University Press, 1993.

Kidd, Kennth K. "Can We Find Genes for Schizophrenia?" *American Journal of Medical Genetics* (Neuropsychiatric Genetics) 74 (1997): 104-111.

Kitwood, Tom. "Towards a Theory of Dementia Care: The Interpersonal Process." *Aging & Society* 13 (1993): 51-67

Koester, Helmut. *Introduction to the New Testament.* 2d edition., vol. 1. New York: Walter de Gruyter, 1995.

Kuhn, Thomas. *The Structure of Scientific Revolution,* 2d edition. Chicago: University of Chicago Press, 1970.

Kuhse, Helga and Singer, Peter. *Should the Baby Live: The Problem of Handicapped Infants.* New York: Oxford University Press, 1985.

Lecky, William E. H. *The History of European Morals from Augustus to Charlemagne.* Vol. 2. New York: George Braziller, 1955 [original 1869].

Lindberg, David C. and Numbers, Ronald L., editors. *God and Nature: Historical Essays on the Encounter between Christianity and Science.* Berkeley and Los Angeles: University of California Press, 1986.

Loehlin, John C. *Genes and Environment in Personality Development.* Newbury Park, Calif.: SAGE Publications, 1992.

Loftus, E. F. "Psychologists in the Eyewitness World." *American Psychologist* 48 (1993): 550-580.

Lovejoy, A. O. *The Great Chain of Being.* Cambridge, Mass.: Harvard University Press, 1936.

Loyola, Ignatius. *The Spiritual Exercises: A Literal Translation and a Contemporary Reading.* Edited and translated by David L. Fleming. St. Louis: Institute of Jesuit Sources, 1978.

Lykken, David, and Tellegen, Auke. "Happiness Is a Stochastic Phenomenon." *Psychological Science* 7 (1996): 186-189.

MacIntyre , Alasdair. *After Virtue*. Notre Dame, Ind.: University of Notre Dame Press, 1981; 1984.

MacKay, D. M. *Behind the Eye*. Oxford: Blackwell, 1991,

MacKay, D. M. *The Open Mind and Other Essays: A Scientist in God's World*. Leicester: InterVarsity, 1991.

MacMullen, Ramsey. *Paganism in the Roman Empire*. New Haven, Conn.:Yale University, 1981.

Malony, H. Newton. "Counseling Body/Soul Persons." In the *International Journal for the Psychology of Religion* 8, no. 3 (1998): 211-216.

Martin, Dale B. *The Corinthian Body*. New Haven, Conn.:Yale University, 1995.

Matlin, M. *Cognition*. Third edition. Fort Worth: Harcourt Brace Publishers, 1994.

Mattill Jr., A. J. *Luke and the Last Things: A Perspective for the Understanding of Lukan Thought*. Dillsboro, N.C.:Western North Carolina, 1979.

McClendon, Jr., James Wm. *Ethics: Systematic Theology, Volume One*. Nashville, Tenn.: Abingdon Press, 1986.

McGue, Matt. "Nature-Nurture and Intelligence." *Nature*. 340 (17 August 1989): 507-508.

McGue, Matt, Bouchard Jr., Thomas J., Iacono, William B. and Lykken, David T. "Behavioral Genetics of Cognitive Ability: A Life-Span Perspective." In *Nature, Nurture, and Psychology*, edited by Robert Plomin and Gerald E. McClearn. Washington, D.C.: American Psychological Association, 1993.

Meyering, Theo. C. *Historical Roots of Cognitive Science: The Rise of a Cognitive Theory of Perception from Antiquity to the Nineteenth Century*. Dordrecht: Kluwer Academic Publishers, 1989.

Midgley, Mary. *Beast and Man: The Roots of Human Nature*. New York: New American Library, 1978.

Milner, B. "Memory and the Temporal Regions of the Brain." In *Biology of Memory*, edited by K. H. Pribram and D. E. Broadbent. New York: Academic Press, 1970.

Milner, B., Corkin, S., and Teuber, H. L. "Further Analysis of the Hippocampal Amnesic Syndrome: 14-year Follow Up Study of H. M." *Neuropsychologia* 6 (1968): 215-234.

Mishkin, M., and Appenzeller, T. "The Anatomy of Memory." *Scientific American* 256, no. 6 (1987): 62-71.

Moore, Thomas. *Care of the Soul: A Guide for Cultivating Depth and Sacredness in Everyday Life*. New York: Harper Collins Publishers, 1992.

Moore, G. E. *Principia Ethica*. Cambridge: Cambridge University Press, 1903.

Müller, Peter. *Der Soma-Begriff bei Paulus: Studien zum paulinischen Menschenbild und seine Bedeutung für unsere Zeit*. Stuttgart: Urachhaus, 1988.

Murphy, Nancey. *Anglo-American Postmodernity: Philosophical Perspectives on Science, Religion, and Ethics.* Boulder, Colo.: Westview Press, 1997.

Murphy, Nancey. *Beyond Liberalism and Fundamentalism: How Modern and Postmodern Philosophy Set the Theological Agenda.* Valley Forge, Pa.: Trinity Press International, 1996.

Murphy, Nancey, and Ellis, George F. R. *On the Moral Nature of the Universe: Theology, Cosmology, and Ethics.* Minneapolis: Fortress Press, 1996.

Murphy, Nancey. "Supervenience and the Nonreducibility of Ethics to Biology." In *Anglo-American Postmodernity: Philosophical Perspectives on Science, Religion, and Ethics.* Boulder, Colo.: Westview Press, 1997.

Murphy, Nancey. *Theology in the Age of Scientific Reasoning.* Ithaca, N.Y.: Cornell University Press, 1990.

Murphy-O'Connor, Jerome. *Becoming Human Together: The Pastoral Anthropology of St. Paul.* Good News Studies 2. Wilmington, Del.: Michael Glazier, 1982.

Nee, Watchman. *The Spiritual Man.* 3 vols. New York: Christian Fellowship, 1968.

Nelkin, Dorothy and Lindee, M. Susan. *The DNA Mystique: The Gene as a Cultural Icon.* New York: W. H. Freeman and Company, 1995.

Nelson, James B. *Between Two Gardens: Reflections on Sexuality and Religious Experience.* New York: Pilgrim Press, 1983.

Nickelsburg Jr., George W. E. *Resurrection, Immortality, and Eternal Life in Intertestamental Judaism.* Harvard Theological Studies 26. Cambridge, Mass.: Harvard University, 1972.

Nielsen, J. T. *Adam and Christ in the Theology of Irenaeus of Lyons.* Assen, The Netherlands: Van Gorcum & Co. N.V., 1968.

Nietzsche, Friedrich. *Twilight of the Idols / The Anti-Christ.* Translated by R. J. Hollingdale. New York: Penguin Books, 1968 [original 1870].

Nilsson, L.G., et al. "Genetic Markers Associated with High Versus Low Performance On Episodic Memory Tasks." *Behavior Genetics* 26 (1996): 555-562.

Norton, Simon Leys, translator. *The Analects of Confucius.* New York: Norton, 1996.

Okin, Susan Moller. *Women in Western Political Thought.* Princeton, N.J.: Princeton University Press, 1979.

Ornstein, P.A., Gordon, B. N., and Baker-Ward, L.W. "Children's Memory for Salient Events: Implications for Testimony." In *Development of Long Term Retention,* edited by M. L. Howe, C. J. Brainerd, and V. F. Reyna. New York: Springer Verlag, 1992.

Otto, Rudolf. *The Idea of the Holy.* Translated by J. W. Harvey. London: Oxford University Press, 1936.

Ozonoff, Sally, Robers, Sally J., and Pennington, Bruce P. "Asperger's Syndrome: Evidence of an Empirical Distinction from High-Functioning Autism." *Journal of Child Psychology and Psychiatry* 32 (1991): 1107-1122.

Palmer, R. E. *Hermeneutics.* Chicago: Northwestern University Press, 1969.

Pannenberg, Wolfhart. *Anthropology in Theological Perspective.* Translated by Matthew J. O'Connell. Philadelphia: Westminster, 1985.

Pannenberg, Wolfhart. *Jesus: God and Man.* Philadelphia: Westminster, 1968.

Parens, Erik. "Taking Behavioral Genetics Seriously." *Hastings Center Report* 26, no. 4 (July-August 1996): 13-18.

Parrinder, Geoffrey. *Sex in the World's Religions.* New York: Oxford University Press, 1980.

Passingham, R. *The Human Primate.* Oxford: Oxford University Press, 1982.

Peacocke, Arthur. *Creation and the World of Science.* Oxford: Clarendon Press, 1979.

Peacocke, Arthur. *Theology for a Scientific Age: Being and Becoming—Natural, Divine, and Human.* 2d enlarged edition. Minneapolis: Fortress Press, 1993.

Peacocke, Arthur. "God's Interaction with the World: The Implications of Deterministic 'Chaos' and of Interconnected and Interdependent Complexity." In *Chaos and Complexity: Scientific Perspectives on Divine Action,* edited by Robert J. Russell, Nancey Murphy, and Arthur R. Peacocke. Vatican City State and Berkeley, Calif.: Vatican Observatory and Center for Theology and the Natural Sciences, 1995.

Peacocke, Arthur. *God and the New Biology.* London: J.M. Dent and Sons, 1986.

Pennington, Bruce F. "Using Genetics to Dissect Cognition." *American Journal of Human Genetics* 60 (1997): 13-16.

Perner, J. and Ruffman, T. "Episodic Memory and Autonoetic Consciousness: Developmental Evidence and a Theory of Childhood Amnesia." *Journal of Experimental Child Psychology* 59 (1995): 516-548.

Persinger, A. "People Who Report Religious Experiences May Also Display Enhanced Temporal Lobe Signs." *Perceptual and Motor Skills* 58 (1984): 163-197.

Persinger, A. "Propensity to Report Paranormal Experiences Is Correlated with Temporal Lobe Signs." *Perceptual and Motor Skills* 59 (1984): 583-586.

Persinger, A. "Religious and Mystical Experiences as Artifacts of Temporal Lobe Function: A General Hypothesis." *Perceptual and Motor Skills* 557 (1983): 1225-1262.

Persinger, A. "Striking EEG Profiles from Single Episodes of Glossalalia and Transcendental Meditation." *Perceptual and Motor Skills* 58 (1984): 127-133.

Pinker, Steven. *The Language Instinct.* New York: William Morrow and Company, 1994.

Polkinghorne, J. C. *One World*. London: SPCK, 1986.

Pope, Alexander. "Essay on Man." In *Poetry of the English-Speaking World*, edited by Richard Aldington. London: Heinemann, 1947.

Posner, M. I., et al. "Localisation of Cognitive Operations in the Human Brain." *Science* 240 (June 17, 1988): 1627–1631.

Post, Stephen G. *The Moral Challenge of Alzheimer Disease*. Baltimore: John Hopkins University Press, 1995.

Post, Stephen G. *Spheres of Love: Toward a New Ethic of the Family*. Dallas, Texas: Southern Methodist University Press, 1994.

Preston, W. Warren, editor. *Principles of Emergent Realism: The Philosophical Essays of Roy Wood Sellar*. St. Louis, Mo.: Warren H. Green, Inc., 1970.

Raff, Martin. "Neural Development: Mysterious No More?" *Science* 274 (1996): 1063.

Reichmann, James. *Philosophy of the Human Person*. Chicago: Loyola University Press, 1985.

Robinson, John A. T. *The Body: A Study in Pauline Theology*. London: SCM, 1952.

Robinson, H. Wheeler. *The Christian Doctrine of Man*. 3d edition. Edinburgh: T. & T. Clark, 1926.

Rorvik, David. *In His Image: The Cloning of a Man*. Philadelphia: J. B. Lippincott Company, 1978.

Rowe, David C. "Genetic Perspectives on Personality." In *Nature, Nurture, and Psychology*, edited by Robert Plomin and Gerald E. McClearn. Washington, D.C.: American Psychological Association, 1993.

Rumbaugh, Duane. "Primate Language and Cognition: Common Ground." *Social Research* 62 (1995): 711–730.

Ruse, M. "Evolutionary Ethics: A Phoenix Arisen." *Zygon* 21 (1986): 95–112.

Ruse, M. *Taking Darwin Seriously: A Naturalistic Approach to Philosophy*. Oxford: Basil Blackwell, 1986.

Ruse, M. and Wilson, E. O. "Moral Philosophy as Applied Science." *Philosophy: Journal of the Royal Institute of Philosophy* 61 (1986): 173–192.

Russell, Robert J., Murphy, Nancey, and Peacocke, Arthur, editors. *Chaos and Complexity: Scientific Perspectives on Divine Action*. Vatican City State and Berkeley, Calif.: Vatican Observatory and Center for Theology and the Natural Sciences, 1995.

Russell, Robert J., Ayala, F. J., Stoeger, William, editors. *Molecular and Evolutionary Biology: Scientific Perspectives on Divine Action*. Vatican City State and Berkeley, Calif.: Vatican Observatory and Center for Theology and the Natural Sciences, forthcoming.

Russell, Robert J., Murphy, Nancey, and Isham, C. J., editors. *Quantum Cosmology and the Laws of Nature: Scientific Perspectives on Divine Action*.

Vatican City State and Berkeley, Calif.:Vatican Observatory and Center for Theology and the Natural Sciences, 1993.

Rutter, Sir Michael. "Concluding Remarks." In *Genetics of Criminal and Antisocial Behaviour,* Ciba Foundation Symposium 194. Chichester:Wiley, 1995.

Ryle, Gilbert. *The Concept of the Mind.* London: Hutchinson, 1949.

Sacks, Oliver. *An Anthropologist on Mars.* New York:Vintage Books, 1995.

Sanders, E. P. *Judaism: Practices and Beliefs (63 BCE—66 CE).* London: SCM; Philadelphia:Trinity, 1992.

Savage-Rumbaugh, Sue and Levin, Roger. *Kanzi: The Ape at the Brink of the Human Mind.* New York: John Wiley and Sons, Inc., 1994.

Scharlemann, Martin N. *What Then Is Man?* St. Louis: Concordian Publishing House, 1958.

Schnelle, Udo. *The Human Condition: Anthropology in the Teachings of Jesus, Paul, and John.* Minneapolis: Fortress, 1996.

Schweizer, Eduard. "Body." In *The Anchor Bible Dictionary,* 6 vols., edited by David Noel Freedman, 1:767–772. New York: Doubleday, 1992.

Sellars, Roy Wood. *The Philosophy of Physical Realism.* New York: Russell and Russell, 1966 [original 1932].

Shelp, Earl E. *Born to Die? Deciding the Fate of the Critically Ill Newborn.* New York: Free Press, 1986.

Sherman, Stephanie L., et al. "Recent Developments in Human Behavioral Genetics: Past Accomplishments and Future Directions." *American Journal of Human Genetics* 60 (1997): 1265–1275.

Spencer, H. *The Principles of Ethics.* London, 1893.

Squire, L. R. *Memory and Brain.* New York: Oxford University Press, 1987.

Stendahl, Krister. "Immortality Is Too Little and Too Much." *Meanings: The Bible as Document and Guide.* Philadelphia: Fortress Press, 1984.

Stent, Gunther S. "That Was the Molecular Biology That Was." *Science* 160 (1968): 390–395.

Strauss, D. F. *The Life of Jesus Critically Examined.* Philadephia: Fortress, 1972 [1835].

Stubbs, Michael. *Discourse Analysis:The Sociolinguistic Analysis of Natural Language.* Chicago: University of Chicago, 1983.

Sweetser, Eve E. *From Etymology to Pragmatics: Metaphorical and Cultural Aspects of Semantic Structure.* Cambridge Studies in Linguistics 54. Cambridge: Cambridge University, 1990.

Tarnas, Richard. *The Passion of the Western Mind: Understanding the Ideas That Have Shaped Our World View.* New York: Ballantine Books, 1991.

Terrace, Herbert, Petito, Laura, Saunders, Richard, and Bever, Tom. "Can an Ape Create a Sentence?" *Science* 206 (1979): 892–902.

Thébert, Yvon. "The Slave." In *The Romans,* edited by Andrea Giardina. Chicago: University of Chicago, 1993.

Theissen, Gerd. *The Miracle Stories of the Early Christian Tradition.* Studies of the New Testament and Its World. Philadelphia: Fortress, 1983.

Theissen, Gerd. *The Social Setting of Pauline Christianity: Essays on Corinth.* Philadelphia: Fortress, 1982.

Torrance, Thomas F. *Divine and Contingent Order.* Oxford: Oxford University Press, 1981.

Torrance, T. F. *Theology and Science at the Frontiers of Science.* Edinburgh: Scottish Academic Press, 1985.

Trevarthen, C., editor. *Essays in Honor of Roger W. Sperry.* Cambridge: Cambridge University Press, 1990.

Truett, K. R., et al. "A Model System for Analysis of Family Resemblance in Extended Kinship of Twins." *Behavior Genetics* 24, no. 1 (1994): 35-49.

Tuinier, S., Verhoeven, W. M. A., et al. "Neuropsychiatric and Biological Characteristics of X-linked MAO-A Deficiency Syndrome: A Single Case Intervention Study." *New Trends in Experimental and Clinical Psychiatry* 95 (1995): 105-106.

Tulving, E. *Elements of Episodic Memory.* Oxford, Clarendon Press, 1983.

Tulving, E. "What Is Episodic Memory?" *Current Directions in Psychological Science* 2 (1993): 67-70.

Turner, Max. "Modern Linguistics and the New Testament." In *Hearing the New Testament: Strategies for Interpretation,* edited by Joel B. Green. Grand Rapids: Carlisle Paternoster, 1995.

Vlastos, Gregory. "Slavery in Plato's Republic." *The Philosophical Review* 50 (1941): 289-304.

Waddington, C. H. *The Ethical Animal.* London: Allen & Unwin, 1960.

Wadell, Paul J. *Friendship and the Moral Life.* Notre Dame, Ind.: University of Notre Dame Press, 1989.

Wallis, Claudia. "Faith & Healing." *Time Magazine,* 147, no. 26 (June 24, 1996).

Walters, LeRoy and Palmer, Julie Gage. *The Ethics of Human Gene Therapy.* New York: Oxford University Press, 1997.

Wanamaker, Charles A. *Commentary on 1 and 2 Thessalonians.* New International Greek Testament Commentary. Grand Rapids: Wm. B. Eerdmans; Exeter: Paternoster, 1990.

Weaver, G.D. "Senile Dementia and Resurrection Theology." *Theology Today* 42, no. 4 (1986): 444-456.

Wenham, Gordon J. *Genesis 1-15.* Word Biblical Commentary 1. Waco, Texas: Word, 1987.

Westermann, Claus. *Genesis 1-11: A Commentary.* Minneapolis: Augsburg, 1984: 147-58.

Weiskrantz, L. *Blindsight: A Case Study and Implications.* Oxford: Oxford University Press, 1986.

Wessels, Anton. *Images of Jesus: How Jesus Is Perceived and Portrayed in Non-European Cultures.* Grand Rapids: Wm. B. Eerdmans, 1990.

Wiles, Maurice. "Religious Authority and Divine Action." In *God's Activity in the World: The Contemporary Problem,* edited by Owen C. Thomas, Chico, Calif.: Scholars Press, 1983.

Willard, D. *The Spirit of the Disciplines.* San Francisco: Harper and Row, 1988.

Williams, Nigel. "Biologists Cut Reductionist Approach Down to Size." *Science* 227 (1997): 476-477.

Wilson, A. C.. and Cann, R. L. "The Recent African Genesis of Humans." *Scientific American* (April 1992): 68-73.

Wilson, E. O. *On Human Nature.* Cambridge, Mass.: Harvard University Press, 1978.

Wilson, E. O. *Sociobiology: The New Synthesis.* Cambridge, Mass.: Harvard University Press, 1975.

Wing, Lorna. "The Continuum of Autistic Characteristics." In *Diagnosis and Assessment in Autism,* edited by E. Schopler and G.B. Mesivob. New York: Plenum, 1988.

Winter, Bruce W., editor. *The Book of Acts in Its First Century Setting.* Vol. 6: *The Book of Acts and Its Theology,* edited by I. Howard Marshall and David Peterson. Grand Rapids: Wm. B. Eerdmans, 1996.

Witherington III, Ben. *Conflict and Community in Corinth: A Socio-Rhetorical Commentary on 1 and 2 Corinthians.* Grand Rapids: Wm. B. Eerdmans; Carlisle: Paternoster, 1995.

Wolf, U. "The Genetic Contribution to the Phenotype." *Human Genetics* 95 (1995): 127-148.

Wolfensberger, Wolf. "The Growing Threat to the Lives of Handicapped People in the Context of Modernistic Values." *Disability & Society* 9(no. 3), (1994): 395-413.

Wolff, Hans Walter. *Anthropology of the Old Testament.* Philadelphia: Fortress, 1974.

Wright, N.T. *Christian Origins and the Question of God.* Vol. 1: *The New Testament and the People of God.* Minneapolis: Fortress, 1992.

Wuthnow, Robert. *Communities of Discourse: Ideology and Social Structure in the Reformation, the Enlightenment, and European Socialism.* Cambridge, Mass.: Harvard University, 1989.

Index

what do we mean by immortality of
↓ the soul? what does the book suggest?
   see 226

Do we use "soul" in a variety of ways?
   a person or event / moment with soul
   are there words we could use instead
   of soul? 175f
meaning 221,177 f, 186, 22   99f very imp
relational 180, 224-5..
Dualism is requisite for ethics 198-200
   ''   not '',   202, 227
   ''   product of gnosticism 184
substance dualism 203

Dementia 201
↑ Life beyond death 177, 226, 187-93, 100

why Do we have to understand human nature?
   controversial 209, 158, 172-3

what is spiritual if there is no soul?
   226 to be in relationship with God
   101-2

agape 212
===

Do the authors take sin seriously enough?
   181-3, 226